Alchemy for Managers

Turning experience into achievement

Tom Reeves

BUTTERWORTH
HEINEMANN

Butterworth-Heinemann Ltd
Linacre House, Jordan Hill, Oxford OX2 8DP
A division of Reed Educational and Professional Publishing Ltd

A member of the Reed Elsevier plc group

OXFORD   BOSTON   JOHANNESBURG
MELBOURNE   NEW DELHI   SINGAPORE

First published as *Managing Effectively: Developing yourself through experience* 1994
Second edition 1997

British Library Cataloguing in Publication Data
A catalogue record for this book is available from the British Library

ISBN 0 7506 3340 9

Composition by Genesis Typesetting, Rochester, Kent
Printed and bound in Great Britain by
Biddles Ltd, Guildford and King's Lynn

Contents

Preface

All managers need to have management development at the centre of their agenda . . .

Make no mistake, management development is not something to be done on the side. It is central to what your work is about . . .

Charles Margerison: *Making Management Development Work*

The enterprise where we work is far and away the most significant business school that managers ever attend.

Gordon Wills: *Your Enterprise School of Management*

In order to develop as a manager, as well as making yourself more practically competent, you may also need to change the way you are – how you think and behave. This book is about the self-transformational aspects of becoming more effective as a manager. Managing effectively demands more than knowing what to do and how to do it. It demands that you draw on your personal qualities – your imagination and creativity, your energy and enthusiasm, your ability to form relationships, your power and persistence. You need also to be able to manage your own psychology; for it is not unknown for a person's ego to be an obstacle to managing effectively.

While books on the professional and practical side of managing abound, much less has been written on the personal side of managing. The purpose of this book is to explore how your everyday experience of managing can be used to develop your personal capabilities to manage effectively. We all learn to improve our management practice from experience; this book aims to show how this natural process can be taken further.

In order to develop yourself as an effective manager you need to have the experience of managing effectively. To create this experience you need to undertake and successfully complete a managerial task as a result of which you achieve some worthwhile purpose.

The experiences that this will entail are essentially the same as those of any management project: setting aims and objectives, involving others in achieving your purpose, team working, dealing with the organization and with relevant people outside it, leading and managing change, keeping control of progress, and evaluating outcomes. In treating these topics, however, the emphasis in this book will be less on the conventional 'how to do' and more on the 'how to' of developing yourself from the experience.

The terms 'self-development' and 'management develop-ment' have a variety of meanings. Management development is usually quite loosely used to refer to any training, education or personal development, including on-the-job experience, designed to improve a manager's knowledge, skills or capabilities.

Self-development in its colloquial usage is similarly all-embracing, meaning any kind of development that you undertake on your own. The objectives of self-development can include:

- Acquiring new skills or knowledge;
- Seeking to improve performance in your job;
- Advancing your career;
- Developing your potential as a person and a manager; and
- Learning to understand and accept yourself.

All these objectives are relevant for this book, which is concerned both with your practical development and devel-oping yourself at a personal level.

The objective is to have you use an experience of managing effectively to develop yourself. You are invited to undertake a special assignment or project in your work that will give you a complete, self-contained experience of managing effectively. You undertake some task which involves you in 'managing effectively' from beginning to end – from deciding on the effect you want through to achieving it. Provided this task has been pitched at a level that stretches you, you learn and develop – both practically and personally.

It is recognized that a book may well not be the best medium for facilitating personal development. There is no opportunity for the author to confront readers with feedback about their behaviour. There is neither opportunity to insist that the reader takes time to reflect, nor for he or she to have the opportunity to talk through how their reflective observations should be acted upon. Accepting, however, that this is a book and not a developmental workshop, readers prepared to exercise a degree of self-honesty will find many pointers for using their experience to gain new insight and develop themselves.

Summarizing therefore, the book has two prime objectives:

- To show how the experience of undertaking a managerial task or project can be utilized to develop effectiveness; and
- To explore what inner resources and personal qualities managers need to call on to be effective.

A further objective is to help develop leadership capabilities. Initiating and seeing through a project of your own at work will involve you in the basic activities of leadership – determining purpose, drawing others into your venture, and directing people and events to the outcome you want. There is much mystique surrounding the concept of leadership. Undertaking a project of your own offers a simple and pragmatic approach to acquiring the essential skills.

The book also deals with issues that face someone becoming a manager for the first time. Professional people – hospital consultants, engineers, head teachers, caterers, social workers – in talking about their prospective role as a manager have highlighted a number of apprehensions.

One is anxiety about handling the professional or technical side of managing, especially the finances. These kinds of anxieties are normally remedied by training. Another is hesitation about taking on what is sometimes seen as an alien role.

A third recurrent theme is a sense that, although they believe they could do it, and often already are doing it, there must be something more to managing than what they are doing. It is hoped that this book will reassure such managers that they may be doing the right things already.

There are of course many books already on different aspects of management development, for example on self-management, creativity, intuition, leadership, action learning. But there is to my knowledge no book which brings together personal development and practical action in the way that is done here.

Most books and courses on self-development are to do with personal skills (usually interpersonal skills) and coping skills (e.g. stress and time management), while 'self-management' tends to be primarily about managing one's external behaviour without necessarily exploring its well-springs.

Although written primarily for managers, especially those who have just become managers, anyone working in a business or organization should be able to use the book to help develop their effectiveness.

Other categories of reader likely to find the book of value include:

- Professional and technical staff who want to prepare themselves for taking on managerial responsibilities;
- Managers on qualificatory courses (e.g. DMS, MBA, IPD), especially where undertaking an action project is required;
- Anyone who 'manages', that is to say involves others in getting things done, regardless of whether or not they have the title of manager;
- People running small businesses who may gain a new perspective on linking personal and business growth;
- Managers on action learning programmes, who could find in this book some new approaches to interpreting and learning from their experience;
- Trainers or managers who are supervising learning projects.

The book is structured to take you through an experience of managing and reflecting upon that experience.

For readers without formal training in management, this book could provide a means of capitalizing on your practical experience. All too often managers who go on a formal training course for the first time have grave doubts that what they have been doing in their managing hitherto is 'right'. They need to be reassured that the purpose of the course is not to show them up as 'wrong', but rather to build on their experience and take it further. This book would help you do this.

Part One explores what is meant by managing effectively, first from a practical, managerial perspective and then looking at what this means in personal terms.

Part Two describes what has to go into a managerial experience in order to give it the potential to be developmental.

Part Three deals with some of the practical issues that you will need to confront in undertaking a developmental task or project – first at the level of the organization, then the group or team, and finally you as an individual trying to get something done.

Part Four concludes by reviewing some of the processes that you may need to work through in order to use your experience as a basis for learning and development.

It is hoped that those who read this book will better understand how to manage effectively by being themselves. If you seriously use the book as a means of developing from experience, as opposed simply to reading it for general interest:

- You should find that you have learned to manage effectively in a way that draws on your own particular personal qualities, vision and creativity.
- You should have acquired greater skill in reflecting on experience, not just for developing professionally, which we all do all the time, but in being able to use insight from experience to develop personally.
- You should have a greater understanding of what it is in yourself that draws others into your ventures.
- You should have gained a sense of accomplishment as well as simply acquiring the lessons of experience.
- Finally, you should have acquired a perspective on managing that looks beyond the immediate day-to-day tasks that any competent manager could carry out to the creative contribution that only you can make.

Each of the four Parts of this book begins with a 'Personal transformation report'. These are case reports by individual managers who have put themselves through the process of undertaking a small but challenging project in their work which has resulted in practical learning and personal development.

The managers undertook these projects as part of a 3-month part-time course entitled 'Effective Management' based around this book. This course formed part of a wider university education programme leading to a Diploma in Management Studies or a Master's Degree in Management. The managers were required to plan and implement some change at work that would improve their effectiveness and write an account of what they did and how they developed as a result.

The four cases presented have been chosen because the managers had a clear story to tell. The case reports are presented in the managers' own words, edited and adapted from the report they wrote for their course assessment. Each report speaks for itself. The managers describe their role, what they did for their project, and how they personally changed as a result of doing it. Each case report well illustrates the main theme of this book: do something challenging in your work and allow yourself to develop from the experience of doing it.

Tom Reeves

Acknowledgements

Writing this book was greatly aided by having a good friend, Claire Nash, Managing Director of Vis-a-Vis Productions, act as a literary mentor. Her smiling or downcast responses to various chapter drafts let me know instantly when I was on or off course. Dr Peter Critten, a long-standing colleague, has been a continuing source of references, ideas and debate. Their comments on my drafts have been gratefully incorporated, and my special thanks go to both of them for their enthusiastic support and encouragement.

My thanks go also to other colleagues who took time to read and comment on the penultimate draft: Mary Hartog, Annabelle Mark, Stephen Hearnden; and also Angela Hills, a Manager with Noble Lowndes. Their comments too have been gratefully heeded.

My employers, Middlesex University, granted me a term's sabbatical leave in which I was able to write the first draft, the University Business School promptly obtained all the books I requested, and Stephen Hearnden deputized in my absence so competently that I was free to concentrate exclusively on writing. Joan Lindeman suggested that I ask for sabbatical leave in the first place.

Jacquie Shanahan and Jonathan Glasspool, my editors at Butterworth-Heinemann, have both made suggestions that have had a creative impact.

Many of the ideas in this book stem from my participation in a series of personal-development workshops run by the former Bellin Partnership (now transformed into Universal Learning). My understanding of how people can develop and change has been deeply influenced by my experiences on those workshops, and their spirit pervades these pages. As neither the Bellin Partnership nor any of its tutors are cited in the references at the end, I acknowledge here their contribution – most especially Graham Browne.

The idea for writing this book came while working at the Hotel and Catering Training Board (now Company). I had the opportunity there to design and run, in association with Kim Parish, a new management development programme based on action learning principles in which managers undertook work-based projects. I acknowledge the contribution of all those managers on that programme and subsequent ones who have demonstrated that project-based experiential learning is a powerful development medium. A few of their experiences and achievements are recounted in the book. Many more have influenced it.

My thanks go to all.

Part One
Setting your Agenda

The manager ... would (welcome) the title of leader: group leader, team leader, project leader, are perfectly acceptable terms ... a lot of managers accept the idea of being a boss quite happily.

Antony Jay; Management and Machiavelli, p 93.

Personal transformation report 1

Achieving effectiveness through becoming an 'informed coordinator'

Before undertaking this project I had never really attempted to define what a manager was supposed to do or achieve. I have worked in various settings, but had never been trained as a 'manager'. Now I feel I am taking on the 'mantle of management'.

I am a Service Manager within the Social Services Department of a London borough. The Service Manager role is a combination of several middle management functions in an attempt to flatten the hierarchy and we are stretched in many directions. It is not uncommon to be representing the local authority at the highest level one moment, then be locked into complex local operational concerns the next.

The project

I was contacted at home by the Director of Social Services and asked to take on the added responsibility of organizing and leading on Disability until a new Principal Occupational Therapist (OT) was appointed. The Director stated that he was 'very comfortable with me doing this'. Well, he might have been; I was terrified, though I conceded.

The opportunity of using this task as my project for the Effective Management course did give me some confidence, however. I have a background of specializing within Children and Families Services, specifically child protection, though part of my responsibilities include an overview of physical disabilities – much against my inclination and understanding given my background.

Disability Services, according to the Director, were 'a mess!' Waiting lists, he told me, were increasing and 'out of control', with many months' waiting prior to an occupational therapist assessment, except for the highest priority cases (life and limb). There was low morale among staff and a lack of uniformity in practice.

What to do ?

My first problem was to define the task more clearly and resolve the problems of managing my time in order to work in two Area Teams at the same time. I spent a few days (and nights) attempting to analyse the situation and then, realizing the task given to me was impossible to resolve as it stood, asked myself: 'How am I to become effective?'

I took on board the comment towards the end of Chapter 1 of this book: 'Ultimately, you have to formulate your own concept of effectiveness and develop your own practice of it. There are no right ways to manage that can be learned. There is no one way to be effective. All that can be done is to experiment in different situations and become a person who is able to discern, for each new situation, what is required to manage it effectively.'

My preliminary assessment of the problem I had to resolve was that there were too few therapists, who worked, fairly isolated in Area Teams, with little administrative support. A meeting with the Director to ask for extra financial resources produced an extra OT locum to reduce tensions in the waiting lists and an agreement to increase the OT establishment in the next financial year. But this was only my 'stream of consciousness' reaction to handle the situation in the short term. I formed a deeper resolve to unravel this problem in a more meaningful fashion.

I came to realize that this was *not* my problem alone. It had been chronic prior to my starting with the department. The National Health Service and Community Care Act 1990 had affected volume and expectations. Unfortunately, the department had not been able to find a satisfactory response. Now the Director was looking to me for a response and a solution. A label had been put on me: I had become the adviser for physical disabilities and as such had to be seen as effective.

Finding a way forward

In order to share the problem I organized a Planning Away Day for the operational staff and their managers in which they could think through their own response to the problems facing them. In order to plan for this I utilized the series of 'crystallizing questions' set out in Box 4.6 of this book:

1 'Why do you want to undertake this project?' For me it was about getting the 'whole' picture, and survival.
2 'What are you going to achieve?' I laid down my aims and objectives with my Area Manager and the facilitator for the Away Day.
3 'How are you going to achieve these aims?' With agreed conclusions and tasks set out from the Away Day.
4 'Who will you need to involve?' An agreed list of participants, central to the perceived problem.
5 'When will the project be completed?' Initially, my idea was that the event itself would conclude the project, though since then further Away Days have been held.
6 'How much is the project going to cost?' Limited budgets were going to entail serious negotiation with the Finance Manager and Director.

The time it all took to set up proved a (controlled) nightmare of logistic operation for me.

Outcomes and achievements

There were a number of valuable outcomes of the Away Day. Probably the most important was that the Disability managers identified a number of practical actions they themselves could take. A further important achievement was that senior managers, led by the Director, attended. This signalled a change of emphasis for these front-line operational workers. It moved OT from the peripheral outer edges into a central theme that had been set for reorganizing the Social Services Department as a whole.

For morale, the Away Day has had a curious effect. The staff are sceptical of its ultimate purpose and, at the same time, relieved that their concerns have been aired to a wider and, hopefully, receptive audience. It says, at the end of Chapter 1 of this book: '. . .it is hard to see how anyone could reasonably be described as having managed effectively if they did not actually achieve anything.' My achievements so far in managing my new responsibility have been both tangible and psychological.

On the tangible side there is locum support and the Director's promise of extra financial resources; the Away Day itself, with senior management present and listening; tasks agreed for managers to undertake; possible further Planning Away Days. On the psychological side, staff know that their concerns are being listened to; they are no longer isolated and responsibility for their problems is being shared; and there is a realization that waiting lists are not the whole problem. To realize these 'changes', I had to negotiate with the Directorate and my peers. The main group, though, was the occupational therapists themselves. Without this group 'on board', the event would have had limited value.

I already had a vision, or 'mental map', of how the Day should be and, in part, its aims and objectives. I feel the two principal developments that I achieved for myself were negotiating and leadership skills.

Once I had identified a way of tackling the problem, and through sharing the concerns, I was able to move away from a feeling of sole ownership to shared responsibility. This has reduced my role to one of 'informed coordination'.

The way in which I realised the Away Day was to define it, not specifically as a Disabilities problem, but as a management task. A manager has to balance the needs of his or her staff within the confines of budgets and efficiency to the service. (Well, that is one view!)

Personal change

The project has led to personal change and new self-knowledge, and a new level of capability. There has been a 'personal transformation'. For example, referring to Box 10.1 of this book:

- 'New insights and self-understanding' - of individuals and their personal agendas (micro politics) and a 'helicopter' understanding of events (macro view).
- 'Relating to others with fewer barriers' - we all need to realize the problem and potential solution. I am *not* the expert; you are! I just coordinate.
- 'Take on the "mantle" of management' - I am a negotiator at different levels, leading by example.

I have come to understand how you can know what is correct and when to do things. I have understood that although you can lead (others expect that), people anticipate compromise at the same time. I realize that events are triggered by the initially agreed change.

The project has allowed me to create a vision based on my interpretation of events. Perhaps it did not change me 'to the soul' but rather fine-tuned skills that were already evident.

The greatest personal change in myself, I feel, has been to temper my own impatience with others and to await a shift in their views to result from events. I realize too that I have to allow people to understand and relate to my 'mental map'.

For the future, I now know I have to be receptive to others. I feel comfortable with this. Not to allow people to challenge or express is not an efficient way to manage. I know from experience now that '. . . There are no right ways to manage that can be learned. There is no one way to be effective. All that can be done is to experiment. . .'

1   Effective action

Introduction

This chapter is about the meaning of effective management and how you might develop your ability to manage more effectively.

It first describes what managers do and looks at how different writers on management have viewed effectiveness, namely as:

* Seeing the whole picture;
* Combining task achievement with maintenance of morale and motivation;
* Initiating one's own projects; and
* Successfully handling roles and processes.

This is followed by guidance on how you might think through your own personal approach to managing effectively. Some principles are culled from 'action learning' as a way of setting in motion an experience of managing effectively for yourself.

The chapter concludes with my own views on what managing effectively might comprise.

A manager's dual role

Managing, as the popular definition goes, is about getting things done through people. It is also about deciding what things ought to be done, and ensuring that what is done is worthwhile.

Books and courses on management advise you on what you should do and how you should do it – the professional knowledge and skills of managing. What they do not and cannot tell you is whether what you actually do as a manager is effective. Only experience can tell you that. Courses and books can help you put together a mix of ingredients for managing a particular situation. But whether this is an effective mix can in the last resort only be judged by the outcomes that result.

Managers basically have to do two overlapping things. They have to keep the existing show on the road – that is to say manage the routine or recurring activities for which they are responsible. They also have to innovate and make improvements – that is to say change the way things are done or which things are done.

Innovation and change have tended to be thought of largely as the prerogative of those at the top of the organizational hierarchy. But the complexity of modern-day organizations and the rapidity of change mean that people at all levels now have opportunities to initiate improvements – indeed may need to if they care about success or survival, whether corporate or personal.

Books on the management of change tend, however, to be addressed to the chief executive, with the assumption that it is the managers down the line who will have to do the implementing. While often this is so, *Alchemy for Managers* is written on the assumption that managers down the line also wish to do some initiating. Indeed, in the present era of 'delayering' and decentralization, having the capability to initiate and lead projects of benefit to the organization is an essential survival skill.

Managers without the title

Many people manage. You may not have the title of 'manager' or even be in employment. You may not think of what you do as 'managing'. But if you are working through other people to achieve a purpose or goal, you are managing.

The removal of levels of middle management means that there are now fewer people in organizations with the title of manager who do little real managing. Opportunities for any member of staff to remain as a 'back-room' person are decreasing.

There are also more people without the title of manager who are now expected to do some managing. There have always been people in organizations who were not formally called managers – secretaries, personal assistants, controllers, supervisors – but who undertook managerial tasks. Changes in organizational size and structure mean that people who, given the choice, perhaps would not have put themselves forward as managers are now being drawn into management roles. This book aims to help all these categories of 'manager' with the personal development they need to handle their role.

The meaning of 'effectiveness'

Effectiveness is, at its most basic, about getting effects. An effective manager is one who is able to get the effects that he or she wants.

As a 'manager', you will almost certainly already have some concept of effectiveness. You may not have your criteria explicitly worked out. But if you were asked 'Why are you doing this? Why are you doing it this way? How do you know you are doing the right thing?', you would probably be able to answer. In all likelihood you would talk about the effects you are achieving.

An 'effect', according to the *Oxford English Dictionary*, means 'something caused or produced, a result, a consequence, something attained or acquired by action, an accomplishment'. 'Effective' in a management context thus means more than simply being efficient; it is about being efficient to good purpose. To manage effectively is to manage in a manner that produces a *desired* effect, a result, an accomplishment.

Writers on management who have attempted to define effectiveness are broadly in accord with this dictionary view of managerial effectiveness. Worthwhile accomplishment, explicitly or implicitly, is a common theme in their definitions.

Writers on management, however, have tended to be less concerned with abstract definitions of effectiveness than with specifying what managers need to do in order to be effective. In many cases it is in fact taken for granted that the meaning of 'effective' is known and all that is needed is to specify the knowledge or skills that are needed for its attainment.

What these skills and knowledge are should have been variously specified. There is no common view of the ingredients of effective management. All writers have their distinctive perspective, based on their own experience, observation or research.

Strategy for becoming effective

This book does not attempt to synthesize these diverse views of effectiveness. I believe that managers can only become effective by working out for themselves what constitutes effectiveness in their particular job.

Principles and theories can help you up to a point. They can provide you with ideas, suggest what things you might look out for, help you analyse situations, indicate possible ways forward. But no theory or principle learned in a book or classroom can tell you precisely what to do in your precise circumstances. That you have to discover for yourself – anew in each fresh situation.

The starting point for effective action, therefore, needs to be an analysis of the situation you are having to manage. This means doing three things:

• Reviewing the world about you;
• Examining your own motives and psychology; and
• Managing, in the sense of handling and directing, both these.

For it is not just external circumstances that are unique; so also is each manager. 'Effectiveness' is not something 'out there' to be picked off the shelf and applied. It is the result of the interaction between, on the one hand, each manager's unique motivation and capabilities and, on the other, the opportunities and constraints present in the situation he or she is managing.

The interaction between the manager's external and internal worlds as the source of effectiveness is a recurrent theme of this book. Through understanding how these two worlds interact in your particular case, you will learn to understand more clearly what is the best way for you to manage.

Critical to your development as an effective manager is actually wanting to be one. You need to want to manage – to want to direct and shape something, to be willing to take responsibility with all that entails – caring about getting outcomes or results, willing to push or lead others to achieve your ends, and not being afraid to take some risks. Not everyone wants to be a manager, and of those who do become manager in title, not all are willing, or are hesitant, to embrace these attitudes. A corollary of this kind of motivation is that managers want to make themselves more effective.

Different views of effectiveness

Six views on what it means to manage effectively are presented below. They have been selected because in each case the writer has attempted to come to grips with the meaning of effectiveness as well as what needs to be done to attain it. Each view is presented in a separate 'box' accompanying the text.

It is fortuitious that there should be so much diversity of view. The objective in a book on learning from experience is not to synthesize all the existing views and provide you with one theoretical ideal of effectiveness to emulate. Rather it is to enable you, drawing on your own experience, to become a better judge of what effectiveness means for you and your particular circumstances. The fact that the boxes accompanying the chapter reflect so many diverse views of effectiveness should impel you to think through your own stance for managing effectively.

Building a cathedral

Let us start with Peter Drucker who has written a book entitled *The Effective Executive* – (see Box 1.1). Drucker sees effectiveness very much from the perspective of the total corporation or organization. It is the managers of that corporation as a whole who have to ensure, through their shared vision of a common goal, that what is done by management and other employees at all levels contributes to overall effectiveness.

Box 1.1   Effective managers 1

Peter Drucker: Cathedral builders

'An effective management', that is to say corporate management, 'must direct the vision and efforts of all managers towards a common goal. It must ensure that the individual manager understands what results are demanded of him.'   The response of the 'effective executive' is illustrated through a parable:

> . . . three stone cutters were asked what they were doing. The first replied: 'I am making a living'. The second kept on hammering while he said: 'I am doing the best job of stone-cutting in the entire county'. The third one looked up with a visionary gleam in his eyes and said: 'I am building a cathedral'.

> . . . it is the definition of a manager that in what he does he takes responsibility for the whole – that, in cutting stone, he 'builds the cathedral'.

Drucker cites five habits of mind for an effective executive:

- Get as much of their time as possible under their own control and manage it systematically.
- Focus on results rather than means.
- Build on strengths – their own and others', plus the possibilities of the situation.
- Concentrate on a few areas where they can make a difference.
- Ensure the effectiveness of their decisions by gearing them to the sequence of steps involved in carrying out their tasks.

A corollary of the five habits of mind is that effective executives attend to their personal development:

> The man who asks himself: 'What is the most important contribution I can make to the performance of this organisation?' asks in effect 'What self-development do I need? What knowledge and skill do I have to acquire to make the contribution I should be making? What strength do I have to put to work? What standards do I have to set myself?'

Adapted from: Drucker (1988: 57; 1989: 120, 124).

Drucker's ideas were very influential in the development of the technique of 'management by objectives' in which the common goal is broken down into discrete, clearly defined and manageable tasks. The risk in practice is that this leads to fragmentation of vision and purpose. But this was far from Drucker's intention. Through his parable of the stonemason, he enjoins a holistic view: all must understand that they are 'building the cathedral'. Taking the metaphor a little further, managing effectively means not only knowing that you are building a cathedral, but also knowing why it is being built and being satisfied that this is an appropriate project for this time and place.

Wagon masters

Another striking image of effective managing comes from J.S. Ninomiya (see Box 1.2). His metaphor of the effective manager as 'wagon master' emphasizes the need to integrate morale-sustaining leadership with competent administration. In view of the spate of books in recent years that attempt to draw an invidious comparison between 'managers' and 'leaders' (e.g. Bennis, 1989; Kotter, 1990), it is useful to have this memorable reminder that to achieve effective management they may need to go hand in hand.

Ninomiya's article was inspired by his observation of:

> ... businesses continuing to promote people into administrative ranks with apparently little consideration for their ability to manage others, their willingness to include subordinates in decision making, or their suitability as teachers and role models for a coming generation of supervisors. Many of these newly promoted managers perform in the managerial styles of a past era, characterized by self-serving attitudes, empire building, and autocratic methods.
> (Ninomiya, 1991: 24, by permission of *Harvard Business Review*)

Ninomiya's analogy of the wagon master having to combine teamwork with survival has considerable relevance to today's world where corporations have to survive in the face of global competition and domestic economic constraints, while at the

Box 1.2   Effective managers 2

J.S. Ninomiya: Wagon masters

Ninomiya developed his ideas on effective management from over a quarter of a century's work as a middle manager in the auto industry (Ford) and from fly-on-the-wall observations when working in a research team that visited colleagues in the oil and auto industries.

Ninomiya draws on the analogy of the wagon masters of the westward movement in North America during the last century – 'some of the most effective managers this country has ever seen'. A wagon master had two jobs:

> He had to keep the wagons moving toward their destination day after day despite all obstacles.

> He also had to maintain harmony and a spirit of teamwork among the members of his party and to resolve daily problems before they became divisive.

> A wagon master's worth was measured by his ability to reach the destination safely and to keep spirits high along the way. He had to do both in order to do either.

Ninomiya sees the skills of effective managers as essentially the same, and he sums them up in seven roles that they play:

- Listener and communicator;
- Teacher;
- Peacemaker;
- Visionary;
- Self-critic;
- Team captain; and
- Leader.

> Wagon masters pushed their wagons toward specific destinations – Oregon, the California goldfields . . . Good managers . . . understand their dual function. Getting the wagons to Oregon without the passengers is no achievement. Keeping everyone in high spirits right up to the moment they perish in the desert is not success.

Extracted from: Ninomiya (1991: 27–29), by permission of *Harvard Business Review*.

same time meet the increasing expectations of staff for a rewarding and satisfying work environment.

Intrapreneurs and project managers

Rosabeth Moss Kanter's use of the metaphor of 'business athletes' (see Box 1.3) to epitomize management effectiveness very much reflects the emergence of 'intrapreneuring' man-

---

Box 1.3 Effective managers 3

Rosabeth Moss Kanter: Business athletes

Kanter's view of effective management was coloured by her original research for *The Change Masters*. She came across two types of manager: the non-innovators who managed the routines, and the 'entrepreneurs' who initiated new ventures. It was the latter, who met the challenge of an 'innovation-stimulating environment', who earned her accolade of managing effectively. She identified three new sets of skills needed for this:

- Power skills – the ability to persuade others to back your initiatives with information, resources and other support.
- Collaborative skills – able to manage and work with teams and to facilitate employee participation.
- Change skills – knowing how to work the levers of change in an organization.

Subsequently, in *When Giants Learn to Dance*, Kanter described these corporate entrepreneurs as 'business athletes'. To be such an athlete seven 'skills and sensibilities' need to be cultivated:

- Operate without dependence on hierarchical authority;
- Compete in a 'win-win' fashion;
- Behave ethically;
- Temper self-confidence with humility;
- Attend equally to the process of implementation and to the result;
- Be versatile, able to adapt to diverse and changing circumstances;
- Find reward in the accomplishment of results.

Adapted from: Kanter (1985: 35–36; 1989: pp 361–364).

---

agers during the 1970s and 1980s. Effectiveness in Kanter's eyes lies in being able to initiate new ventures within an organization. As we shall see in a later chapter, she heaps scorn on managers who do no more than mind the routines and never embark on any projects which would break them out of their rut. Nevertheless, her specification of skills for a business athlete has an applicability to effective managing that need not be confined to intrapreneuring.

Tom Peters' perspective (see Box 1.4) is not dissimilar in that he too extols the intrapreneur. Strangely perhaps for someone who has offered so many prescriptions as to what managers ought to do, Peters has nowhere in his writings brought together a specification of an effective manager. The closest he comes to doing this is in his book *Liberation Management* (1992), where he recommends turning all management into the management of projects. The effective manager is thus someone who is able to cultivate the autonomy needed to create and manage projects. Peters too does not endorse the view that leadership and managing are separate.

Box 1.4   Effective managers 4

Tom Peters: Search for excellence and thrive on chaos

Peters is a long-standing critic of traditional styles of management. His prescriptions for effectiveness in the future include:

- Have the mental and emotional flexibility to manage paradox and ambiguity;
- Get close to customers and be highly responsive to their needs;
- Stay close to the action – have a hands-on approach and empower people to be productive;
- Never lose sight of values and purpose;
- Get initiative and entrepreneurship (i.e. leadership) to emanate from all levels; and
- Manage everything as if it were a project.

Extracted from: Peters and Waterman (1982) and Peters (1989; 1992).

In Peters' view, it is only managers who lead projects who add value. He is openly contemptuous of 'middle managers', by whom he means functionaries and intermediaries in personnel, information processing, financial control, etc., who coordinate and control without adding value. He in fact sees little future for this type of manager, already an endangered species as the spreading use of information technology makes their role redundant, and as firms 'delayer' in their drive to 'leanness'. His advice to those remaining, if they want to survive, is to find a line position where they can be involved with a value-adding project.

At the core of Peters' perspective is the ability to be able to handle the paradox of managing projects. On the one hand, one needs voluntary co-operation, while at the same time one needs to be able to exercise the toughness and single-mindedness necessary to achieve results. This is a recurring theme in his writings. Box 1.4 summarizes, from the plethora of prescriptions that pervade his books, what I regard to be his central principles.

More than once in this book there will be occasion to draw attention to the distinction between managing change and managing routines. From the point of view of designing experiential learning projects, introducing change or managing innovation is likely to prove more challenging and therefore more fruitful as a learning experience than will the management of routine operations. Projects that are essentially corrective action for a routine operation may also lack developmental potential. This is not to disparage the importance of the management skills needed for managing the routines, but simply to point out where the developmental challenges are likely to be greatest.

Role and processes

Another approach to effectiveness is through the processes necessary to achieve it. Roger Plant, writing in the context of managing change, sees managers as having a 'potential effectiveness' which can only be realized if they create appropriate circumstances. He makes the common-sense observation that, while job knowledge, skills and technical competence are necessary, they are not enough if your role does not allow you to use your competences. Plant identifies ten aspects of a role that can impinge on your potential for effectiveness (see Box 1.5).

Malcolm Leary and associates address the processes of managing effectively in a rather different way. They note that

---

Box 1.5   Effective managers 5

Roger Plant: Role management

Plant sees managerial effectiveness as resulting from your potential effectiveness and the role you perform. It is the integration of the two that ensures effective role performance. Managers need to work on their role to allow their potential effectiveness to flourish. Plant identifies ten dimensions of role that are critical for effectiveness:

- Centrality – carry out activities that are central rather than peripheral to the organization's mainstream.
- Integration – deploy your particular strengths, e.g. experience, technical training and special skills, in your role.
- Proactivity – take some initiative; a reactive style of managing allows less scope for being effective.
- Creativity – find opportunities for trying out new or unconventional ways of doing things or solving problems.
- Connections – if your own role is connected to other roles there will be more opportunity for joint understanding, joint approaches and joint problem-solving.
- Giving and receiving help – self-evidently increases effectiveness.
- Wider organizational value – if you feel that you are contributing to a wider purpose you are likely to function more effectively.
- Influence – self-evidently necessary for effectiveness (likely to be enhanced if your activities have wider organizational value).
- Personal growth – scope to grow and develop in your role will contribute greatly to your effectiveness in it.
- Confronting problems – facing interpersonal problems and searching for solutions enhances effectiveness; avoiding problems, denying them, shifting them to someone else to solve, or referring them to superiors reduces it.

Adapted from: Plant (1987: 45–50) by permission of the publisher, HarperCollins.

Box 1.6 Effective managers 6

Malcolm Leary and associates: Inputs, processes and outputs
Leary and associates identify three areas of effectiveness. All three
need to be brought together to achieve a holistic, integrated approach:

- Input effectiveness – what managers put into their activities and
  tasks.
- Process effectiveness – how they carry out their work (particularly
  that involving others).
- Output effectiveness – what contribution the output makes to their
  explicit or implicit objectives.

The relationship between the three areas of effectiveness is
illustrated in the diagram below.

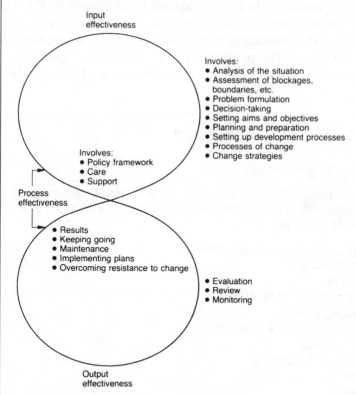

Input
effectiveness

Involves:
- Analysis of the situation
- Assessment of blockages,
  boundaries, etc.
- Problem formulation
- Decision-taking
- Setting aims and objectives
- Planning and preparation
- Setting up development processes
- Processes of change
- Change strategies

Involves:
- Policy framework
- Care
- Support

Process
effectiveness

- Results
- Keeping going
- Maintenance
- Implementing plans
- Overcoming resistance to change

- Evaluation
- Review
- Monitoring

Output
effectiveness

Adapted from: Leary *et al.* (1986).
Research carried out by Transform/Sheffield City Polytechnic and
sponsored by The Manpower Services Commission. Quoted with
permission.

some approaches to effectiveness stress getting the 'inputs' right, while others emphasize the 'outputs' – in terms of the metaphors in the boxes above, either hoping that sound wagons and strong horses will see you through, or that keeping the vision of the cathedral in mind will give you all the direction you need.

Straddling inputs and outputs are of course the *processes* of managing, as indicated in the central section of the diagram in Box 1.6. This diagram gives a useful picture of the totality of managing effectively.

A middle manager view

It may be illuminating to conclude this brief overview of what constitutes managing effectively with a list of the responses of a group of middle managers employed in a large manufacturing corporation to the question 'What is effectiveness here?' Their responses, shown in Box 1.7, are a mix of things they

---

Box 1.7   Effective managers 7

A middle management view

Answers to the question 'What is effectiveness here?' by a group of middle managers in an automotive parts manufacturing plant of an international company, 1992:

- Setting goals and achieving them.
- Communicating.
- Delegating.
- Making best use of resources.
- Developing people.
- Doing better than the competition.
- Inspiring others.
- Being good at planning.
- Leadership.
- Flexibility.
- Managing your time.
- Team building.
- Not putting your foot in it.
- Humour.

---

had to do and qualities they had to have. Some, for example being better than the competition, are corporate level concepts. Others, for example not putting your foot in it, are individual level concepts.

Taken as a whole, the list, upon which all the managers in the group agreed, makes a statement about the management culture which they worked in, and their view of what was expected of them.

Your own concept of effectiveness

Research into management practice has greatly extended our knowledge of what managers do. It has not, however, led to any agreed understanding of what managers have to do to be effective. Henry Mintzberg, probably the most reputed of the researchers into what managers do, has commented:

> It must be one of the great ironies of our age that amid all the courses telling people how to manage, and all the consultants and publications telling them how to manage better, we have yet to produce a widely-accepted conceptual understanding of what managers actually do and have no serious theory at all on what constitutes effectiveness in the practice of management!
>
> (Mintzberg, 1991)

A universal theory of what constitutes managerial effectiveness may perhaps never be reached. So much depends on circumstances and the individual manager. Each organization has its own concepts of effectiveness in relation to its particular goals and policies. In undertaking a managerial task you will need to formulate your own concepts of effectiveness that are appropriate to the context in which you are operating. In doing so, it is hoped that you will find useful the various attempts to define managerial effectiveness that have been described above.

Agendas and networks

One further description of the effective manager, which has inspired the title for this Part of the book, may help. Reporting on his research into how effective general managers approach their jobs, John P. Kotter (1986) observed that they do two fundamental things. They:

- Set agendas: they figure out 'what to do despite uncertainty, great diversity, and an enormous amount of potentially relevant information'.
- Build networks: they get 'things done through a large and diverse set of people despite having little direct control over most of them'.

Although writing about managers who were the chief executive of their division or unit, the need to set an agenda and build networks applies to any manager who wants to influence events in his or her organization.

Ultimately you have to formulate your own concept of effectiveness and develop your own practice of it. There are no right ways to manage that can be learned. There is no one way to be effective. All that can be done is to experiment in different situations and become a person who is able to discern, for each new situation, what is required to manage it effectively.

An experience of managing effectively

To gain a comprehensive experience of managing effectively you need to manage a task or project from initial conception of the idea through to its realization in an accomplished goal or outcome, as shown in Figure 1.1.

You start with the impetus for action – a problem or a vision of change. You progress through overlapping stages in which you explore and test possibilities. You take the action needed to bring about the desired result. Finally you review your achievements, which may in turn lead to yet new directions and another cycle of action. The path from original purpose to final outcome is of course rarely as smooth as the diagram might imply; there will be hesitations, deviations, repetitions, setbacks, reappraisals of purpose and direction.

The cycle of purpose–action–accomplishment depicted in Figure 1.1 is of course essentially the same as that of many management projects. The elements in the cycle could

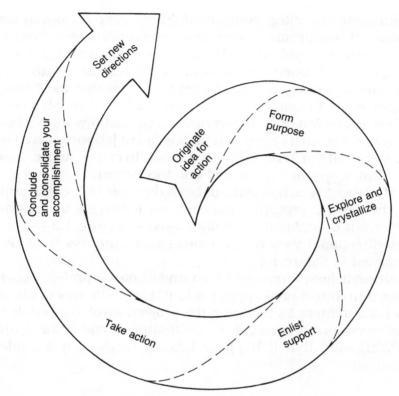

Figure 1.1 The purpose–action–accomplishment cycle

equally well have been described as: project brief, research on problem definition and solution, recommendations, implementation, review. The difference lies in the fact that the kind of project being advocated here will be specifically designed to bring about learning and development as well as achieve a corporate outcome. It will also be very different in scope to the kind of large-scale construction project that most books on project management are concerned with.

Alternative view of managing

The purpose–action–accomplishment cycle could perhaps be criticized for being tied too closely to the conventional view of management as comprising planning–organizing–co-ordinating–commanding–controlling. Those time-honoured elements of management were first propounded by a Frenchman, Henry Fayol, in 1916, although not translated into English until much later (Fayol, 1949). Research into what managers actually do has, however, shown that most managers do not in fact spend their time working through a cycle of set goal–plan–monitor–review. Organizations as a whole may operate such cycles, but management jobs are carved up in ways that cut across these activities. In consequence, their work may appear fragmented and incoherent.

Mintzberg, who has perhaps been the most influential critic of the Fayol perspective, instead sees managers as creating order out of ambiguity, as illustrated in Figure 1.2 – a less uni-directional view of the management process than that depicted in Figure 1.1.

Nevertheless, a manager who undertakes a project, has to take a unidirectional approach to it. He or she has to attend to such matters as planning the project, involving people in its execution (organizing, co-ordinating, commanding) and making sure that it happens broadly in the way intended (control).

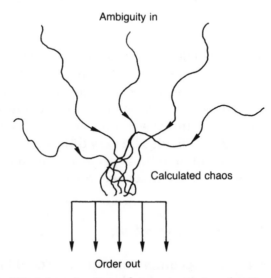

Figure 1.2 Mintzberg's view of a manager's role. From: Mintzberg (1991)

Many years ago I was employed as a research assistant to carry out research into managerial control systems. I and my fellow research assistants soon discovered that if we asked managers how they planned and controlled, we all too often got bemused reactions or theoretically correct but obviously unreal answers. Realizing that many managers did not think about their work in the theoretical terminology of planning and control systems, we began instead to ask more pragmatic questions, such as 'How do you decide what to do next?', 'How do you know when things have gone wrong?', 'What do you do then?' Answers to these questions revealed fascinating and often dramatic accounts of how the managers discharged, or sometimes failed to discharge, their planning and control functions (Reeves, 1970; Reeves and Turner, 1972).

The Figure 1.1 view of management, pursuing a purpose, and the Figure 1.2 view, creating order out of ambiguity, provide complementary perspectives on the manager's role. However, as a guide to action the Figure 1.1 view may offer a more helpful model.

Action learning

The experience of a project along the lines in Figure 1.1 has the potential to provide a complete self-development experience. Working to achieve a worthwhile purpose can precipitate learning opportunities for you in virtually all the key aspects of managing effectively. You learn from having to find out how to do something you may never have done before. You learn from the actual doing. You learn from reflection on the experience. Attaining a new level of achievement develops you. The personal insight gained from the experience enables you to develop. But above all, you develop from attaining a new level of achievement.

The approach to learning from experience taken in this book owes much to the ideas of 'action learning' (Revans, 1971, 1983; McGill and Beatie, 1992; Pedler, 1991). It dispenses, though, with many of the procedures one might expect to find on many orthodox action-learning programmes.

An important feature of action learning, or indeed any experiential learning is that you place yourself in a situation where you have to learn by finding out for yourself, where you may have to question received wisdom, and where you most certainly cannot expect to rely on general theories and principles as your guide to action. This is at the core of action learning, which is more than simply learning from experience. It is more aptly described as learning from active discovery when faced with inescapable problems and challenges.

The term 'action learning' has come to be loosely used for any form of management learning from experience. In its precise usage, however, action learning is more focused than that. It is a means of learning in which the starting point for learning is not a predefined syllabus, but a real-life problem or task which the action learner has to tackle. Identification of what needs to be learned arises from the demands of the task.

But 'action learning' is not confined just to drawing out the lessons from experience of undertaking the task or resolving the problem. Genuine action learning goes wider than that, and the action learner is expected to draw on any possible sources of knowledge. Books, courses, workshops, and also research may all form part of an action learning programme. The essential point is that the starting point for what is learned is the learning needs of the learner as defined by the project or task.

Reg Revans, the progenitor of action learning, held that for effective learning, managers needed to combine programmed knowledge (i.e. standardized learning that is dispensed through books or courses) which he called P, with questioning insight (i.e. customized learning that is acquired as a result of having to tackle real problems in an organization), which he called Q. His formula for managerial learning (L) was $L = P + Q$.

Revans also held, and action learning practitioners still largely follow this protocol, that experiential Q learning should normally precede P learning. In that way P learning is given relevance, is likely to be pursued more assiduously, and be more lastingly absorbed.

For many readers of this book the starting point for learning may not be an experiential learning project but a course on which they acquired, or are currently acquiring, *P* learning which they wish to apply in their work. There is no good reason that I can see why '*P* learning' should not precede '*Q* learning'. Indeed this happens on many orthodox action learning programmes, including some of those Revans himself ran. The notion, prevalent in some action learning circles, that one's starting point should always be an identified organization or business problem risks missing out on opportunities to introduce new thinking or practices that have developed elsewhere.

Complete learning

There has been a debate over many years in management development circles over the relative merits and demerits of learning from on-the-job experience as opposed to more structured and possibly more broadly educative off-the-job learning. Caricaturing the debate somewhat, the issues reduce broadly to:

- 'Theoretical' classroom or book learning is rarely relevant to any actual situations that managers have to manage and, even when it is, there are often insuperable difficulties in importing new ideas to solve problems that other managers do not recognize as existing.
- On-the-job learning too often wastes managers' time by having them re-invent wheels that they could learn about much more readily in a classroom or from a book. Moreover, since any competent management educator knows what these 'wheels' are, why get managers to go beating about the bush of experience in order to learn?

As far as developing the self and learning to manage effectively is concerned, the debate is largely irrelevant. Practical managerial competence can only be acquired through experience. Some principles and theoretical understanding will be useful in providing initial guidance, but ultimately it is only through practice and experimentation that personal development can occur.

Using the project approach

Projects have long been used as a means of management development. You do something that tests you in the capacities you wish to develop and you reflect on the experience and learn from it.

The issue for readers of this book is whether you undertake a complete project of the kind depicted in Figure 1.1. Certainly, in order to gain a complete experience of managing effectively you would need to do so. On the other hand, you could treat the book as another piece of background reading on management.

The concern of many readers may simply be to learn how to manage effectively their compartmentalized share of the whole. Others may feel their work is too closely tied to the management of routine or recurring operations for them to be able to get involved with the development of innovation or the management of change.

Indeed, undertaking a complete project may not always be realistic. Some managers, particularly when employed in a large organization, rarely if ever have the opportunity to manage a complete cycle of activities of the kind depicted in Figure 1.1.

Although this book focuses on a 'complete' project, it does not mean that you have slavishly to follow through all the steps of a project in order to benefit from it. How far you involve yourself in the total project cycle, or even use this book as a basis for experiential learning, is a matter for you to decide in the light of your particular needs and circumstances. You could:

- Undertake a special project as a development exercise – realistically, you are unlikely to do this unless required to do so as part of a course or development programme.
- Apply some concepts from this book to a complete project you are required to undertake in any event as part of your management job.
- Use concepts from the book in an *ad hoc* way to guide selected aspects of your everyday managing.
- Superimpose the project concept on your managing – the framework of a project can be applied to virtually any task.

- Reflect on previous experiences of managing effectively to distil further learning from them. However, reflection on past experience will not advance your development to anything like the extent that would be possible were you to undertake a new stretching challenge.

The scope of development

To develop as a manager you have to attend to both the personal and professional sides – who you are as well as what you know and can do. Peter Drucker has observed that 'development is always self-development' (1989: 184). An educational course in, say, marketing, finance, personnel, operations scheduling, quality management, economics, business policy or business ethics will develop you personally as well as intellectually. New understanding is a transforming experience.

While ignorance or incompetence may undermine your ability to manage effectively, the possession of knowledge or skills can be no surety of being effective.

Self-development is thus in part about improving your knowledge and skills. It is also about improving your capacity to use them in an effective way. It is learning more about how your world of work functions and how you can affect it. It is also learning more about yourself – how you perform in your world of work and how you might need to change in order to be more effective.

Conclusion on effectiveness

Drawing the threads of this chapter together, to manage effectively you need to:

- Have a purpose to accomplish, and actually to accomplish it – it is hard to see how anyone could reasonably be described as having managed effectively if they did not actually achieve anything. The purpose needs to be a worthwhile one, combining corporate and personal aspirations.

- Take responsibility for successful achievement of the purpose. You really need to make it your own personal venture, thus committing yourself to seeing it through to a conclusion. To this end, you will need a personal sense of purpose, mission even – a view of how you want to shape your bit of the world and leave it different to how you found it.
- Ensure you are sufficiently knowledgeable and competent for what you are doing – or be able to find people who are.
- Apply your personal capabilities to your managerial tasks, and not to allow self- doubt, or unwarranted self-criticism, to stand in the way of your doing so.
- Ensure that what you are doing contributes to a wider whole.
- Draw in the support you need – people, money, equipment, authorizations – to achieve your purposes. Without the involvement of others you might effectively carry out a professional or technical task, but you probably would not be managing.
- Be true to yourself; be authentic in what you do. Some non-managers believe that to become a manager is to sell your soul to the devil. Once you have, so to speak, taken the managerial shilling, you have compromised your integrity as an individual of moral standing. Managing can be a thorny path to tread, and there are sometimes invidious decisions to be made or executed that affect people. Managing effectively is often about maintaining your integrity in the face of difficult ethical choices.

To be personally effective as a manager, therefore, means to have a sense of purpose, a view of how you want to shape your bit of the world, and the knowledge and skills to be able to leave it different to how you found it.

Your vision does not necessarily have to be original. It can be equally valuable to see the potential for application of an idea encountered elsewhere, perhaps on a visit to another organization or learned on a course, and to make yourself the 'champion' for this cause. It is hard to see how you can be successful in such a venture, however, unless you are willing to put yourself fully into realizing your purposes.

That means more than simply performing at your present level of competence. It means remedying any lack of knowledge or skill and handling any inner or outer block that is an impediment to achievement. It means deploying your talents and capabilities to best advantage. All this may require considerable self-searching, which is the subject of the next chapter.

Action and reflection points

- Think through what managing effectively means for you in your job. Write it down for future reference.
- How well do your views on effectiveness as you have just formulated them fit with the organizational culture you are working in? If they do not fit, will that be a problem for you?
- Consider how you will use this book
  - to support an identified task or special project, or
  - as a general guide to making sense of your managerial experience.

2   Being effective

Introduction

The previous chapter reviewed the external constituents of effective managerial action. This chapter reviews the inner or personal side of the equation: how you need to think, feel and behave in order to perform effectively.

First, a number of views of what being an effective person entails are presented. These are based on:

- Self-awareness and self-understanding;
- The 'character' to produce results and go on doing so;
- A set of positive and negative traits; and
- A set of personal competences.

The chapter then goes on to review the psychological processes that you need to be aware of and manage in order to be personally effective:

- Your preferences, which may cause you to pursue 'comfortable' rather than effective behaviours.
- Your perceptions and beliefs, which may distort your view of the world and of yourself.
- Your needs and motives, which can cause you to engage in counter-productive management behaviours.
- Your emotions and feelings, which can reinforce or undermine your intentions.

The chapter concludes by reviewing what is involved in being effective and being yourself, and what is entailed in this kind of personal development.

The personal side of managing

To be effective you must be a person who can achieve your purposes. The importance of this personal side of managing is reflected in much contemporary management jargon: 'having vision', 'being proactive', 'owning', 'taking responsibility', 'being a champion' or 'having passion' (for a cause), 'committing yourself', 'being resilient', 'empowering' (yourself or others), 'being a role model'. One could poke fun at the language used in some cases, but all these words and phrases have been coined to describe a key aspect of managing – the manager's personal input into the management process.

In managing, what you are is often far more important than what you know or what you can do. As anyone who has ever managed or been managed knows, the person who is doing the managing makes all the difference.

As a manager you have to be able to display enthusiasm, be sociable, exercise persuasion, use your imagination, think laterally, draw on your knowledge or experience, handle your motivation, muster your psychological energy, create commitment, be empathetic, make choices, take responsibility for your decisions, be willing to do mundane tasks, and overcome dismay when things do not go according to plan. How you manage reflects your personal qualities, the kind of things you prefer doing, your view of the world, the needs and motives that drive you, and how you feel about other people and what is required of you. Moreover, your attitudes, and how you manage, will affect the way others around you work and perform.

But, just as there is no one right way to manage effectively, so there is no one right way of being effective. We each have to work out our own version of personal effectiveness. The objective, as in the previous chapter, is not to hold up theoretical ideals as to how you should 'be' as a person, but rather to make you aware of factors that could affect your capacity to perform as effectively as you would wish.

Personal competence

To be effective, your managerial behaviour needs to be consciously directed and controlled. Putting that the other way round, managerial action should not normally be directed by unconscious motives. Managers should know why they are doing what they are doing. Nor should they allow unconscious or inappropriate drives or emotions to deflect them from their purposes or draw them into political 'game-playing'. Everyone has probably had experience of managers who on occasion seem out of touch with them-selves. Their actions do not tie up with their overt pronounce-ments. Unwittingly they are capricious.

Inability to understand oneself and one's actions, when it results in failure to realize intentions, is tantamount to personal incompetence. Having self-insight and being able to act on one's insight are prerequisites of being personally competent.

'Managing yourself' is increasingly a topic of management courses and books. The focus, however, tends to be on managing one's behaviour rather than on exploring the inner psychology that gives rise to it. Flamholtz and Randle, authors of *The Inner Game of Management* (1989), a book designed to remedy this neglect, observe that:

> . . . the dimension of managers . . . managing their own psychology and mindset in order to be more effective in their roles . . . is rarely recognized and even more rarely discussed . . . (Although) it is critical to the success of individuals and the organizations that employ them, it is not taught even in the most prestigious MBA programmes.

This kind of personal development is likely to be of increasing importance for managers. Changing social values are making it less and less acceptable, both in the conduct of manager–staff relations and for a corporation's public image, for management practice and decisions to be distorted by inept personal idiosyncracies or the irrational expression of inappropriate emotion or unregulated power needs. There have been several notorious examples of such distorted behaviour at the top of major corporations in recent years. The case of Robert Maxwell, and the nefarious dealings that came to light after his death, is perhaps the most well known. Anyone who works in an organization will no doubt be aware of less public or less gross examples.

Models of personal effectiveness

Four approaches to describing what it means to be effective have been selected for presentation here. The first two, described in Boxes 2.1 and 2.2, start with a concept of what personal effectiveness is and then suggest what a person needs to be or do in order to attain this concept of effectiveness.

Box 2.1

Dorothy Rowe: The successful 'self'

Rowe sees a 'successful self' as based around awareness and understanding.

> *Awareness* means using our ability to act, feel and think while observing our actions, feelings and thoughts. It means responding to other people's actions while wondering what thoughts and actions lie behind such actions.

> *Understanding* means becoming aware of how we explain why people behave as they do, checking our theory about people against what we observe, and then modifying or changing our theory.

No two 'successful selves' are the same. However, 'successful selves' can be defined in a very general way as:

- Feeling valuable, self-accepting and self-confident.
- Not engaged in a constant battle to preserve their *persona* intact – pride does not block them from changing
- Flexible and creative in developing themselves, in ways that are congruent with their sense of who they are and their purpose in life.
- Using their model or view of the world as a basis for making their own decisions and being creative.
- Having developed the skills to understand and work with other models or views of the world.
- Having created a life story for themselves that gives a sense of progress – past events are interpreted in a positive light and are seen as leading to a positive future.

Adapted from: Rowe (1988: 9–41).

Dorothy Rowe's book *The Successful Self* (1988) arose from her work as a psychotherapist. She sees society as made up of people doing one of three kinds of things:

- Accepting and valuing themselves, secure in themselves, neither burdened nor driven, being freely themselves. They are the 'successful selves'.
  or
- Working hard at being good at overcoming a sense of inadequacy or badness. They may be outwardly successful, but they are driven and burdened, and worry about how well they are coping.
  or
- Not coping very well with their lives – holding a poor self-image of themselves, experiencing depression and possibly displaying symptoms of mental illness.

Other books that Rowe has written have been about the problems of people who fall into her third category – people

---

Box 2.2

Stephen Covey: Habits of effective people

Covey postulates seven habits of 'highly effective people' which form the basis of their character. The seven habits are:

- Habits of independence
  1. Be proactive;
  2. Do things with an end in mind; and
  3. Manage your personal priorities.

- Habits of interdependence:
  4. Operate on a win-win basis;
  5. Empathize – first understand, then be understood; and
  6. Work to create synergy.

- The habit of renewal:
  7. Preserve and enhance your productive capacity – physical, social/emotional, mental and spiritual.

Adapted from: Covey (1992).

not coping very well with their lives. In *The Successful Self*, however, she looks at the opposite end of the spectrum – the successful or effective person.

Rowe's 'successful self' is built around:

- Awareness – not just insight into oneself but also into others.
- Understanding – both having theories about the causes of events and people's behaviour and being aware of how we come to form these theories.

Rowe proposes six characteristics of a successful self, which complement these core elements of awareness and understanding (see Box 2.1).

Stephen Covey's popular book, *The Seven Habits of Highly Effective People* (1992), is underpinned by a concept of effectiveness based on 'character'. However, he does not see character as innate, but as something that is developed through practising the 'seven habits' described in Box 2.2. These form:

> . . . the basis of a person's character, creating an empowering centre of correct maps from which an individual can effectively solve problems, maximise opportunities, and continually learn and integrate other principles in an upward spiral of growth.

Such persons will have created a sense of personal autonomy and direction coupled with an ability to get things done and go on getting them done.

The core of their character is an ability to maintain a balance or harmony between:

- 'Production' – the ability to lay golden eggs; and
- 'Productive capacity' – the ability to survive as a goose that lays golden eggs.

Six of Covey's effective habits are about what is needed to get things done. His final and seventh habit is about keeping yourself renewed so that you can go on producing.

Norms of effective behaviour

Another approach to defining personal effectiveness is to compare one's own behaviour with that of others who have been judged effective by some objective criteria. The 'Verax model' of personal effectiveness presented in Box 2.3 is of this kind.

Drawing on an extensive review of the psychological literature, J. Clayton Lafferty, founder of psychological consultants Human Synergistics-Verax, identified twelve dimensions of behaviour or 'style' presumed to be relevant to effectiveness. These twelve dimensions form the basis of a questionnaire used by Human Synergistics-Verax, for diagnosing a manager's 'life-style'.

Central to the Verax approach is that the questionnaire results do not pigeon-hole you. Instead they provide a starting point for change. All twelve facets or dimensions are to do with one's thoughts or self-image. These impact on your performance. By changing your thoughts or your view of your self, you can increase your effectiveness.

The point on each dimension above or below which one might be deemed to be effective is then established by reference to the scores of managers with high salary levels, job responsibilities and professional success, and who expressed feelings of satisfaction and well-being. The positive traits, which common sense would associate with effectiveness, have in fact been shown to be so by research.

Practical competence

A fourth view of personal effectiveness is that it is to possess a range of personal competences.

Boyatzis (1982), who many would regard as the founding father of the competency approach to management development, defined job competency as:

> . . . an underlying characteristic of a person which results in effective and/or superior performance in a job. (It may be) a motive, trait, skill, aspect of one's self image or social role or body of knowledge.

Box 2.3

J. Clayton Lafferty and Human Synergistics-Verax: Life-style

A manager's 'life-style profile' is measured on twelve dimensions of behaviour. Positive and negative traits for each of the twelve dimensions include:

Positive traits	*Negative traits*

In relation to people:

• Active and open	vs • passive and defensive
– self-reliant	– needing approval
– open to new ideas	– conforming to rules
– independent	– dependent
– confident.	– self-condemning/ apprehensive.

In relation to tasks and performance:

• Constructive	vs • aggressive or defensive
– accommodating/tolerant	– critical/sceptical
– adaptable	– domineering
– co-operative	– competitive
– accepting.	– perfectionist.

In relation to developing potential:

• Committed	vs • Uninvolved/alienated
– takes on challenges	– underachieving
– concerned for and supportive of others	– preoccupied with own concerns
– involved with others	– reserved and distant from others
– fulfilling self.	– dissatisfied with self

Adapted from: Human Synergistics-Verax (1989) by permission.

What is interesting about that definition is that it so clearly identifies practical competence with inner qualities.

In Britain, competence is being used as a basis for assessing junior and middle managers towards a National (or Scottish) Vocational Qualification (NVQ or SVQ). Standards for assessing competence have been defined by the MCI (Management Charter Initiative), a body that has established itself as the official specifier of standards for management education and development. Among their competence standards is a model of 'personal competence', shown in Box 2.4.

Box 2.4

The MCI personal competence model

This model of personal competence is based around four areas or 'clusters' of competence, all geared to 'optimizing results':

- Planning to achieve results
  - show concern for excellence,
  - set and prioritize objectives, and
  - monitor and respond to actual events in light of plan.

- Managing others:
  - show sensitivity to their needs, and able to
  - relate to them,
  - obtain their commitment, and
  - present oneself positively to them.

- Manage oneself:
  - show self-confidence and personal drive,
  - manage personal emotions and stress, and
  - manage personal learning and development.

- Use intellect:
  - collect and organize information,
  - identify and apply concepts, and
  - take decisions

Adapted from: MCI (1990).

This list of personal competences could be seen as no more than a set of practical skills. Indeed, in an earlier book in this series (Murdock and Scutt, 1993), the MCI's model of personal competence has been used in just this way – as a framework for describing the practice of personal effectiveness. The boundary between a personal quality and a practical competence is not always clear. To a large extent who we are is defined by what we do.

The personal competences in Box 2.4 presume the existence of underlying qualities, namely:

- Conscientiousness,
- Motivation,
- Awareness,
- Sensitivity,
- Sociability,
- Leadership,
- Positive self-image,
- Self-confidence and energy,
- Emotional resilience,
- Inquiring mind and ambition,
- Capacity for analysis,
- Conceptual thinking, and
- Resolution.

Whether acquiring outward competence ensures managerial effectiveness is another matter; although obviously incompetence can detract from effectiveness. Without some overall concept of effectiveness, it is unclear how proficiency in a range of competences is any guarantor of a person actually being effective. Possessing competences is perhaps best regarded as a 'hygiene factor'. It is necessary to have them, but in themselves they do not create effectiveness.

The competency approach has been disparaged because of this limitation. Certainly an approach to developing oneself solely by this route could be overly mechanistic, a Leggo-brick or painting-by-numbers approach to managing, which could result in some kind of rudderless super-manager: proficient in everything and effective in nothing. But, if combined with clear ideas about what constitutes managerial and personal effectiveness, the competence approach need not result in this dire outcome. In fact current approaches to the assessment of competence do demand evidence of achievement.

Personal qualities

The kind of person we are is undoubtedly a key driver of our managerial performance. The question arises whether you need to be born with certain sorts of qualities in order to manage effectively. How far is it possible to acquire personal qualities or traits that you believe you lack?

Specifying the traits a manager ought to possess is the traditional approach to assessing a manager's potential for effectiveness. If you ask managers what kind of character-istics or qualities managers ought to possess, a considerable part of their answer is likely to be expressed in terms of traits – 'leadership' qualities, drive, sensitivity, honesty, enthu-siasm, confidence, imagination, independence of mind, and so on. We can all probably generate such lists, and they can form a useful agenda for specific self-development. Most traits, however innate they might seem at first sight, can probably be developed to some degree.

A sample of managers studied by John Burgoyne and Roger Stuart (1976) regarded their mental agility, their creativity, their proactivity and their emotional resilience largely as innate characteristics. Whether these managers were right in their belief is highly questionable. In a mature person innate qualities and experience, education and training interact to such a degree that it is futile to attempt to disentangle which abilities and characteristics are attributable to nature and which to nurture.

Managing your personal psychology

'Being effective' has many parallels with 'effective action' discussed in the preceding chapter. You need to know what you want for yourself and be able to achieve it.

To some extent this is a matter of developing yourself in deficient personal competences and qualities. In this regard

Box 2.4 could be a good starting point for formulating an agenda for your personal development. But being effective depends on more than possessing the right traits or acquiring competences. You need also to be able to manage your own psychology.

This does not mean engaging in some kind of therapeutic self-help. The starting point for managing your psychology does not have to be a diagnosis that there is something 'wrong' with you that needs fixing. Nor does developing your self mean resolving some deep-seated personal problem for which therapy or counselling would normally be indicated.

Your starting point can simply be that you want to be more effective at managing the processes that mediate between your 'inner self' and your outward behaviour – to keep in check any psychological forces that might manifest themselves in the kind of personal incompetence or unwitting capriciousness described earlier in this chapter. You need too to be able to deal with any inner blocks to what you want to accomplish.

Four aspects of our psychology that can, with a modicum of self-awareness, be fairly readily managed will be discussed here:

- What we prefer doing – our behavioural repertoire.
- How we see things – our perceptions and beliefs.
- What drives us – our needs and motives.
- How we feel – our emotions and feelings.

We may not always be conscious of these aspects of ourselves. But conscious or not they are always there, shaping what we do as managers. These aspects of our self can be envisaged, as depicted in Figure 2.1, as coalescing in a single driving force that results in managerial action.

Preferences

Everyone has preferred behaviours. All things being equal, we tend to do the things that we are most comfortable with doing and avoid doing the things that come less naturally to us. The most obvious example is our innate right- or left-handedness. If one lost the use of one's dominant hand, one would, with

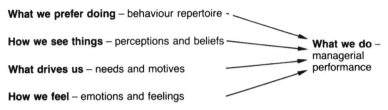

Figure 2.1   Components of the inner manager. Modified version of framework in Reeves, 1992

practice, acquire considerable facility with one's non-domi-
nant hand. But it is not something one would normally
choose to do. What we do in our daily lives is highly
influenced by our preferences, whether innate or acquired.

An example of a model of behavioural preferences that
many managers will be familiar with is Belbin's classification
of team roles, for example chairman, resource investigator,
company worker, plant, finisher (Belbin, 1981). Measuring
people's preferences for team roles has become part of the
normal routine of team building. Successful teams need a
balance of roles, which in turn means that a balance of
preferences needs to exist among the team members. If it
does not exist and the team is to function effectively, some
members may need to engage in styles of behaviour that do
not come naturally.

Of much wider relevance to human behaviour, however, is
the model of preferences that underpins the Myers–Briggs
Personality Type Indicator (Myers, 1980). The 'indicator' is a
questionnaire which diagnoses your 'personality type' on the
basis of four fundamental preferences. It is increasingly being
used as a tool for diagnostic purposes in personnel selection,
counselling and management development.

What your personality type might be is less relevant in the
context of developing yourself than understanding the nature
of your preferences. According to the Myers–Briggs model we
have preferences for:

- Perceiving our world, through either
  – our five senses of sight, hearing, taste, touch and smell,
  or
  – our intuition or sixth sense.

We also have preferences for

- Judging or reaching a conclusion about what we have perceived, either
  – by thinking, using logical and rational processes,
  or
  – on the basis of feelings or values.

These preferences or choices are illustrated in Figure 2.2.

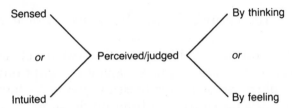

Figure 2.2 Myers–Briggs preferences in knowing one's worlds

The Myers–Briggs model is based on Jungian psychology, which postulates two 'worlds' that we need to relate to:

- Our outer world of physical objects, people and events; and
- Our inner world of thoughts, ideas and imaginings.

Some people prefer to focus their energy and attention on their outer world, which in Jungian terms makes them extrovert, and some on their inner world making them introvert (see Figure 2.3).

It should be noted that these meanings are not the same as in some more colloquial uses. 'Extrovert' in this context does not necessarily imply someone who is hearty and outgoing, nor does 'introvert' imply someone who is timid and withdrawn. It is quite possible to be a shy extrovert or a sociable introvert. The same goes for a manager – contrary to popular belief, you do not need to be an extrovert in order to be effective. But you will need to exercise some extrovert skills.

Indeed, most introverts, unless a compete recluse, normally develop very good extrovert skills in the course of their life. However strong someone's preference for putting their

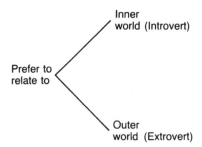

Figure 2.3   Jungian preferences in relating to one's worlds

energy into their inner world, they have to deal with their outer world.

The same cannot be said, however, of extroverts developing skills of introspection. Unless extroverts experience some significant life event which causes them to look inward, they may never have pressures on them to do so.

We all can be classified in terms of the factors depicted in Figures 2.2 and 2.3. We will have a preference to sense or to intuit, to perceive or to judge, to think or to feel, to relate to our inner or outer world.

In managing we need to be competent in all of these facilities, regardless of preference. Intuiting–perceiving skills are needed for vision and creativity in identifying new directions. Judging skills, using both thinking and feeling, are needed to determine which new possibilities should be pursued. Sensing–perceiving skills are needed for environmental scanning and for detecting problems that need attention. Intuition is needed to draw imaginatively on your resourcefulness and ingenuity. Thinking skills are, of course, so widely needed in management as to hardly need mentioning – although the extent to which they are always used in practice is another matter. Natural intuiters particularly need to draw on thinking skills to translate their initial ideas into workable plans.

Introversion-extroversion

The inner–outer world preference affects even more significantly how we manage. Most obviously it affects the way we relate to others – our interest in interacting with other people and establishing relationships with them.

Extroversion skills are continually called for in managing: in everyday interactions with staff, in networking, making presentations, enlisting support for projects, in dealing with conflict and opposition, and in encouraging and enthusing people.

Introversion skills are no less important, though not always obviously displayed: in understanding how you can use your personality and inner qualities to influence situations and events; in recognizing when your ego rather than the requirements of a task is dominating what you do; in recognizing overconfidence or an excess of diffidence; in managing your motivation in the face of setbacks.

Dorothy Rowe, whose model of the 'successful self' was presented in Box 2.1, sees the effects as even more pervasive than this. She believes the introversion–extroversion dimension to be the dominant force in people's lives, besides which the perceiving–judging dimensions depicted in Figure 2.2 are inconsequential.

To the extrovert, according to Rowe, the external world actually seems more real than the inner world; while to the introvert the inner world seems the more real. These differences in perception profoundly influence how we evaluate situations and set our priorities. It is the ability to switch between the introversion and the extroversion perspectives that Rowe is primarily referring to in the 'successful self' being able to understand and work with other models or views of the world.

Perhaps one of the most valuable aspects of experiential learning is making us aware not only our own preferences but also those of other people. But this cannot be achieved without some reflection and introspection, which may come more easily to the introvert than to the extrovert.

Perceptions and beliefs

How we see our outer and inner worlds inevitably determines much of what we do; our perceptions and beliefs are the premises on which we act. For present purposes, the terms 'perception' and 'belief' can be regarded as virtually synonymous. What is meant by them are ideas that we have about:

- Our external world:
  - beliefs about things and events, and
  - perceptions of people.
- Our internal world (self-image):
  - perceptions of what we are like, and
  - beliefs about our capabilities.

Changing one's beliefs or perceptions is a simple but extremely profound way of developing. Once you have made the shift things are never the same again.

The communication of new and different ideas about things and events in our external world is of course what most of education and training is about. Development occurs when we modify our theories about how it works, what is cause and what is effect. Indeed, it is commonplace for managers on educational courses to talk about how they have changed as a result of what they have learned.

Team building is as often as not about changing people's perceptions of others, bringing them into line with reality. If one comes to see other people in a different way, it is likely that behaviour in dealing with them will change too.

Team-building exercises can also create heightened awareness of our own behaviour in teams. It is often the interaction between changed perceptions of others and of our self that brings about changed behaviour.

Information about the external world tends to be conveyed on educational courses, if not quite as definitive objective truth, at least as hypotheses or theories about a possible objective truth. This is a far cry from treating the world as a set of subjective perceptions. From this subjective perspective, there is no 'truth'. Everyone has their own unique view of the world around them. If we change the way we see, for example, the organization we work in then we will change the way we relate to it and can manage it.

This subjective, perceptual approach to understanding the world around us is at the core of Gareth Morgan's book,

Imaginization (1993). Morgan urges us to consider the organization we work in as a set of images (for example, to see managers as 'termites' that build, or organizational structures as tentacled 'spider plants') rather than to attempt to define its objective reality.

His contention is that if we can only 'imaginize' our external world in new ways, we will improve our ability to see and understand situations and to deal with them. Awareness of the metaphors that we use, explicitly or implicitly to think about our colleagues and our organization, can break us out of stereotyped patterns of thinking and break down blocks to mutual understanding. Developing new metaphors can, in Morgan's experience, be used as a creative force for reshaping the future.

Self-perception

A great deal of management development is about attempting to change a person's self-image, the individual's perception of their inner world. Success in doing this can often bring about quite dramatic and noticeable change.

The typical strategy is first to generate accurate self-knowledge, and then to build on that to remedy weaknesses or develop strengths further. The simple fact of knowing yourself and accepting what you see can often change you almost without you being conscious of the process. Experiential events such as outdoor exercises, management games, simulations and projects are widely used for this purpose. The objective is to generate feedback that is so unequivocal that the person receiving it feels compelled to accept it and act upon it.

In these kinds of experiential event, however, there will normally be a tutor on hand to make the necessary feedback explicit should the participant fail to perceive it, and perhaps too to confront him or her with its significance. This kind of external prompt to insight and action is of course missing in most everyday management. One of the objectives of this book is to help managers to heighten their awareness of their behaviour and its consequences. In other words, to learn the art of self-feedback from experience.

A project which takes you beyond your self-perceived limits, and thereby results in a new level of achievement, can help you in this. Reflection on what you have done and what has happened is, however, critical. You need to understand what you have achieved and its significance for you. Later chapters will deal extensively with this process.

Motives and needs

Our motives and needs, the third factor in the list of inner drives in Figure 2.1, can be a powerful source for some of our most productive and counter-productive behaviours.

Most writings on motivation at work are concerned with why we work, what brings us satisfaction and reward from doing so, and what might induce us to be more productive or conscientious. Macgregor's Theory X and Theory Y, Herzberg's hygiene factors and motivators, and Maslow's hierarchy of needs, are theories that most managers are probably familiar with. Here, however, we are considering needs from a rather different perspective, i.e. not to identify possible inducements or sources of job satisfaction, but what individuals can do to manage their motives and needs – their driving forces – more effectively.

Human Synergistics-Verax based their life-styles profile (see Box 2.3) on how we respond to twelve basic human needs identified by motivational and psychological theorists. These twelve needs are to:

- Be liked,
- Conform,
- Depend on others,
- Be secure,
- Attack,
- Control,
- Win,
- Excel,
- Achieve,
- Support others,
- Belong, and
- Fulfil oneself.

None of the needs above are good or bad in themselves. As Box 2.3 shows, each dimension of behaviour can have positive and negative aspects. Our need for control, for example, is normally constructive. It enables us to regulate our lives, gain autonomy and give us a sense of identity. But it can also, if allowed to become too dominant a force, drive us to seek total control over events or people. Similarly, a drive to excel can, in an unconstructive manifestation, turn into an obsessional search for perfection, getting in the way of prioritizing and delegating.

Flamholtz and Randle, authors of *The Inner Game of Management* (1989) quoted earlier, have identified a whole range of distorted managerial behaviours that can result from failing to manage just three needs:

- For control,
- To be liked, and
- For self-esteem.

Syndromes of inappropriate behaviour that can result from managers failing to manage one or more of these needs are

---

Box 2.5

Syndromes of managerial behaviour resulting from failure to manage inner needs (for control, self-esteem and to be liked)

- Doer
- Imposter:
  - superperson
  - ugly duckling
- Godfather:
  - malevolent,
  - benevolent
- Napoleon.
- Salesperson.
- Hamlet:
  - information-seeker,
  - buck-passer,
  - agonizer.

Adapted from: Flamholtz and Randle (1989).

---

presented in Box 2.5. You may recognize some of the syndromes in Box 2.5, perhaps in less extreme form, in managers you know, or even possibly in yourself.

In the 'doer' syndrome, a person's self-esteem is so bound up with their professional or technical proficiency that they are unable on promotion to management to let go of doing those things that have always given them their psychological rewards. So they carry on doing what they were doing before promotion to management. If they were good at selling or at working with computers that is what they carry on doing. People are usually promoted because they are good at their job. But dabbling in one's previous job after promotion, however helpful one may believe this to be, is likely to be seen as interference by those being 'helped'. Such managers have to learn how to let go of doing these things and derive satisfaction instead from the things they have to do in their role as a manager.

'Imposters' seek to prove themselves either as a 'super-person' or, as an 'ugly duckling', they fail to appreciate that they are really swans.

'Godfathers' derive satisfaction from their control over people, either by dominating or looking after them.

'Napoleons' are driven by a sense of low self-esteem so strong that it could be regarded as an inferiority complex. But, unlike godfathers, they have no concern to be liked by the people they control, and thus lack the redeeming feature of caring for others.

The 'salesperson' syndrome takes its name from Arthur Miller's play, *Death of a Salesman*, in which the principal character is obsessed with being liked and hence is continually driven to please others.

The 'Hamlet' syndrome, even without knowing the play, should be self-explanatory from the brief description in the Box. Robert Johnson (1991) has described Hamlet as a forerunner of the 'modern, worrying, anxious man'. He 'makes chaos and failure of everything he touches'. Johnson quotes R.H. Blyth:

> Hamlet is the Zen-less man, whose energy, like a mouse in a wheel, goes round and round inside him and issues, not in action, but in talking.

Johnson comments that Hamlet is:

> . . . wise enough to see but not strong enough to accomplish. He is caught between vision and practicality and fails in both regards. In this he is the prototype of so many modern men who see a noble world in their imaginations but don't have the means to accomplish it.

Recognizing need-driven behaviour

Possible practical consequences that can result when managers adopt any of the syndromes depicted in Box 2.5. are presented in Box 2.6. You may recognize some of the foregoing syndromes and their symptoms in managers you know, for example a manager who:

- Seems incapable of delegating (a need to control or a failure of self-esteem).
- Does not confront people who are failing to deliver (a need to be liked or lack of an adequate need to control).

Box 2.6

Practical symptoms of failure to manage inner needs

- Tendency to emphasize own performance:
  - At expense of supervising, managing or leading;
  - By failing to delegate tasks or decision-making responsibility;
  - By surrounding oneself with people less interpersonally skilled or less technically competent than oneself;
  - By competing for the position of expert or technical guru;
  - By ensuring that one's own performance gets recognized and failing to give recognition to that of others.
- Tendency to avoid rather than deal with conflict.
- Inability or unwillingness to make decisions.
- Inability to deal with the ambiguous nature of the managerial role.
- Desire to be recognized as a powerful person.

Adapted from: Flamholtz and Randle (1989: 174–175).

- Seems incapable of refraining from offering criticism at every opportunity (the need to attack).
- Never acts without first checking out whether they are likely to meet with approval (a need to be liked or a need to be dependent).

It is important to note the alternative interpretations in the brackets above of what the driving need might be. There could be more. It is unwise to jump to a conclusion about someone's inner motives on the basis of their observed behaviour alone. You need corroborating evidence from their own insights into what drives them.

Similarly, in the case of your own self-observations you need to reflect on what is really going on inside and not mislead yourself by imposing some facile, but comfortable interpretation on your behaviour.

Certain patterns of behaviour become important supports to our ego; we can then be disinclined to admit to them even to ourselves, let alone be willing to modify them although we can see they may be counter-productive. Sometimes too, when we feel that we are being successful enough as we are, we may feel disinclined to enquire too closely into what is going on inside lest self-consciousness undermines one's creative and constructive driving forces.

Emotions

 The last of the four driving forces are our emotions. These can be both a glue which keeps us stuck and a solvent which enables us to create and commit ourselves to do new things.

Feelings and emotions are so closely related as often to be treated as synonymous. An emotion is defined by the *Oxford English Dictionary* as 'a strong feeling', and a feeling, among other definitions, as 'an intense emotion'.

In terms of the Myers–Briggs and Jungian model of preferences in Figure 2.2, feeling is the ability to value: to see things as good or bad, liked or disliked, attractive or unattractive. An emotion, by contrast, is a physical or psychological sensation, which can be pleasurable, such as excitement, joy or love; or upsetting or disturbing, such as sadness, anger or fear.

It is our anticipation of the emotional effects that future events will have on us – people we expect to encounter, actions that we know we will have to take, issues we shall have to confront – which drives us in certain directions and makes us avoid others. When there is a discrepancy between the experience we have intended for ourselves and what is actually happening, or that we believe will happen, we experience those visceral or other physical sensations known as emotions.

A trait often cited as needed by managers is 'emotional resilience'. By this seems to be meant the ability to withstand one's emotions, not to allow oneself to be unduly upset by them, and not to be deterred from action by the anticipation of unpleasant emotion.

Displaying resilience is one way we might deal with our emotions. It is not necessarily the most appropriate way. It is particularly difficult for women who want to retain their femininity as a manager and not appear hardened. For a sensitive man too, suppressing display of emotions can produce inner stress. Resilience may lead to suppression of emotions which could, if expressed, be a valuable driving or influential force.

The expression of emotion can be constructive. Indeed, the experience of being upset or disturbed can often be an indicator that one has embarked on a process of learning.

There are strong inhibitions in Western society about expressing emotions in any public situation. At work we are expected to keep a tight rein on our emotions. Expression of positive emotion, for example elation over an achievement, can sometimes be acceptable. But expression of what are regarded as negative emotions, for example fear or anger, is not normally acceptable. Nevertheless, letting people know how you feel can be a powerful way of getting them to take notice and give attention to your concerns. I am not suggesting that you let your emotions all hang out. But the controlled and directed expression of emotion may on occasion be an appropriate and effective way of communicating.

It is certainly important to be aware of one's emotions, and know how they are affecting one's behaviour. It is also important to know how to let go of or work through an emotion which may be blocking you from action. This is not always easy. We all too often allow negative emotions to fester, and allow their significance to grow, rather than become more predisposed with time to let go of them.

An emotion can be an especially negative force if you allow it to attach you to a particular viewpoint, perception or stance. Changing a perception or belief, even in the face of irrefutable contradictory evidence, may then be resisted.

When a shift of view demands the acceptance of critical feedback, it is understandable that it be met with resistance or denial; blame for failure laid elsewhere. More curious perhaps is the case of people with a poor self-image who respond to positive feedback with denial of its validity, attributing their success to luck or the efforts of others. Or even denying that there has been a success. Emotional attachments to feeling not okay can sometimes be very powerful.

The attachment may serve an inner need to hold this negative self-image. But it is often possible for a person to move forward simply by letting go of a belief or perception that has lost whatever usefulness it once may have had, although this is easier said than done.

One theory of the cause of emotion is that it is triggered by discrepancy. Thus, people may have an emotional reaction when confronted with feedback or evidence that contradicts their self-image. A step in the process of personal development is to recognize this emotion and accept it. Doing so can have quite transforming effects on your perception of who you are.

An effective person

If effective action is unique for each individual manager, *being* effective is even more so. The first part of this chapter set out a range of views of what goes into personal effectiveness. But as with effective action you have to work out for yourself what comprises being effective for you.

Essentially you need to be able to manage yourself in such a way that your behaviour corresponds with your intentions. The dynamics of this process has been the subject of the second part of the chapter. Approaching the process of personal self-management via the four driving forces described above should help you break it into manageable parts.

In reality, of course, these driving forces are not as separate as implied. You do not just bring your behavioural preferences, perceptions, needs and emotions together, add your personal qualities, and perform as an effective manager. There has to be an integrative process. Each individual, whether consciously or unconsciously, has to reconcile these forces, not just intellectually but psychologically, so that he or she may function effectively. Acting from the position of a complete, integrated person is fundamental to being effective.

Being yourself

A key element in a manager's development has to be to find an appropriate fit between his or her 'self' and what it is he or she has to do as a manager. This may seem so obvious as to be trite. Nevertheless managers, at least on initially becoming a manager, do seem to worry about whether it is okay to be themselves in their new role. They may even put on an act, culled from popular images of how a manager should behave, which they may not be comfortable with but which they believe is expected of them. Managers can have enough difficulties preventing their ego from interfering with their effectiveness without additionally taking on board what might be called a 'normative ego'.

There is another aspect to being true to yourself that goes somewhat deeper than adherence to values or principles. It is about doing things in a way that is consistent with your personality, about not losing sight of the kind of person you are. You may appear chameleon-like on the surface, presenting different facets of yourself to different people for different occasions; you may change your stance on issues, adapt your opinions, compromise, change your mind. But you should be able to do all this without being 'phoney'. But if you behave phonily, out of character and out of touch with yourself, I do not see how you could be said to be managing effectively.

Even managers who are mature and wise enough not to be tempted into putting on any act can nevertheless be anxious lest they are not doing 'the right thing'. If they have not had any management training they may believe that there must be something missing, something that is less than professional in their managing.

Introspection

How well or otherwise you manage, the fit between your self and your managing will be very much affected by your skill in managing the different aspects of the inner self described above. Introverted people are more likely to be aware of their psychological processes than extroverts. Yet both types risk being unwittingly incompetent if they do not engage in some introspection.

There are now a growing number of management courses where participants are encouraged to be introspective. Outdoor exercises, role plays, diagnostic questionnaires, management games are among the devices used for highlighting how you behave and think, and to encourage self-reflection.

This process can sometimes seem intrusive, prying into your psyche, perhaps provoking realizations that trigger an upsetting or disturbing emotional response. It is therefore only appropriate to invite this kind of self-searching when managers have explicitly signed up for a process of personal exploration. It is not suggested that this book is going to provoke you to an emotional response. But episodes in the course of your experience of managing may well do so. As a manager you have signed up for that possibility.

Developing

Personal change can be said to have taken place when new self-knowledge is combined with the ability to act upon it or, vice-versa, a new level of capability or performance is coupled with appreciation of its significance. Either way we are talking about both insight and action as ingredients of personal growth.

This kind of self-development may be contrasted with the kind of development that you derive from vocational or general education aimed at enhancing knowledge, understanding and analytical capabilities. Or with the development that comes from practical training in job competences such as team working, delegating, negotiating, or communicating.

Developing your 'self' is about fitting yourself to be able to manage all the different kinds of situations you encounter in your life and work. It involves:

- Knowing yourself and being aware of your behaviour and its effects;
- Seeing things differently and feeling differently;
- Learning to adapt to different roles and expectations;
- Evolving your attitudes and your values in the light of your self-knowledge and experience; and
- Being able to use your versatility and self-knowledge in practical accomplishments.

Reflection and action points

- Use the concepts and models in this chapter to draw an honest portrait of yourself. What does this tell you about your development needs?
- How far does your actual behaviour as a manager match your desired self-image? A trusted friend or mentor may be helpful to you getting to the truth on this matter.
- Review your skills in managing your psychological processes:
  - Emotions: do you suppress them or do you harness them – use them to create energy and drive?
  - Perceptions and beliefs: do you validate them or act on misplaced beliefs?
  - Preferences: do you confine yourself to preferred behaviours or have you extended your repertoire?

- Needs and motives: how conscious are you of how they drive you and do you succeed in managing them?
- Traits and qualities: how well do you draw on your strengths and compensate for your less strong points?

- In doing the foregoing tasks, did you gain any fresh insight? If not, do you feel the need to do so? What will you do to get it?

Part Two
A Developmental Experience

Fare forward, you who think you are voyaging;
You are not those who saw the harbour
Receding or those who will disembark.
Here between the hither and farther shore
While time is withdrawn, consider the future
And the past with an equal mind . . .

T.S. Eliot: *Four Quartets*

Personal transformation report 2

Achieving effectiveness through becoming a 'time maker'

A hospital's bed manager is at the focal point of its operations. All requests for admission are made through the bed manager who is contacted via the bleep system.

The role is one in which sudden, unexpected events can require immediate decisions and rapid action. One process may be interrupted by one of greater priority and the bed manager has to keep a number of issues in play together.

I was appointed to the position of Bed Manager within a large National Health Service hospital with 450 beds just over two years ago. This was a recently created, nursing-grade post. The purpose of my job is to ensure that the hospital's bed stock is managed efficiently and effectively. All admissions to the hospital, both emergency and elective, are coordinated by me.

My workload can be quite unpredictable and cannot be subjected to any set routine. The consequence of this is that I find it most difficult to manage my time at work effectively. Operational demands leave little time during working hours to plan and prepare work-related projects, and prepare for meetings and general administration.

My project

I decided therefore for my project on the Effective Management course to see whether a way could be found of organizing the work so that I did not have to spend my personal time on these matters. Within the 3-month time scale allowed my aims were to:

1 Determine the amount of time spent on various activities at work through an activity analysis, identifying in particular the time taken up by bleeper related activity.
2 As a result decide where changes need to be made.
3 Determine where blocks of time could be allocated to carry out work-related projects and meetings.

My long-term aim is to facilitate change by making better use of my time at work. Improved time management would prevent arrears of work accumulating and would assist in the planning of my workload within the constraints of the unpredictable demands. This in turn, I hope, will lead to increased personal efficiency and enhanced job satisfaction.

Starting point

I set off to keep a diary for one week of how I spent my time at work. In fact I found myself under such operational pressures that I did not even have time to do this fully!

In the end I summarized the number of admission requests I had had to deal with from my daily paperwork, and counted the number of times I was bleeped, which varied between nineteen and seventy times a day. But my sketchy activity analysis did highlight the proportion of my time spent on ancillary, non-professional   duties, which could perhaps be delegated, reduced or done differently.

The management action I took as a result of my analysis was that I:

- Encouraged nursing staff in the Accident and Emergency Department to streamline their requests for admission
- Argued the case for trialling a daily one-hour 'bleep-free' period, as the medical staff already had, to allow time free of interruptions for work-related projects
- Started to 'educate' the switchboard to direct patient enquiries for admission to the appropriate admission clerk thus avoiding misuse of my time
- Set about organizing project meetings for Fridays when there were fewer elective admissions to deal with
- Made the case for my filing and similar ancillary duties to be delegated to secretarial support.

Personal outcomes

The ultimate purpose of this project was to plan and implement some change in what I did at work that would improve my managerial effectiveness. I have experienced both practical and personal learning while doing it. I have learnt more about how my work functions and how it affects me. I have learnt about myself and how I need to change in order to be more effective as a manager. This was partly a matter of time management, but I also learned from the actual experience of the project itself.

Following the 'purpose–action–accomplishment cycle' described in Figure 1.1 of this book, I started off with a simple idea for action – to keep a diary for a week. The experience of working through the whole cycle has certainly evoked new skills and understandings. It has given me a greater under-standing of my present workload and has enabled me to see the picture as a whole. It has made me realize that my own perceptions and beliefs can distort the picture. For example, I initially felt that I did not have time to prepare projects within my working day. Through my explorations, however, I have identified ways to achieve this.

The project also highlighted that my preference previously was to pursue comfortable rather than effective behaviours. For example, it was easier to work on projects after hours as I would not then be interrupted, and to do my own filing as this would be easier to do myself. Thus my need for 'comfort' may have been causing me to do things that were counter-productive.

Doing the project gave me a sense of commitment which carried me through from initiating it in the first place, not just to its immediate completion, but beyond that to setting new directions for future tasks and projects at work. This, along with what I feel to be my greater personal efficiency, will, I believe, enhance my working relationships with colleagues and help me to adapt when I encounter different situations.

3   Managing and leading

Introduction

'Leading' is a concept that is hedged about with a considerable amount of mystique. Leadership qualities are often thought of as something you either have or do not have. There have been attempts to look at leadership in other ways, for example as a function of the task or situation, but these approaches can still leave managers bemused as to whether they have what it takes to 'lead' in their particular circumstances. The purpose of this chapter is to show how leading can be a feasible activity for any manager.

The chapter starts by suggesting that much managerial leadership is not something special or extraordinary, but something that a manager can do quite naturally in the course of carrying out a project. It then looks at the kind of attitudes that you may need to have in order to lead, and the distinctive approach some women managers are taking to leading.

Alleged differences between 'managing' and 'leading' are examined, and the distinction shown to be artificial. Leading follows whenever managers pursue new initiatives. Initiative, and hence leadership, can be displayed in a wide variety of management contexts.

The chapter then takes a look at so-called 'charismatic' leadership to see how this too can be translated into everyday activities that a manager can do. The skills of 'intrapreneuring' are also reviewed to show how managers can best go about pursuing their initiatives in an organizational context.

The chapter concludes where it began, by emphasizing that leadership, although it involves practical skills, is in the last resort a matter of attitude. You have to want to do it.

Leading your projects

Only when you have an achievement that you can look back on can you be truly certain that you have managed effectively. To achieve something demands undertaking a task – a project – even though it may not be formally defined as such. The notion of a 'project' can be applied to virtually anything we do that has a purpose and results in an outcome. In this sense, washing up can be thought of as a project, driving to work is a project. At work, we in effect embark on a new project every time we decide on our next task and get started on it. Managers undertake projects all the time. Whether we define what we are doing literally as a 'project' is immaterial. What counts is working towards an outcome and achieving it.

To be in charge of a project and see it through from beginning to end will not just give you practice in managing effectively. It will also, inevitably, involve you in 'leading'.

Attitude of leadership

Although leading is in large part doing, it also demands a certain way of thinking, a certain attitude to the world. Warren Bennis, on the basis of interviews with 'great' leaders, has characterized this attitude of mind in terms of four dimensions:

- Guiding vision,
- Passion,
- Integrity, and
- Curiosity and daring.

What Bennis means by these terms is set out in Box 3.1. You may feel that Bennis' vignette of a leader's state of mind does not encapsulate exactly the kind of attitudes you need or wish to cultivate for yourself. The point, however, is that you do need to think differently if you are to create and see through new projects rather than remain an implementer of directives and instructions.

Women and men's styles

A survey by Judy Rosener (1990) has compared women's and men's styles of leadership. Her findings suggest that women

---

Box 3.1

Attitudinal ingredients of leadership

- Guiding vision
  - Clear idea of what he/she wants to do – professionally and personally, and strength to persist in face of setbacks, even failure.

- Passion
  - For the promises of life, vocation, profession, a course of action.
  - Loves what he/she does and loves doing it.

- Integrity – the basis of trust
  - Self-knowledge: candour with self.
  - Candour: honesty of thought and action, steadfast devotion to principle, wholeness, soundness.
  - Maturity: learning to be dedicated, observant, capable of working with and learning from others, never servile, always truthful. Locates these qualities in self, then encourages them in others.

- Curiosity and daring
  - Wonders about everything, wants to learn as much as he/she can, willing to take risks, experiment, try new things.
  - Does not worry about failure. Learns from adversity.

Adapted from Bennis (1989: 39–41).

---

may naturally lean towards using a 'transformational' style of leadership and men a 'transactional' style.

By the latter is meant that the manager or leader sees getting people to do things as a matter of effecting 'transactions'. Rewards are given for services rendered and sanctions used to penalize poor performance. Deals may be struck. Transformational leaders, on the other hand, work to change the attitudes of the people they wish to influence, getting them to 'transform' their immediate self-interest and concern themselves with the wider common good.

The women in Rosener's survey tended to cultivate participative methods of influence and sought to share power. But,

Rosener observed, their self-description of their leadership style went beyond the usual definitions of participation:

> Much of what they described were attempts to enhance other people's sense of self-worth and to energize followers. In general, these leaders believe that people perform best when they feel good about themselves and their work, and they try to create situations that contribute to that feeling.

The interesting point, however, about Rosener's conclusions is not that women and men necessarily lead in different ways, but that women's success in using a 'transformational' style of leadership is pointing the way to a revision of traditional definitions of effective leadership.

This very much accords with the emphasis in the previous chapter on not allowing oneself to be locked into one's natural preferences. While many men may be more at home with a traditional style of transactional leadership, there is no reason why they should not experiment with alternative styles that women have been showing to work effectively.

Managers who lead

Certain writers on leadership draw an invidious distinction between managing and leading. Leading is presented as the heroic role; with mere managing to be left to the administrative hacks. Whether this distinction was ever valid is questionable. Certainly it can have scant validity today when managers at all levels – and often non-managers too – are expected to initiate improvements in operations or service and lead projects and teams to bring them about. Both Henry Mintzberg and Tom Peters, two researchers who can claim to know more than most about what managers do, find the distinction between managing and leading artificial, even odd.

The objective of this part of the chapter is to set managing and leading, proactivity and reactivity, in context so that you can discern how you might best utilize a project to develop yourself in all these aspects of managing effectively.

Project leadership may not, by some definitions, be regarded as 'true' leadership. But it certainly demands many of the qualities typically associated with leadership – imagination and vision, tenacity and often audacity, to say nothing of influencing and personal skills.

Bennis, whose conclusions on the attitudes of a leader are reported in Box 3.1, belongs to the school that sees a distinction between the roles of managers and leaders. As can be seen from his depiction of the distinction, presented in Box 3.2, virtually all of the leadership activities he lists could be covered in the course of managing a project.

Willingness to take an initiative, or to take on board someone else's initiative and see it through as if it were your

---

Box 3.2

Alleged differences between a manager and a leader

Manager	Leader
Administers	Innovates
A copy	An original
Maintains	Develops
Focuses on systems and structure	Focuses on people
Relies on control	Inspires trust
Has a short range view	Has a long range perspective
Asks how and when	Asks what and why
Has his or her eye always on the bottom line	Has his or her eye on the horizon
Imitates	Originates
Accepts the status quo	Challenges the status quo
Is the good, classic deliverer	Is his or her own person
Does things right	Does the right things

Taken from: Bennis (1989: 45).

own, demands a certain attitude or approach to managing, which can be summed up as being prepared to act 'proactively' or creatively – as opposed to solely 'reactively'. Box 3.3 sets out a comparison of the way these two are reflected in styles of managing.

'Proactivity' and 'reactivity' are again two terms much bandied about in contemporary management writings, usually with the implication that, like managing and leading, a reactive manager is somehow inferior to a proactive one.

In their introduction to the book *Transforming Leadership* (1986), John Adams and Sabina Spencer have argued that a manager has to be adept in each style. Both reactivity and proactivity are needed for effective managing:

> . . . there is nothing fundamentally wrong with a reactive style. On the contrary, we would argue that this way of thinking is necessary in today's world and that it would be foolhardy to rebel against it. It is so characteristic of management today in most parts of the world that we could also suggest that it forms the basis for the majority of managerial operating premises. Quick problem-solving, maintaining the status quo, operating rationally, and taking corrective actions are part and parcel of what management is about. We need to 'mind the store' on a day-to-day basis and be responsive to shifting conditions around us.

But managers also need to be able to rise above the pressures that keep them perpetually reacting to events: the need to keep the workflow flowing, respond to instructions and requests, attend meetings, and deal with the myriad of other events and problems that conspire to exclude proactive initiatives from managers' agendas.

Similarly, managers of small businesses, where 'minding the store' can become all-consuming, cannot afford to be solely reactive, but must be continually proactive in attending to the long-term future of their company.

In large organizations, however, it might be possible for managers in middle and lower echelons to remain preoccupied with reactive agendas. But this may be less feasible today in a corporate world undergoing continual change.

Moreover, there is a new ethos emerging, reflected in management development programmes, which emphasizes

Box 3.3

Managerial operating styles

Reactive		**Pro-active/creative**
Work to others' goals	*vs*	Envisage your desired outcomes
Assume constraints on action		Assume no limitations on what is possible
Think logically within the parameters of a logical framework		Use intuitive inspiration (though checked out through investigation and analysis)
React to situations as they occur		Anticipate trends and tendencies and adopt preventative stance
Dwell on the lessons from the past		Emphasize desired future
Rely on authority or 'the system' to get things done		Catalyse energy towards making the future happen
See the organization as fragmented with incoherent parts (a tactical perspective)		See the organization holistically and understand the relation of its many different parts (a systematic perspective)
Staying stuck in the belief that one cannot change one's self		Expanding one's horizons in the belief that one can grow and develop
Allow one's self to be victim of (organizational) circumstances in the belief that you cannot make a difference		Actively shape one's (organizational) environment in the belief that one can make a difference
Feeling of lack of control both over the environment and one's responses to it ('it/they are to blame')		Sense of personal mastery over events coupled with a very high degree of self or inner control ('I am responsible')

Adapted from: Adams and Spencer (1986) and from their Organizational Transformation Workshop, Brunel University, 1987.

creativity and initiative, and the management of one's time to make this possible. Proactivity is seen as a critical dimension in any human being's ability to be in charge of their life, to give it the direction they want, and to shape their own destiny.

A state of consciousness

Robert Fritz is one of the most forceful exponents of this viewpoint, though the word he uses is not proactivity but 'creativity' which he contrasts with the 'responsive–reactive' orientation. The difference between the two orientations are highlighted in Box 3.4 by means of selected quotations from Fritz's book *The Path of Least Resistance* (1989).

A creative orientation has to be cultivated by altering one's attitudes, one's 'state of consciousness'. The responsive–reactive orientation is more clearly characterized by the quotations in Box 3.4 than is the creative orientation. The outcomes of being creative are infinitely diverse and cannot be so readily pinned down into a brief caricature. Creative thinking emanates from a different state of mind to that which produces reactive thinking. The creative thinker has a different way of perceiving the world.

Adams and Spencer associate the reactive mode of thinking with 'managing' and creativity with 'leading'. They emphasize, however, that the same individual may both manage and lead:

> While it is the manager's responsibility to direct, control, and maintain his or her part of the organization, it is the leader who expands, crosses boundaries, innovates, and brings about changes in how the organization operates. Since these are . . . states of mind, anyone, including formal managers, can choose to adopt a creative perspective at any time.

Leadership opportunities for managers

Opportunities for leading in the management of projects are depicted in Figure 3.1. The vertical axis in the diagram

Box 3.4

Reactive and creative states of mind

The reactive-responsive orientation

> One way or another, *most* people believe circumstances are the driving force in their life.

> When circumstances are central to your life, you may feel you have only two types of choices: either to *respond* to the circumstances or to *react* against the circumstances. You can be either the 'fair-haired boy' or the 'last angry man'.

> Reacting or responding is more than just a policy of how to live your life. It becomes a way of life, a life orientation. I call this the *reactive-responsive orientation*. In this orientation you take action based on the circumstances in which you find yourself, or might find yourself in the future . . .

> Instead of responding to circumstances, some people rebelliously oppose society's version of how life is portrayed . . .

> If you are reactive, you also believe that circumstances are the driving force of life. But you believe that circumstances are not necessarily the way society presents them.

> Reactive behaviour may take the form of cynicism, or you may have a chronic chip on your shoulder . . . You may hold conspiracy theories about people in power or subscribe to a political or religious philosophy that reacts against injustice or evil. (pp. 18–19)

The creative response

> Creating is completely different from reacting or responding to the circumstances you are in. The process of creating is generated . . . by the creation itself. (p. 48)

> . . . life as a creator is . . . hard to describe to a person in the reactive-responsive orientation. Not only are the same events understood differently, but the possibilities and actualities of life are completely different.

> A creator creates in order to bring the creation into being. People in the reactive-responsive mode often have trouble understanding this sensibility: to create for the sake of the creation itself. Not for the praise, not for the 'return on investment', not for what it may say about you, *but for its own sake*. (pp. 57–8)

Extracted from: Fritz (1989). Quoted with permission of the author.

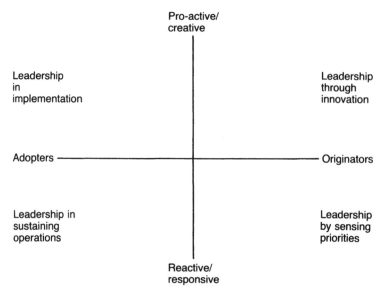

Figure 3.1 Types of leadership in managing

represents one's tendency to be proactive or reactive, while the horizontal axis whether or not one is the originator of one's project or has adopted someone else's idea. The purpose of the diagram is to illustrate the point that with the application of creativity, a manager can exercise leadership functions from any of the cells.

The top right hand cell in Figure 3.1, 'leadership through innovation', represents what is probably most usually regarded as 'leadership': the proactive, creative initiation of change.

Lest it be thought that proactive origination is invariably a state one should aspire to, it should be borne in mind that it can have a less desirable side. Proactive origination can provide the wellspring for aggression or the leading of 'political' attacks.

Reactive managers, however, can also lead. As originators (bottom right-hand cell) they are the people who keep in touch with the environment, stay close to the customers, watch the quality, monitor the efficiency of operations. They exercise leadership by sensing priorities. They are defenders and leaders of counter-attacks.

The notion of a reactive adopter (bottom left-hand cell) being a leader might seem a contradiction in terms. But day-to-day 'minding the store' can call for the exercise of creativity in ensuring that operations run smoothly, that crises are handled, that staff stay motivated, that quality service is delivered. One can of course debate whether it is legitimate to classify creativity in sustaining the operations as leadership. But, whatever the name, there are opportunities in this cell for the display of imagination, creativity and flair, even though what you do may be disparaged as mere 'managing' as opposed to the more revered 'leading'.

Proactive adopters (top left-hand cell) exercise leadership in their implementation of other people's ideas. They are the people who can see the value in the germ of an idea, take it on board and work with it as if it were their own, give it form, develop and extend it, and lead it to an outcome that the originator may never have dreamed of.

The foregoing classification of leadership opportunities fits with John Kotter's view of effective leadership, which he sees as concerned with both constructive and adaptive change (Kotter, 1990). In either case, effective leadership:

> . . . moves people to a better place in which they and those who depend on them are genuinely better off, and . . . does so without trampling on the rights of others.

Kotter, incidentally, is another writer who draws a distinction between leading and managing.

Charismatic leadership

So far leadership has been presented as something you do rather than something you are. Charismatic leadership, in which the leader commands his or her followers by what seems to be force of personality, may fall outside this 'doing' or behavioural approach. On the other hand, there have been several attempts to describe charismatic leadership in behavioural terms.

Alan Bryman (1992), for example, has defined charismatic leadership as:

> . . . concerned with relationships between leaders and their followers in which, by virtue of both the extraordinary qualities that followers attribute to the leader and the latter's mission, the charismatic leader is regarded by his or her followers with a mixture of reverence, unflinching dedication and awe. (p. 41)

J. A. Conger and R. N. Kanungo (1988a), who describe charisma simply as 'an extraordinary talent for influence or leadership', question whether there is such a person as a 'pure' charismatic leader who could be charismatic in any circumstances. Charismatics observed by researchers, they conclude, have been observed to go about transforming a situation in a special way for which they are accorded the attribute of 'charisma'. Their summary of charismatic leaders' observable behaviour discerned by research is presented in Box 3.5.

If Conger and Kanungo's view of charismatic leadership is correct, then it is something that can be learned and practised. With a cautionary note, and not I suspect without tongue a little in cheek, they postulate the following five skill areas that someone would need to work on in order to develop her or himself as a charismatic leader (1988b: 313–319):

- Critical evaluation and problem detection and defining skills, in order that as leader you can:
  - be sensitive to crisis and serious problem situations, being more perceptive than others of deficiencies in the status quo;
  - use this time of transition to facilitate the emergence of your charisma, being prepared if necessary to formulate a crisis by actually searching out potential problems to use as a springboard.
- Visioning skills.
- Communication skills:
  - speech and articulation;
  - interpersonal sensitivity;
  - emotional expressiveness.

Box 3.5

What charismatic leaders do

Charismatic leaders have been observed to do the following things:

- Go with the flow; they move when the time and circumstances are right.
- Capitalize on potential followers' disenchantment or distress with the status quo; they may even induce this disenchantment.
- Act as reformers or agents of radical change.
- Promote a vision that is a radical alternative to the status quo, but attractive, acceptable and feasible.
- Lead through assertive behaviour, self-confidence, expertise, unconventionality, and concern for followers' needs.
- Be self-sacrificing, taking personal risks to achieve the shared vision.
- Use unconventional or extraordinary means.
- Engage in novel, unconventional and counter-normative behaviour.
- Use personal rather than position power.
- Exert this power through elitist, entrepreneurial and exemplary behaviour rather than through consensus-seeking and directive behaviour.

Adapted from: Conger and Kanungo (1988a: 92–93) by permission.

- Personal exemplary behaviour and impression management skills:
  - modelling;
  - appearance;
  - body language;
  - verbal (able to use rhetoric, metaphors, analogies).
- Empowering skills:
  - create conditions for heightened motivation through development of a strong sense of personal efficacy.

How far one might seek to develop these skills through a project must be left to your discretion. Conger and Kanungo believe these notions of charisma are probably too radical for a corporation to wish to build their prescriptions into an official training programme. But corporate conservatism should not deter an individual manager developing along these lines.

Intrapreneuring

Indeed, it is this kind of revolutionary bent that is at the heart of the much vaunted notion of 'intrapreneuring' – the notion that managers can lead commercial business initiatives from within their employing organization.

Rosabeth Moss Kanter, as a result of her research into managers' managing, has dramatically contrasted the things that 'innovating' and 'non-innovating' managers do. The way Kanter describes their roles suggests that the non-innovating managers had little or no experience that might have provided a developmental challenge:

> They repeat what is already known, though sometimes a little faster or better . . .

> The accomplishments nonentrepreneurial managers recount, for example, generally involve beating their own record, advancing their own careers, smoothing friction with subordinates, or adding incrementally to an ongoing process, rather than introducing anything, changing anything, or redirecting or reorienting their area. They rarely describe orientation to a specific goal, a drive toward concrete achievement or a tangible project . . . (1985: 213)

Kanter goes on to observe that she found the interviews with non-innovators 'dull and lifeless':

> They had little to say about what they had done; their achievements were modest, and there was no real story. (1985: 213)

Kanter attributed this to the lack of excitement in these managers' work:

Routine jobs, after all, lack the adventure associated with carrying out specific projects and watching results pile up – a clear 'something' where there was 'nothing', order out of chaos. There is none of the drama and even romance inherent in overcoming obstacles, in proving something, in jumping hurdles. (1985: 213)

The message is clear: a manager seeking to develop from everyday experience needs to bring some imagination to bear on what might otherwise be lifeless, stuck-in-the-rut activities.

George Pinchot III (1985) in his book on intrapreneuring has identified a number of characteristics of the in-house business person; summarized in Box 3.6.

Box 3.6

Characteristics of an intrapreneur

- More interested in making things work better than maintaining the way they are.
- Excited about what they are doing at work; think about their ideas outside work.
- Able to visualize concrete steps for action when they have an idea.
- Unconcerned about consequences of exceeding their authority.
- Work out realistic ideas for implementation rather than announce half-baked ideas.
- Able to push through bleak times when success seems remote.
- Attract an entourage of fans and critics.
- Attract a network of friends who can be counted upon for help.
- Annoyed when others incompetently attempt to implement portions of their ideas.
- Able to overcome natural perfectionist tendency to do all work themselves; able to share responsibility for ideas with a team.
- Would be willing to have part of salary linked to success in order to have opportunity to try out own ideas.

Adapted from: Pinchot (1985: 31).

'Freedom finders'

Pinchot goes on to specify ten 'freedom factors' which a corporation ought to cultivate if it wants to encourage intrapreneuring. Here, these ten factors are stood on their head and presented from the perspective of a middle manager who seeks to create freedom for himself or herself to take independent action within a corporation. The ten 'freedom finders' are:

- Put yourself and your ideas forward.
  If you wait to be asked or appointed to implement an innovation you may wait for ever.
- See it through.
  Stick with your idea until the very end. If you allow responsibility for implementing your idea to be handed over to someone else after you have initiated the first stages of action, you may find it has passed into the hands of people less committed to its success than you, its originator.
- Make your own decisions.
  Do not allow critical decisions to be made, or even approved if you can avoid it, by people higher up who do not appreciate what you are attempting or the issue involved.
- Find time and resources.
  Can you get approval for diverting some of your time? Can you get some budget earmarked as discretionary expenditure? Look for slack in the system.
- Go for modest aims.
  A small-scale project on a shoe-string budget may be the best way into finding freedom to innovate.
- Be prepared for false starts and mistakes.
  Experiment and take a few risks. Write off any failures to experience.
- Live with a long time-scale.
  This may mean having to ward off attempts to terminate your project because you have not got quick results. If you are thwarted initially, realize you can live to fight another day. You may have to accept being judged adversely because you have failed to deliver on deadlines or other targets that you were required to promise, however unrealistic.

- Be willing to encroach on other people's territory.
  Others may be more concerned with defending their patch than with supporting a new idea and you will have to find ways of dealing with such obstructiveness.
- Work across the functions.
  Build a team with the necessary skills and talents regardless of where in the organization they are located. Your team will need to share your vision and be willing to commit themselves to helping you realize it.
- Use the best services.
  You may be expected to use the organization's internal specialist services to support your project. But if the people concerned do not have the vision or skills to realize your aims, using their services may not serve your project well.

Your willingness to lead

Whether you are the originator or adopter of a project, an essential condition for enthusing others and carrying them with you, is your own conviction that the activity which you are leading is something that you want to see happen, one that you believe in fully. It is curious how advice to managers on how to generate the commitment of their staff always seems to take for granted that the managers themselves are committed. A crucial part of self-management is being able, first to generate, and then to keep renewed, your own motivation and enthusiasm.

It means too, however preoccupied you may be with 'minding the shop', cultivating the attitude of mind of a creative leader. You need to be able to move freely between the reactive and proactive modes of managing.

Your ability to develop from a project will only in part come from the way you design it in practical terms. Much of your scope for development will flow from the spirit with which you enter into it. The underlying purpose of this chapter has been to present the attitudinal possibilities.

How radical and innovative you want to be must of course be your choice in the light of what is appropriate in your circumstances and your aspirations. The point is that what you get out of doing your project will depend on the frame of mind with which you approach the action – hesitantly and diffidently, or adventurously and with commitment to change not just yourself but also a bit of the world around you.

Reflection points

- Review what 'leading' you do already. Would it now be appropriate for you to extend your leadership activities?
- Thinking about any new initiative you might be embarking on, what will be its 'managerial' and 'leadership' components? How do you feel about the leadership aspects? Are you ready to take them on? Will you?
- What do you need to do to develop your leadership skills, and your confidence in leading?
- When you have actually done something that has extended your leadership skills, reflect on how this has affected you as a person. How have you changed?

4   Creating a project

Introduction

Previous chapters have advocated using projects as a basis for development, in order to gain the comprehensive opportunities for development that come from seeing a project through from beginning to end. This chapter describes the process of identifying an actual project that you could use for this purpose. It deals in turn with:

- The pros and cons of originating an entirely new project of your own versus adopting someone else's idea;
- The creative process of searching for ideas;
- The steps and thought processes involved in originating a project;
- Linking your developmental project to your personal career aspirations;
- Crystallizing your ideas into a concrete proposal for action.

Many readers, who are not in a position to set up a special development project, or who do not wish to do so, will be using this book simply as an aid to learning from their experience of everyday management tasks. You should nevertheless find this chapter relevant to developing your creative ability to start up any new venture – a normal part of the management process if you are not to remain trapped in routine.

There are two aspects to creating a suitable developmental project. One is to do with starting up a new project, which is the subject of the present chapter. The second is to build features into your project that will enhance its developmental potential. That is the subject of Chapter 5.

Sources of ideas

One approach to finding a developmental project would be adopt one that you have to do anyhow as part of your job.

Perhaps a project that is currently low on your list of priorities may be suitable. In which case it is simply a matter of bringing it forward and tackling it now. On the other hand it may be the case that you have nothing that you feel is suitable on your present agenda. In which case you will need to identify a project from scratch.

Management students required to undertake development projects on courses that I tutor often press me to give them ideas as to what they might do. I usually resist this pressure, since I think that giving suggestions can create a mindset that is limiting. It is better, in my view, to face the challenge of inventing something to do completely for yourself. When I have succumbed to the pressure and supplied a list of selected past projects I have doubted that it has been of much help. They had to create their own project out of their own job and work environment. In the end there is no escaping having to discover for yourself what would be a worthwhile venture.

Adopting projects

You could of course ask your boss or a work colleague to suggest a project. That is acceptable, though it does mean of course that you lose the opportunity of originating an idea for yourself, which is an important part of the development of any manager who seeks to be proactive and lead. To have ideas, to be able to see what needs to be done, what problems need tackling, to develop a vision for future directions, is at the heart of managing effectively.

On the other hand, if you choose to adopt someone else's idea, you get to handle the challenge of taking it on board and working with it virtually as if it were your own. Being able to do this is also an important management skill; adapting Drucker's metaphor (Box 1.1), you do not have to be the originator of the idea of a cathedral in order to build it. Or indeed to have a mission to build it.

The choice of originating versus adopting a project may of course not be open to you. Junior managers in some organizations, or young managers at the outset of their career may not be allowed to take much initiative.

It is possible that something could be lost from a developmental point of view if the experiential learning process is not entirely self-directed. But this is more a matter of how the project is handled than to do with whether or not you are the originator of the idea.

Taking up a cause

An example that I like to quote to illustrate how someone can turn a project adopted from someone else's idea into a personal mission is that of the nineteenth-century pioneer of maritime safety, Samuel Plimsoll. When Plimsoll was first elected to Parliament for an inland midlands constituency, he had had no contact with seafaring and knew nothing about shipping matters. He simply had an aspiration to pursue a worthwhile cause. He at first spent some time pursuing the cause of pit-head safety at collieries until a chance conversation alerted him to the scandal of ships sinking through overloading. His life-time's pursuit of this cause parallels many of the points that will be made in this chapter.

In search of a project, Plimsoll experimented with possibilities. His false starts eventually led him to a cause he could identify with. His commitment to it grew from his progressive involvement. Critics claimed that his motive was less safety at sea than making a name for himself. This he certainly succeeded in doing – ships today are still painted on their sides with a Plimsoll Line to mark how deeply they may be loaded. But whether his ultimate motive was to be of service or self-aggrandizement is largely irrelevant. What he did was to achieve something on the basis of an idea that was given to him. He succeeded, by whatever means, in gearing his motivation towards his purposes, which is what managers have to do all the time.

Perhaps this example may seem far removed from the world of management in the 1990s. I do not think so. I believe it dramatizes exactly what a contemporary manager has to do to be effective. Today's causes include: the pursuit of excellence, total quality, continual improvement, superb customer service, and empowering staff. Professionalism in management is to be able to take on board appropriate contemporary causes and make them your own – to do a good job regardless of whether you or someone else is the originator of the idea to be pursued.

Originating

The most fruitful phase for learning about yourself, and assessing your confidence in your capabilities, can be at this initial creative point of identifying a project. This is the time when you can make decisions that are largely determined by your own inclinations. Although your choices will be constrained by circumstances, what you do at this stage will reflect your particular interests and purposes, your beliefs and feelings, and self-confidence. Even if you are adopting someone else's idea for what you do, the resulting project will inevitably be your own production.

Reflection on this process can reveal how you perceive your strengths and limitations. You will probably be aware of many of the factors that lead you to shape your venture the way you do; some you will be less aware of. Critical self-reflection on your choices at a later stage may be necessary to bring these less conscious influences to light.

Ideas for projects do not normally spring fully fledged out of the air, nor for that matter out of one's head. They emerge – usually gradually, but occasionally in a flash – from prior thinking about the topic, problem or area. There is no such thing as originating an idea from a clean slate; you always start from somewhere.

It is a mistake to think of the process of creating a project in linear terms: first you have the idea, then you work out the idea in terms that can be actioned, then you plan the implementation stage, and so on. The creative process is usually a fairly jumbled one, with steps in the seeming logical sequence occurring simultaneously or in reverse order, and many iterations between steps.

Identifying ideas or problems for action is so much part and parcel of any manager's job that it is easy to take the creative process for granted. Alternatively, when confronted with the need to develop more ambitious or complex ideas, one may fear that one is not up to being creative at this level. You think that the creative process must involve more than what you are doing. The remainder of this chapter is intended to help you bring this creative originating process into consciousness, and hence enable you to have greater control over it.

Being creative

Producing and developing new ideas does not hinge on you being a 'creative person' whatever that may mean – popular images of the creative artist or writer tend to surround the creative process with a great deal of mystique. Inspiration, like lightning, may strike; but while waiting it is more fruitful to get on with the job of generating your own electricity. It is this practical side that current books on creativity largely focus on.

Roger Evans and Peter Russell (1990) have most usefully dissected creativity into a number of actions while at the same time not losing sight of the need to draw on one's intuition and allow unconscious processes to work for you. A summary of their guidelines for 'being creative' is presented in Box 4.1.

Another angle on steering yourself through the creative process is to be aware of the different types of creativity. A classification by Alison Hardingham is presented in Box 4.2. It is interesting to note that she disposes of so-called 'pure' creativity as a fiction.

Exploratory and normative creativity

Simon Majaro (1992), in a wide-ranging book on harnessing creativity to business ends, sees creativity as dividing into two broad types:

• Exploratory, and
• Normative.

Exploratory creativity is where ideas are generated to develop future opportunities. One is trying to extrapolate from present-day knowledge and technology towards some

Box 4.1

The process of creative action

- Take time for preparation;
  - Obtain new information;
  - Work hard with the conscious mind;
  - Don't go too quickly for a solution; spend enough time defining and redefining your problem;
  - Spend time questioning your assumptions; and
  - Avoid impatience and premature closure; explore issue to depth required before moving to working out phase.

- Recognize and accept frustration as part of the creative process:
  - Listen to what is trying to come through;
  - Talk to someone about your feelings;
  - Don't push on hoping you can break through; take a break; think about something else for a while;
  - Don't take it out on others;
  - Don't believe you are not up to the task;
  - Don't give up.

- Allow time for incubation and insight:
  - Notice in what situations insights tend to come to you; don't dismiss them.

- Listen to your unconscious (especially in sleep and dreams):
  - Open yourself to the mystery behind the creative process.

- Trust yourself, your ideas and insights:
  - Don't look for security in the past or in techniques.

- Work out idea or insight in the following form:
  Stage One: Test the insight
  - Will it work? Will it satisfy the original requirements? Is it really the answer? How will it look in practice?
  Stage Two: Implementation
  - Plan and organize in detail. Carry through your ideas. Monitor and get feedback. Be prepared to re-enter the creative loops as you deal with all the problems and issues this stage throws up.

- Learn from the process as a whole.

Adapted from: Evans and Russell (1990: Chapter 3) by permission.

Box 4.2

Types of creativity

- Pure or 'true' creativity:
  - This is when you create something out of absolutely nothing. Apart from the alleged creation of the world in seven days, this kind of creativity has probably never occurred. It is a myth.

- Linking creativity:
  - New connections made between two or more existing practices, concepts, objects, people. For example, choosing the mix for a new team in a way that creates synergy.
  - Seeing new possibilities, for example how an established method could be used in a new context.

- Reconciling or transformational creativity:
  - Using the opportunity or energy generated by conflict (for example between people, goals, ideas) to create an innovative solution. The solution reconciles or transcends the conflict. This is an extension of linking creativity.

- Extending or building creativity:
  - This creativity takes other people's ideas and gives them shape and form, ensures they have impact.

- Craziness creativity:
  - This is the kind of creativity that gets people out of their rut. It uses humour, playfulness, breaking of rules. People who play the clown at meetings, make irreverent comments, may well be stimulating craziness creativity.

Adapted from: Hardingham, A. (1992). *Making Change Work for You.* Sheldon Press by permission of the publisher, SPCK.

---

futuristic scenario. You are not necessarily tied to known requirements or current demands, though these could be taken into account and your explorations could include a search for problems which ought to be dealt with. Success criteria in exploratory creativity are to do with, as Majaro puts it, 'breaking the mould of present day thinking and identifying unorthodox opportunities'.

If one were to attempt to use techniques for idea generation in exploratory creativity, they would need to be relatively unstructured, for example free-ranging brain-storming sessions, 'scenario' writing, even simple daydreaming, and what Majaro calls 'creativity circles' – building networks to identify and develop ideas.

Normative creativity, by contrast, is the process of applying your thinking towards the solving of a problem. It is 'normative' in the sense that the creativity is in response to a defined goal, need, desire or mission. You know there is a problem because you are aware of some deviation occurring between what is actually happening and what ought to be happening. Majaro suggests that this type of creativity could equally well be called 'creativity by objectives'. The measure of success is that the problem is solved or the innovation attained.

The key to success in normative creativity lies in the identification of the precise nature and causes of the problem. You know what the deviation is; it is a matter of discovering how to determine its cause and take the corrective action. The creative action needed will lead you down the well-trodden path of collecting data, analysis, diagnosis of causes until eventually you are in a position to generate ideas for solution.

Although the steps involved in normative creativity are likely to follow a fairly standard pattern, many points in the process demand an imaginative input. But because the normative creative process is usually well structured, it is possible, Majaro suggests, to utilize structured idea generation techniques, for example brain-storming sessions. He also lists 'quality circles' as among the structured techniques appropriate for use in this context.

To summarize the differences between these two modes of creativity, in normative creativity idea generation is focused on a defined problem. It is results oriented. In exploratory creativity, by contrast, the idea generation process is directed outward towards a 'futuristic dream world with the hope of striking gold at the end of the cycle'.

Serendipity

There is a third type of creativity, which probably all readers are familiar with, which cuts across both normative and exploratory creativity. This is serendipity, when one stumbles across a new idea seemingly by chance.

Serendip was the former name of Sri Lanka. The word 'serendipity', according to the *Oxford English Dictionary*, was 'formed by Horace Walpole upon the title of the fairy-tale The Three Princes of Serendip, the heroes of which "were always making discoveries, by accidents and sagacity, of things they were not in quest of"'. Its meaning is defined as 'the faculty of making happy and unexpected discoveries by accident'. Archimedes' discovery in his bath of the principle of the displacement of water and then running naked through the streets of ancient Syracuse shouting 'Eureka' ('I have it') is often cited as an example of discovery by serendipity.

By definition the operation of serendipity happens by chance. But serendipitous discoveries are probably not entirely accidental. As one researcher once wrote in defence of another who had been criticized for having arrived at her research findings by serendipity: 'Only those who have their feet on the ground stumble across anything'. Although Archimedes was not at the time trying to discover laws of fluid mechanics, his mind was highly concentrated, under pain of extreme penalty for failure, on finding a way of ascertaining whether the King of Syracuse's new golden crown was alloyed with baser metals.

Box 4.3

Characteristics of a creative person

- Conceptual fluency;
- Mental flexibility;
- Originality (i.e. novel thinking);
- Suspension of judgement;
- Impulse acceptance (i.e. listening to your intuition);
- A certain attitude towards authority (i.e. a low belief in the invincibility of a superior's wisdom); and
- Tolerance.

Adapted from: Majaro (1992).

Characteristics of the creative person

The purpose of looking at creativity from the point of view of processes and action has been to show that it is not an arcane art. Any manager can do the things needed to create and develop ideas. However, it may help to cultivate certain characteristics. Box 4.3 lists characteristics of the creative person that have been identified by Majaro. Majaro points out that these characteristics centre around the traditional elements of training and education: knowledge, skills and attitudes – all amenable to development rather than innate.

Processes of origination

Identifying a suitable developmental project requires that you apply creative processes to originating a specific idea for improvement or change and translating it into a practical plan of action. Figure 4.1 sets out the principal steps involved. Referring to Figure 4.1:

- The two initial stages of 'becoming aware' and 'evaluating awareness' parallel the central features of the Myers–Briggs model of how we get to know our worlds (see Chapter 2).

  To recapitulate, awareness (or 'perceiving' in Myers–Briggs' terms) can be developed either through 'sensing' – using one's five senses, or by 'intuiting' – using one's sixth

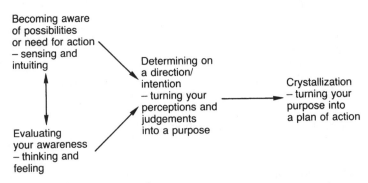

Figure 4.1 The process of originating an action project

sense. Evaluating (or 'judging' in Myers–Briggs' terms) can be effected either through 'thinking' – using logical processes, or through 'feeling' – drawing on one's values and sentiments.

Becoming aware of one's world and evaluating it do not take place independently of each other. They perpetually interact, with evaluations generating searches for new awareness, and vice versa.

- 'Determining direction' is the process of drawing together all the prior strands of 'awareness' and 'evaluation' in order to decide on a purpose, a way forward. It is a stage beyond the processes dealt with in the Myers–Briggs model that is concerned solely with the initial processes of relating to your worlds. Nevertheless, it is highly coloured by those former processes and one's behavioural preferences. It is important therefore to be aware of these and not allow them to distort your view of the world.
- All the foregoing processes have had but one aim: 'crystallization' into a plan to realize a new aim, a new task or problem, a new direction. This is the point of setting action objectives.

The subsequent sections will review each of these stages in turn.

Becoming aware

Most managers already have a considerable awareness of the world around them, indeed they have to in order to do their job. They are aware too of the need for action in certain areas. This awareness can of course form the starting point of a development project. But if you want to explore something entirely new you will have to extend your awareness. The stages in this process are set out in Figure 4.2, which essentially is an elaboration of the Myers–Briggs process of 'perceiving'.

People have different ways in which they get to know their world. Women are reputed to know it subjectively (i.e. intuitively and feelingly) and men objectively (i.e. through senses and logical thought). While there are cultural expectations that tend to create this relationship, it is far from

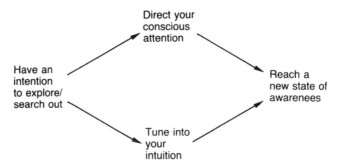

Figure 4.2   The process of becoming aware

universal. For the purpose of personal development, it is more useful for each individual to examine their own particular preferences without making gender-based assumptions. One of the great advantages of the Myers–Briggs classification of behavioural types is that it allows you to do precisely this.

The nature of your intentions towards making yourself more aware can be critical. With a positive intent you will be active in picking up clues, searching out what you need to find. With an indifferent or half-hearted intent you risk inadequately briefing yourself about possibilities and pitfalls. A negative approach, or searching without an open mind, and you risk blinding yourself to essential information, which you may deny or block off from your consciousness.

Where to look

Books on project management tend to take for granted that a project has been defined and discuss only how to put a given project in train. But these projects had to start somewhere.

Finding a project could mean selecting a problem, exploring its origins and ramifications, identifying a suitable solution, and implementing it. Or it could mean identifying some innovatory idea and applying it in your job or organization to develop a new product or service or to improve operations.

If you are simply seeking a project for developmental purposes, it is not usually difficult to find one. There is

always something that needs doing on most managers'
agendas or, if not, on their boss's agenda. Alternatively, as
a starting point one might carry out a review of customer
attitudes or market opportunities, or an internal review of
staff attitudes or look for other problems needing attention.
The possible starting points for a project are numerous and
the practicalities of finding one are not normally difficult. A
check-list of possible starting points, or 'areas that can
benefit from creativity' as Majaro puts it, is given in Box 4.4.
It covers all the main functions of management – production, marketing, finance and control, research and
development.

There is a training pack called *A Question of Service* (Nash,
1988) in which a video shows a group of employees in a public
swimming pool, a hotel equipped to take disabled residents,
and a National Trust house, taking on the role of customers
in order to experience from that perspective their own
services and facilities, i.e. 'the service journey'. They start at
the beginning of the customers' experience, in the car-park or
at the entrance or even prior to that, and put themselves
through everything a customer would experience. At the end
of the journey, they had identified significant needs or gaps in
the service. The changes to deal with them took considerable
discussion: more convenient arrangements for mothers with
small babies at the swimming pool, moving the car-park at
the National Trust house, making fire doors in the hotel
easier to open for people in a wheelchair. The point being
made is that to find starting points for projects you have to
look about you. How you do this is limited only by your
imagination.

Becoming aware of the world around us is something that
is so automatic that it is easy to take it for granted. What is
being emphasized here is that it should be tackled
creatively.

Active seeking out of information should be supplemented
by all the pointers and cues you can pick up in an incidental
fashion. Intuition will be critical here. This is probably the
major value of 'management by walk about': gleaning ideas,
learning about problems, seeing what is going well and what
is going wrong, getting to know people's concerns, understanding the potential obstacles. It requires good listening

Box 4.4

Starting points for creative ideas

Production
- Purchasing policies and practice.
- Scheduling and logistics.
- Manufacturing productivity.
- Quality control.
- Technology and layout.
- Industrial relations policies

Marketing
- Market intelligence and research.
- Market strategies.
- Product development.
- Market-testing procedures.
- Pricing.
- Distribution systems.
- Promotional activities (advertising, sales promotion, publicity).
- Organization and effectiveness of sales force

Personnel/human resources
- Employee relations.
- Remuneration and reward strategies and practice.
- Recruitment methods.
- Employee turnover.
- Motivation and morale.
- Employee communications.
- Training and development

Finance and control
- Management accounting systems.
- Presentation of information.
- Communications with other departments.
- Style and speed of response to requests for information.
- Audit arrangements.
- Format and content of Annual Report

Research and development
- Selection of R&D projects.
- Links to market.
- Technical and innovative capabilities.
- Value of R&D outcomes.
- Cost consciousness amongst R&D staff.
- Public image of department and its impact on recruitment of creative, talented staff.

Adapted from: Majaro (1992) by permission.

skills, and skill also in interpreting what you see and hear – being able to decode oblique messages.

In searching out your information you obviously need to make sufficient investigation of an area to be credible when you draw on this information in order to convince others of the validity of your ideas. This is often a key to influencing others.

But you should not allow yourself to be drawn into unnecessarily complicated research. Some managers seem to have a curious belief that only information discovered by means of a formal research method can be used in evidence when making a case. In this strange view, a casual conversation with someone in the key position to know, from which you obtain an appraisal of a situation or problem, does not count as legitimate information. You may, of course, need to check this information out further, but information it is. Remember too that at this exploratory stage, you do not need to have all the information you need in order to progress a potential project to a conclusion. Part of the plan for realizing your aims can be the collection of more comprehensive information. In other words do not allow the necessary task of developing your awareness to develop into procrastination.

Evaluating awareness

The process of evaluating what you have become aware of is illustrated in Figure 4.3. The diagram parallels the Myers–Briggs model of reaching a judgement by logical analysis and by feeling. Added, however, is the notion of 'assembling' as a precursor to the process, to enable you to weigh up your options.

The diagram again emphasizes the need to bring into play each polarity of the Myers–Briggs choices, both thinking and feelings, and not to allow preference for one or the other to distort one's judgement.

The first step in the evaluative process is to assemble all the information and ideas that we want to give consideration to in order to reach a conclusion. While it is possible to do this in your head, I suggest you make a written list.

'Assembling' is critical to the effectiveness of the creative process. We need information and past experience and

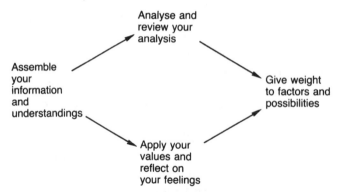

Figure 4.3   The process of evaluating

existing ideas to be creative. What we find to assemble, and what we screen out from our assembly is perhaps one of the most significant steps in the whole creative process. You can only be creative with what you have to build with. These building blocks can of course be in your conscious or unconscious mind – intuition can play as large a part in the evaluation process as it does in developing awareness.

It is important at this stage that you do not allow your vision to be blinkered in any way, thus closing your mind to potentially fruitful avenues.

Information about your external world that you are aware of will obviously be brought into your 'assembly'. Less obviously perhaps, also information from your internal world: your beliefs about your capabilities, your perceptions of the obstacles to achievement, your feelings about your ability to succeed, your feelings about working with others.

Information about your external world will not be entirely objective and neutral. You will have beliefs about the way the world works, and therefore about what you need to do in order to achieve your ends within it. Part of the process of resolving your awarenesses and judgements will be to see whether you can come closer to reality.

This model of evaluating is intended to reflect a more deliberately creative process than that described by the Myers–Briggs model of judging through thinking and feeling. It identifies what you need to do, or need to work through, in order to reach a judgement or conclusion. Thus you do not just use your feelings in making your evaluation; you may need to work through feelings, 'letting go' of outmoded sentiments, in order to progress. You may need to substitute feeling for analysis, and vice versa. What you do should not be determined solely by your innate preferences. Rather you should manage them in the way that your purposes demand.

Determining direction

Although in Figure 4.1 determining a direction is shown as an intermediate stage, this can in fact be a starting point. As already noted, the creative process never starts with a clean slate. The seemingly prior processes of becoming aware and evaluating awareness may in fact be no more than activities undertaken to supplement present perceptions and understandings.

Figure 4.4 depicts the processes involved in this 'chicken and egg' stage of determining direction. If your developmental experience is to be driven by a personal purpose, it makes sense to start the process of determining direction with a review of your personal agenda. This agenda may relate to your external or internal world.

Most of the foregoing discussion has focused on the former. But if your starting point for development is, for example, to deal with a personal shortcoming of which you are aware, or to present a new image to your boss or colleagues, then a first stage may be to work through the blocks which have hitherto held you back.

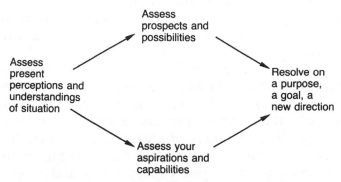

Figure 4.4 The process of determining a new direction

Telling the truth

In assessing your present perceptions and understandings, it is critical that you should get as close as you can to reality with regard to both your internal and external worlds. You certainly should not be the dupe of any 'organizationally correct' fictions about what is going on or what is claimed to have been achieved, for example going along with official pronouncements about customer satisfaction with excellent standards of service when you yourself can see shortcomings in that service.

Realistic scrutiny requires introverts to overcome any diffidence they may have about engaging with their external world and extroverts to overcome any inhibitions they may have about exploring their internal world. It is important too, as observed earlier, not to stereotype yourself according to assumed gender differences.

Fritz (1989), in describing how to be proactive in order to create and realize one's visions, emphasizes the great importance of 'telling the truth' about 'current reality'. Without that truth you sabotage your prospects of reaching the land you promise yourself. The process of developing awareness will be instrumental in enabling you to get this accurate picture. This is the time for checking perceptions, beliefs and assumptions against objective reality in so far as this is possible.

'Assessing prospects and possibilities' relates to your perception of your corporate world: what support, authorization, collaboration, resources, information, and so on, are likely to be available to you.

'Assessing aspirations and capabilities' parallels this, but with regard to yourself. This is about your perception of what you are capable of doing, and your feelings about what you wish to do.

This personal assessment can sometimes usefully be aided by drawing your 'career line' – where you have come from, where you are now, and where you would like to be going. A procedure for doing this is described in Box 4.5.

Thinking ahead to where you want to be, it may be worth experimenting with several time-scales, ranging from a few weeks or months to a few years. A developmental project needs to fit as far as possible with your long-term aspirations.

Box 4.5

Your career life line

This exercise is designed to help you look forward from your past career in order to determine future directions for yourself at work.

First draw your 'career line' up to the present time. To do this take a suitable starting point in your life, say your late teens, and draw a line to represent the progression of your career to date.

(Use a large piece of paper and keep your line within approximately the left-hand two-thirds of the page in order to allow room for extending it into the future later.)

Put in peaks and troughs to represent high and low points.

You may wish to draw two lines: one to represent your career and another your personal life.

Consider your line(s):

- Can you single out any particularly significant experiences or decisions?
- What were your important successes? How did you bring these about?
- Where did you attain satisfaction and fulfilment? What were the sources of this?
- Were there any significant disappointments or setbacks? How did these occur?
- What have been your major driving interests?
- Did anyone have a particular influence on you and how?
- Overall, how have you managed your life at work? Have you got what you wanted from it? If not, can you identify why – external circumstances or factors within yourself?

Next consider the 'here and now' point on your line:

- Where are you now?
- Are you satisfied with this?
- How well do you think you are doing? Would others agree?
- How do you feel about the way your capabilities are being used?
- What do you value about your work? What do you really enjoy?
- Is there anything that you would fear doing, or would feel particularly apprehensive about? Is this an area for development?
- What do you consider to be the benefit to yourself and to your organization of you being in your present job?

When you have answered these questions, extend your career line as far as you reasonably can into the future, say about five years if you can.

Be realistic but at the same time do not allow your imagining to be overly constrained. The exercise is about you deciding what you really want for yourself, not about the constraints of your present job, or difficulties of changing jobs, or in getting requalified.

Then, thinking ahead to this future point, flesh out what it means for you:

- What do you want for yourself?
- What kind of contribution would you like to make over this period?
- Where do you want to be?
- By when?
- Is there any capability or skill you will need to develop in order to do this?
- What will you need to do? Or acquire?
- Who can help you?
- What will 'success' mean for you?

Next, decide whether you intend to move to this future or leave it as fantasy. If the latter, consider why you do not want to attempt to realize the future you would like for yourself.

- What is stopping you?
- Are you stopping yourself, and if so, why?

Finally, consider what this long-term purpose you have for yourself implies for the kind of developmental experiences you might now wish to engage in.

Tips for doing this exercise

- It is not meant to be an intellectual working out of goals and means; it is intended to be an aid to getting in touch with purposes and values you already have; so allow your feelings free play.
- Do it when you know you will not be distracted.
- Take time over it; answer the questions (or invent others to answer if these are not quite apt) as honestly as you can; tell the truth about yourself to yourself.
- It will help if you make sure you are fully relaxed before starting the exercise; you will probably also find it helpful to close your eyes for a short period before drawing your career line and while thinking about your responses to the questions.

A complementary approach advocated by Covey (1992), would be to work on developing one's own personal mission statement, in which you set out your values and guiding principles for directing your life. You may be comfortable with neither of these approaches, which are only suggestions for your self-assessment. The point is to find some way of formulating your own sense of direction.

Both the foregoing steps, assessing your internal and external worlds, are concerned with the considerations that you put into the equation in formulating your ideas for action. Often this is done perfunctorily, even unconsciously. 'I fancy doing that'. 'That would go down well'. 'I could never do that'. 'They would never agree'. 'There wouldn't be the money'. In the process of originating an idea you should take a serious look at the assumptions you are making about yourself and your external world and not let them go unquestioned.

A good mentor or learning group would make you confront your untested assumptions. A book can only draw your attention to the possibility that you may be needlessly limiting your horizons unless you take a few risks and test your assumptions about your inner and external realities. You need too to question the value of solutions that have worked reliably in the past. Over-ready resort to tried and tested solutions can limit creative thinking for the present problem.

Practitioners of action learning abound with stories of managers plucking up their courage to tilt at windmills that proved non-existent. But sometimes of course they are real, and you need to know this so that you can plan your tilting carefully. It is your beliefs about what is possible and what you are capable of, perhaps more than anything else in the originating process, that will shape the production of your venture – as cautious or ambitious, as keeping within your known bounds or as extending yourself.

Crystallizing

The final step in the sequence of originating an idea for action is to crystallize one's intentions into a concrete plan. Box 4.1, describing the creative process could be a useful guideline. It is often, however, worthwhile at this point to resort to those hackneyed questions: Why? What? How? and When? Adding

Box 4.6

Crystallizing questions

WHY do you want to undertake this project?

- What problem will it be tackling?

or

- Why do you want to change things?
- Why is this action or change needed?

WHAT are you going to achieve?

- What are your objectives?
- What, if anything, has already been done?
- What still needs to be done?
- What will be the end result – recommendations or changes introduced?
- What will the outcome look like?
- How will you know when you've achieved them?

HOW are you going to achieve your aims?

- What information will you need?
- How will you obtain and analyse it?
- What action do you plan?

WHO will you need to involve?

- What is the precise nature of the support you will need?
- Who do you have in mind?
- How will you get them involved?

WHEN will the project be completed?

- When will intermediate tasks be complete?
- What might delay these estimates?
- Do you have any contingency plans?

HOW MUCH is the project going to cost?

- In terms of money?
- In terms of time?
- How do you justify this expenditure?
- How do you intend to get it authorized?

also: Who? and How much? These basic questions are elaborated in Box 4.6.

Even if the precise questions in Box 4.6 are not appropriate for you, you should try to work systematically through some comparable questions. It is all too easy, working in your head, to think that you have attended to everything. At the very least you should try to talk your ideas and plans through with somebody. You may of course need to submit a written proposal or make a presentation. The value of writing down

---

Box 4.7

Adopting a project: four golden rules

1 Ask relevant questions

- How clear is my brief?
- What is the required result?
- Why is it being sought?
- Is it feasible?
- Who does what?
- What are likely to be the repercussions?
- What is the completion deadline and why?
- How should I organize my role?
- Who has authority for selecting staff/spending money?
- How much is the budget?
- What is more important – time or money?

2 Never assume anything

- Clarify everything.
- Remember that wrong assumptions waste time, money and effort.

3 Keep asking about the project's purpose

- Identify clearly what is the need for it, not just what actions are required.

4 Identify its effects, externally as well as internally.

Adapted from: Burton and Michael (1992).

what you intend, even if only to yourself, cannot be overemphasized.

Moreover, having a document that can be circulated not only facilitates discussion, but also enables any misunderstandings to be identified and clarified. This is especially important if you have adopted someone else's idea. If you set out on paper your understanding of your brief, you create an opportunity for any misunderstandings to be dealt with at an early stage. The four 'golden rules' to follow when adopting a project in Box 4.7 emphasize further this need for clarifying devices.

These discussions of course can be an additional input to the creative process. This process does not stop with the generation of an original idea; that is often the least of it. The major elements of creativity, in management as in other spheres, are in the realization of the idea in practice – in the actual change that is brought about. The process of implementation feeds back to the conception.

The process of introducing change should ideally be organic, not just allowing unforeseen circumstances to be accommodated, but also allowing the original conception to be further evolved. The journey should be part of the process of discovering where one is going, but without this degenerating into muddling through. Which is why a clear proposal at the outset can be so critical.

Writing a proposal

If you do have to submit a formal written proposal or make a presentation, even though it may have to conform to a prescribed house style, it will probably need to be ordered around certain broad headings as described in Box 4.8.

The grammarian, Fowler, in his *Dictionary of Modern English Usage* described the colon as having the 'special function of delivering the goods that have been invoiced in the preceding words'. At the end of the introduction and objectives sections comes an invisible colon. What follows should be an explanation that flows on naturally of how the objectives will be delivered. Reassure your audience that the action you are recommending is the best way forward. You

---

Box 4.8

Format for a project proposal

- *Introduction* – including background to the proposed project, rationale for it and any work done to date.

  The objective should be to make the proposal a self-contained, self-explanatory document without the need of supplementary memos to further explain it.

- *Objectives* – this is where you nail your colours to the mast and declare what it is you hope to achieve.

  Watch out for any means masquerading as ends – it is easily done.

- *Proposed plan of action* – detailed enough to be credible, and to provide you yourself with guidelines and benchmarks.

  But without so boxing yourself in that you will lack freedom of action to deal with contingencies or adjust direction.

- *Resources needed* – money, facilities, people, and your justification for these requests.

  Nail down precise collaboration needed from senior managers and managers in other departments; remember the petty cash – printing, travel, entertainment.

- *Timing* – allow as much slack as you can get away with. Highlight bottleneck points dependent on others' collaboration.

- *Anticipated outcomes* – these are your promises that you use to sell your project and which one day you will have to deliver.

- *An executive summary* – writing this will be the acid test for discovering whether your ideas really are sorted out. This is written last but placed at the beginning.

---

have made the case that something needs to be done. Is what you are proposing the right something?

A particular issue your audience may need reassurance on is 'wheels', and their concern either that you may be re-inventing them, or failing to make use of perfectly good existing ones. Are you recommending rollers in ignorance of the availability of wheels? Are you recommending the production of customized wheels when you could be buying into a quite satisfactory off-the-shelf wheels package? Or are you recommending wheels because you are unaware of caterpillar tracks? The points that these somewhat fanciful metaphors are making is, firstly, that your homework at the developing awareness stage should have been as thorough as possible, and, secondly, if you are ignorant of an area, acknowledge it and build remedying it into your plan of action.

Whatever the precise format, the objective must be to put over the essence of your 'story': what the project is about, the benefits of doing it, how it is feasible, and – most critically – what you want the recipients of your proposal to do (Give you permission? Give you resources? Both?). Your objective in the process is to be persuasive, carry conviction, appear credible, to make your priority their priority, and convey your own enthusiasm in a manner that will elicit support and commitment.

At this stage, you need to be on your guard against unwarranted criticism. Other managers may need to be helped to the point of unblinkered, open vision that you have painstakingly achieved for yourself.

What is happening at this crystallization stage is that you are making an imaginative leap from where you are now to where you want to be. If you can see it in your mind's eye and capture it in words, you make its attainment seem more realizable.

Action and reflection points

- The action you need to take if you are going to set up a developmental project is self-evident: use the guidance in the chapter to do so. You will also need to refer to the next chapter which describes how to shape your project in a way that will maximize its potential for developing you.
- If you are not going to set up a special project, review the elements of your role that call on your creativity. Are you as innovative in your thinking and on as many occasions as you might be?
- Think of what you have to do in your work as a series of 'projects'. Use the creative processes described in this chapter to enhance the way you go about these 'projects'.

5   Shaping your experience

Introduction

Managers learn and develop from experience all the time. In order, however, to be assured of doing so effectively, it is sensible to have some developmental objectives in mind in advance of the experience, to be aware of them as it unfolds, and subsequently to reflect consciously and systematically on events.

This chapter discusses how you might design an experience or 'developmental project' to facilitate these processes and thus enhance its potential for personal development. It deals with:

- Experiences that precipitate development;
- Strategies for developing from experience;
- Factors that will add a developmental dimension to your projects;
- Examples of developmental projects;
- How development can result from achievement;
- Styles of learning and their implications for learning from experience; and
- Learning in the course of action.

The chapter concludes by reviewing key dilemmas that managers need to resolve in implementing their plans, and consequent personal development issues.

Occasions of development

Development as a person is something that takes place as a result of experience in real life. It does not always need conscious intervention on our part for it to occur. Much of the time it is spontaneous, an automatic response to sudden insights. More often it is a slow, steady, evolutionary process that accompanies our progress through life and our development in our jobs. One is often scarcely aware that one has developed until one looks back and takes stock of how one has changed.

Alternatively, development occurs as a result of a particular event. This could be an achievement which makes you realize that you are capable of more than you thought, or a set-back which causes you to re-appraise basic assumptions about yourself and the way you manage your job or indeed your life.

Development and growth can, however, be consciously facilitated. The practice of such facilitation is the basis of counselling, psychotherapy, much management development and all the many personal development techniques that are on offer today to people seeking to improve themselves. Indeed, this book, advocating the use of experience as a basis for personal development, must be counted amongst this genre.

Which self?

'Personal development' is a phrase that is loosely used to describe a whole host of personal and interpersonal skills: leadership, team working, time management, communication and presentation, conflict handling, appraisal, mentoring, creativity, managing stress, and so on. A look through any management training brochure will illustrate the range.

The impact of these forms of personal development on development of the self, your growth as a person, is however uncertain. That is to say, as a result of this development you change your attitudes to people or to the world, alter your preferred way of doing things, are better able to handle the needs and motives that drive your behaviour, re-appraise your view of your self, even perhaps change your values. All education and training has the potential to do this. But more often than not this kind of personal development takes place incidentally; it is not addressed directly in the training.

The 'self' that this book invites you to develop is not easily definable. At its most basic, 'self' means our sense of identity, our sense of being an individual separate from all other individuals. When we attempt to describe this self of ours there are many different categories we can use: personality, character, personal qualities and traits, abilities, likes and dislikes, values and beliefs, and physical or emotional characteristics.

In fact there is no single, definitive self, but many selves, which we deploy in different circumstances. Nowhere is this more so than in managing. Indeed, it could be said that appropriate and controlled presentation of different aspects of oneself in differing circumstances while still retaining one's integrity is the hallmark of the truly skilled manager.

Developmental strategies

Development from experience can be deliberate or inadvertent. For deliberate development you need to do two things:

* Design or structure your experience with the intention of learning from it (as opposed to leaving developmental experiences to occur haphazardly – a *'laissez-faire'* approach).
* Reflect on that experience systematically (as opposed to occasional, random reflection on events – an *'ad hoc'* approach).

These two dimensions are depicted in Figure 5.1. The horizontal axis represents one's approach to shaping experience – 'with intent' or *'laissez-faire'*; while the vertical axis represents one's approach to reflecting on that experience – 'systematic' or *'ad hoc'*.

The bottom left-hand cell in Figure 5.1 thus represents managers for whom development is inadvertent. They leave their experience to unfold as the dictates of their job demand and subsequently only reflect on such experiences as they feel warrant attention. For these managers, lessons from experience are more often than not tacitly rather than explicitly drawn. This is the normal everyday learning from everyday experience that we are all no doubt familiar with.

By contrast, in the top right-hand cell are the managers for whom experiential development is deliberate. These managers will specially design an experience or project to meet

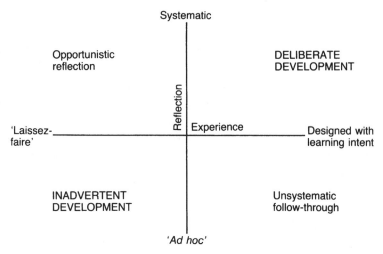

Figure 5.1 Approaches to experiential learning and development

developmental objectives and conscientiously ensure that they reflect systematically upon it.

This kind of deliberate development most typically occurs when a manager is on a course where some kind of action-research or action-learning project is a requirement. But it could of course be engineered quite independently of any formal course.

The in-between position (top left-hand cell), that of managers taking a *laissez-faire* stance with regard to shaping their experience, but nevertheless reflecting systematically upon it, offers a pragmatic strategy for capitalizing on experience without undertaking a special developmental project. It is a strategy that many readers of this book will no doubt wish to pursue. Accreditation of prior experiential learning (APEL), the procedure whereby some academic institutions allow candidates to present evidence from their past work experience in order to gain credit towards a qualification, could be said to fall into this category of opportunistic experiential development.

There is a second in-between position (bottom right-hand cell) which is the case of the manager who designs a learning experience but fails to follow it through with systematic reflection. This is a not uncommon experience of managers who find themselves subjected to unexpected new pressures, or who move to another job.

Setting up a developmental project

A developmental project is of course, by definition, 'deliberate development'. The value of using a project as a basis for your developmental experience is that a project has the potential to involve you in virtually all the key elements of managing.

You need to initiate and plan, relate your objectives to wider corporate goals, which means thinking strategically, enlist the co-operation and support of others, handle the organization politics, monitor progress and take any corrective action, and finally to assess the outcome and determine where you should go from there.

In summary, you are involved, within a fairly condensed time scale, in a full cycle of goal-setting, planning, execution and control of the kind expounded in any standard textbook on management. With the right project you may also lead and manage change.

There are a number of ways of structuring a developmental project. You can:

- Identify your specific learning and development needs and set up a project or task that will enable you to meet them.
- Set starting conditions for project, then leave things open for development opportunities to occur naturally during planning and action phases.
- Set starting conditions, coupled with subsequent structured arrangements for reflection and learning.

Each of these options is discussed below. But first a cautionary note.

The foregoing options, and what follows, relate only to the development aspects of a project. You should not allow concern for your own development to cause you to neglect such essential matters as organizational purposes or how the project will impact on others. You also need to be prepared for contingencies. Unexpected events, people's reactions and views, changing circumstances, will need to be accommodated as the project unfolds.

Identify development needs

A review of your own development needs is an obvious starting point for a developmental project. You carry out some form of self-diagnosis of your strengths and weaknesses, and seek out a project opportunity that will involve you in managing in an area that you want to develop. For example, to develop yourself in the area of interpersonal relations you might choose a project that involves you in setting up arrangements for interdepartmental collaboration.

The success of such a developmental project will depend on the validity of the original diagnosis of your needs and on the project in fact challenging you in the area intended. Projects do not always turn out as predicted. In the hypothetical example just cited, the interdepartmental collaboration could take off so smoothly that no challenge, and hence no significant learning or development, is entailed.

Also, in trying to build a project around your known development needs you may be led to design a project that is too narrow in scope. You do not always know what you need to practise until confronted by the challenge of having to do something.

Building a project around development needs would be satisfactory if all you wanted to do was to get practice in specific competences. But if you are looking to the much broader development objective of learning to manage effectively, then you need a different starting point – one that builds in corporate and personal achievement. Meeting your specific development needs is then incidental to this, and you have to trust that your project will throw up opportunities relevant to your needs. Any management project is likely to follow an uncertain path, with no guarantee that it will throw up any of the development opportunities you have planned for.

Setting starting conditions

The alternative is to design your development project around certain starting conditions. These would be expected to make the project demanding and stretching and lead to fruitful development opportunities. Having set the starting conditions the project may then be allowed to run its course with an open approach to identifying learning opportunities and reflecting upon them.

Provided that the project reflects a personal venture for you, this is not an unsatisfactory way of proceeding. In these circumstances you will be looking to make best use of the opportunities afforded by the project. The art is in recognizing the learning and development opportunities and knowing how to make use of them.

Possible starting conditions that you might wish to set for your project are reviewed below.

Personal venture

One critical starting condition for a development project is that you treat it as a personal venture. The task or project should be something that you want to do, that you believe is worthwhile and which achieves some outcome that you care about.

What you do could be your idea or someone else's. The important thing is that – to use a bit of contemporary jargon – you 'own' it. If your development task or project does not meet this condition your learning from it will inevitably be diminished.

If you are working to achieve an objective you care about, the challenges you will be prepared to confront will be that much greater. You will be more concerned to reflect on what happened, and less likely to avoid confronting the lessons of experience. Also it is more motivating and enjoyable to do something that you want to do; and you are more likely to learn in such circumstances.

The distinction between a personal venture and a manager's normal duties is a fuzzy one. Most managers have an 'agenda' that they work to which guides their priorities and decision-making. Part of this agenda will be given, in the sense that you will have taken much of it on board as part of the job. But, to a greater or lesser degree, part of this agenda will be determined by your own values, interests and aims. In particular, it will include your career aspirations, with particular jobs, and projects within jobs, all contributing to the realization of your ambitions.

Managerial

A project to develop you as a manager would also need to be 'managerial'. Achieving this in practice is not always straightforward.

You need to pitch the project at a strategic or organizational level; it should not be concerned with issues that are trivial or mundane. Certainly it should not be at the level of supervising routine activities, nor should it be of a clerical nature, nor exclusively technical or professional. Ideally it should involve the bringing about of change. Ideally you need to tackle a problem that has organizational ramifications.

The project should not be confined to problem-solving, and simply terminate in recommendations for someone else to act upon. Such an experience may develop you as an effective functional specialist, or as an effective consultant, but would be seriously limiting in developing you as an effective manager.

A managerial project should involve others; it should fulfil the notion of managing as getting things done through people. But these people do not necessarily have to be subordinates; they could be peers or superiors.

Leading

Learning from a development project will almost certainly be more profound if you are its leader. This means that if not the actual originator of the project, you should at least have adopted it yourself at an early stage and made it psychologically your own.

You need to be emancipated from dependence on other people's approval and sanction, so that what happens on the project is an outcome of your own decisions. In this way you will have been responsible for creating the experiences from which you are learning. You cannot then evade responsibility for the lessons to be drawn.

Accountability

A developmental project should also have built into it an element of accountability. Firstly, you need to establish that someone else besides yourself cares about the project or venture; and, secondly, that you are personally on the line to deliver a result. This second factor is not just a motivator, though that is important, but a key aspect of managing; it serves to make your project 'managerial'.

If you are the only person who cares about whether or not an outcome is achieved, and the nature of that outcome, there is a risk that your personal venture will not be meeting any recognized corporate goal. You should therefore consider having a 'client' for your project. This could be your boss, or another senior manager. Or it could be the people who report to you.

It is becoming quite usual these days for junior and middle managers to have a 'mentor', someone with whom they can talk through their managerial problems and who may advise them on their development. Such a person could also be a suitable client for one's project.

Having a client can certainly introduce an element of accountability into what you do. It puts you on the line to deliver a result. It can also help to ensure that the project has corporate value. On the other hand, your own commitment to a personal venture that brings about a corporate benefit should also ensure that. An indirect way of creating a sense of accountability is to make your project 'public', for example by publishing your project plan with a clear explanation of what you are trying to achieve, and perhaps also committing yourself to make a presentation or circulate a report about the outcome.

Holistic

A management development project needs to be viewed holistically. Ideally it should take you through the complete cycle of activities depicted in Figure 1.1. While this may not be possible for everyone, it is important always to have sight of the whole, in Drucker's metaphor to know that you are 'building a cathedral'. Without a holistic perspective, whether undertaking a complete or a partial project, large or small scale, your activities are unlikely to match up to any reasonable criteria of managing effectively. Also without a holistic perspective constantly in mind you risk being deflected from your main purpose to attend to tangential issues.

Stretch

The final starting condition that a development project must have built into it is 'stretch'. If what you do does not challenge you and take you beyond your present levels of performance then it is unlikely to develop you very much.

The standard 'action learning' principle for achieving this is that one should tackle an unfamiliar problem or task in an unfamiliar setting, what Revans described as 'maximum stretch'.

In his original programmes, Revans had managers with a background in one function undertaking a project in a different function in a different, 'host' organization. Thus, a marketing person from, say, the oil industry would work on a personnel problem in consumer goods manufacturing. This is certainly the kind of situation in which a high degree of ignorance and incompetence is likely to be revealed and hopefully a commensurate degree of learning and development occur.

Revans' prescription for maximum stretch, although persuasive, has been more honoured in the breach than the observance. Many action-learning programmes are run in which the project is drawn from the programme participant's own organization and very often from his or her own job.

This not only has the obvious advantage of doing something of immediate usefulness for one's own organization, it also avoids some of the key disadvantages of working in a host organization.

One of these is of course the sheer difficulty of finding a suitable host who will be tolerant of an action learner and supply a project for him or her to work on. Working in a host organization may also mean – though not necessarily – casting oneself in the role of external consultant who is confined to making recommendations for others to act on. The limitations of this for management development have already been commented upon.

It is of course hard to know in advance what project will throw up suitable learning challenges. But tackling a familiar problem that is confined completely within your existing sphere of responsibility is unlikely to present much stretch. The project should involve you in crossing organizational boundaries in order to obtain agreements from, collaborate with, and gain commitment of colleagues.

It should ideally involve, as already mentioned, some kind of public commitment on your part. This may not be a necessary ingredient for managing effectively, but it is an important device for facilitating development. Without the sure knowledge that you will eventually have to report to someone about what you have achieved, then you will not have the stretch that comes from knowing that you are on the line to produce a result, nor the motivation that comes from wanting to give of your best in these circumstances.

Structured follow-through

In addition to setting starting conditions for one's development project, it is also possible to set up structured arrangements to facilitate the developmental processes during the course of the project and to ensure that development opportunities are fully capitalized upon. These structured arrangements would include the use of such devices as regular workshops, discussion fora, and meetings of a mutual support group.

In standard action-learning programmes, the learners normally meet in small groups or 'sets' of other managers carrying out similar projects. As well as providing mutual support for undertaking the project, these sets provide a catalyst for questioning and reflection. The set is able to probe, challenge and offer moral support which facilitates learning in a way that is often not possible for a manager ploughing a lone development furrow.

The sets may be supported by a 'set adviser' whose role is to facilitate learning within the group and to guide set members to learning resources outside the group. There are pros and cons of having a set adviser, and 'unfacilitated sets' are now an accepted variant of orthodox action learning (see McGill and Beaty, 1992).

Action learning without a support group or set would probably be regarded by most practitioners as falling outside the bounds of true action learning. This means that many potential action learners, deterred by the time and expense of regular group meetings, may find themselves excluded from the opportunity to undertake an action-learning programme. An objective of this book, as already noted, is to set out the learning processes associated with an action project whereby the lone learner may learn.

Nevertheless, it is important that the lone learner should seek out opportunities, although not necessarily within a formal action-learning programme, whereby he or she can exchange ideas and experience. Without this, approaches to problem-solving and to your role as your manager risk remaining overly constrained by traditional thoughtways and current employer expectations.

Project guidelines

The criteria for setting up a development project outlined above are in wide use on action-learning programmes. An example of their use for work-based projects at Sundridge Park Management Centre is presented in Box 5.1. These guidelines succinctly reflect the general principles discussed above, except perhaps there is more emphasis in this book on actually getting to the action rather than allowing an ending to occur at the point of recommendations 'and action where appropriate'. Nor does the project necessarily have to start with a 'problem' as might be inferred from the Sundridge guidelines, although of course the term 'problem' can be interpreted extremely broadly.

It used to be fashionable in some management and consultancy circles to respond to ideas for change with: 'What problem is it solving?' or 'Is this a solution in search of a problem?' These may be useful questions to ask, but they can also pour cold water on potential innovation. Who knows where ideas may lead, as the numerous case histories reported by Tom Peters and others of 'intrapreneurial' initiatives bear witness. Awareness of new forms of 'best practice' could also be a starting point for change even though your own current practice is not throwing up any recognized problems.

Box 5.1

Work-based project guidelines in use at Sundridge Park Management Centre

- There should be agreement with the participant's manager on a common understanding, objective and interest.
- Regular communication with the manager should be established.
- The time requirement should be protected so the participant does not get frustrated, demoralized or fail.
- The participant should have a strong interest in the subject of the project.
- The project should be as clearly defined as possible.

The following criteria should be applied when choosing a project

- It should offer challenge, provide stretch and should not be a set of tedious clerical routines.
- It should not be a puzzle to which there is a known solution.
- It should be concerned with a major problem whose solution would give broad understanding of the organization.
- It is likely to contain a people element.
- It should require involvement, co-operation and commitment of other colleagues.
- It should have the possiblity for real impact to be made on the problem within the timescale.
- It should include diagnosis of the problem, recommendations and action where appropriate.
- It should not be a problem incapable of solution or too complicated for one individual to tackle.
- It should be linked to some planned or on-going change.
- Though primarily a learning vehicle it should yield some worthwhile benefits for the organization.

From: Smith (1993) by permission.

Finding a suitable project

In my experience of asking managers on courses to identify a suitable project around these kind of guidelines, most are able to do so without too much difficulty. The problems largely arise when the manager is in transition from one job to another, is running a one-person business, is not currently in employment or is not in a managerial role in their job. Some of these difficulties are more imagined than real.

The one-person business manager may simply need reassurance that it is okay to make their business the project. For the person in transition the difficulties focus around timing, and perhaps the tail-end of an old job is not the best time to be committing oneself to a new initiative. For the person not in employment, work in voluntary organizations may offer opportunities, as could also an assignment in a willing host organization – though this could tend more to consultancy than management. The person not in a managerial role could of course seek to be given a managerial assignment, but that could suffer from the same shortcomings as working in a host organization – you are not given an opportunity to get involved in any real managerial action.

Planning August

An example of a project where a 'managerial' dimension could be readily foreseen is afforded by the case of a deputy general manager of a large city centre hotel who set himself the task of making the hotel break even in August. It had always been accepted that the hotel would lose money in this period, it being in a metropolitan area more noted for business visitors than tourists.

This project could have taken the form of simply trying to drum up extra business to fill the empty beds, a fairly hopeless task given its location. He did do this, but primarily he looked at work schedules, holiday rosters, scheduled purchases and in fact every conceivable item of expenditure that could be temporarily adjusted during this one month. He then negotiated with all the other managers and staff concerned with these activities to get their agreement to change their time-honoured practices. So, by dint of skilful internal management well in advance of the time, he cut the deficit very nearly to the break-even point.

Planning Christmas

In another example I actually tried to divert the manager concerned from undertaking his proposed project on the grounds that I believed it would not offer any managerial stretch. The manager was about to take up the post of general manager of a country house hotel belonging to a major chain. He said that for his project he would 'plan Christmas'. I argued with him in vain that he had the opportunity to make a project out of taking over the management of a hotel; planning Christmas would only involve him in technical matters such as the design of menus and functions. I could not have been more wrong, and although I suspect the manager had a better idea of what might be in store for him in planning Christmas than I did, I do not think he had any inkling of what would actually result from embarking on this seemingly straightforward and routine task.

It transpired that the previous manager had never properly planned Christmas. Staff left every year in early December in order to avoid the shambles of muddling through without adequate pre-planning. Some would drift back in January; other were lost for ever. Christmas itself was run with largely temporary staff which aggravated the shambles. So when the new manager announced on taking up his post in August that he was about to start on planning Christmas, such long term staff as were left from this process of annual attrition expressed their amazement and delight – and presented the foregoing scenario. In the event 'planning Christmas' turned into a process of organizational development in which the new general manager not only won the loyalty of the staff and their commitment to stay over Christmas, but a whole new style of participation and involvement was embarked upon.

Managerial action for non-managers

There will be some people seeking to develop their managerial capabilities through project work who are not yet in managerial positions. Most of their everyday experience, while it might be suitable for some developmental purposes, is unlikely to be suitable for management development purposes.

This problem was faced on a diploma course I was involved in running, where local government officials, not yet promoted to management, were required to undertake a work-based project as part of a module on management effective-ness. They could have been allowed to undertake an investigatory style project. This would have prepared them for promotion by developing them in the professional skills of management, but would not have developed them in manage-rial effectiveness.

What was done was to get these officials to review their present job, most particularly any problems they faced in managing their time, in relating to colleagues, in adequacy of resources, or in quality of their outputs. They were then asked to identify what they could do to bring about an improvement in a significant problem area of their job.

Initial reactions to this task tended to be a depressing recitation of the barriers to doing anything about their lot. They all had too much to do in a culture of non-support. They could not do any more than they were doing at present which was their best. But they agreed to take a fresh look at their circumstances and explore the possibility that things might be different. In doing this, they were particularly asked to focus attention on organizational constraints that might need to be modified and opportunities that could be taken advantage of.

Some of the outcomes from these projects were dramatic. These 'non-managers' proved imaginative and forceful in taking initiatives to bring about changes in their job environment.

Court action

One of the most memorable of these projects was that undertaken by a debt counsellor for a local authority. She had explained to us in the initial review of her job how impossible it was to manage her time since she was at the beck and call of the magistrates courts. If one of her clients was appearing in court she had to give top priority to attending the court to represent her client. The court schedules proceeded without regard to the priorities of those who might be called to attend, and although there was some advance notification of cases, court schedules were fre-quently changed at the last moment to suit the court's convenience. She had already done everything she could to

plan her workloads within the constraints of these unpredictable demands. But she agreed to explore further.

Her explorations revealed that her assumptions about the
inexorability of the court demands were unfounded. The
courts' schedules had to accommodate the availability of the
prosecutors, otherwise no case could be brought. The prosecutors in her cases were legal officials employed by another
branch of the same local authority.

She organized meetings of all the debt counsellors and
others who were also subject to the vagaries of the court
schedules and collectively they documented the inefficiencies
that resulted. Then she convened a meeting with officials
from the departments involved in making the prosecutions.
And she got agreement – they did not like it she said, but she
had manipulated some pressures on them from higher
management – that these officials would order their schedule
of prosecutions to fit in with the working needs of officials
representing defendants.

Perhaps not a major strategic project for the local authority,
but several staff in more than one department benefited in
terms of greater freedom to schedule their work. The debt
counsellor herself had been able to enlarge the scope of her
job and start doing things that she had long believed ought to
be done but she had never had the time for. But the main
point about the project was that this 'non-manager' had had
an experience of managing. And she knew that she had been
effective; at her presentation she was justifiably delighted in
her achievement.

Achievement as development

The management literature is full of exhortations about the
importance of managers having freedom to learn from their
mistakes. Learning from the experience of an achievement is
an equally satisfactory – and much more gratifying – way of
learning and developing. A failure may precipitate much
salutary reflection. But development eventually needs to be
consolidated by success.

The original inspiration for writing a book about self-
development and achievement came from the first occasion of
running a new management development course for middle

managers in the hotel and catering industry. A central part of the course was that the participant managers had to under-take short work-based action projects and report on their learning from the experience.

Several managers felt that they had done more than learn in a cognitive sense; they felt they had gained a new insight into themselves and their capabilities. There was talk among some of them having got 'it', which mystified those other managers on the course who had not yet got 'it'. However, as the significance of what he or she had attained sank in, one by one the remaining managers were also able excitedly to announce 'I've got it!' Eventually all were on a 'high'.

The 'it' they had got, while probably not quite the same for each of them, was essentially to do with their realization that they had achieved more than they had thought possible. Some of them had sensed too that this achievement was more than a one-off event; they knew they could do the same or better in the future. They had gained in self-confidence. They had developed.

The highs, the 'eureka' effects, did not last. Later the managers were to say it had been 'fleeting'; it had 'evap-orated'. This is only to be expected. But the new self-perception of what one is capable of doing is usually lasting. Once you have seen yourself and your potential with new eyes it is virtually impossible to revert to your old vision.

Since that initial course I and colleagues have run many similar ones in which managers have undertaken work-based action projects as a basis for development. On these courses, for reasons of cost, time, and in some cases geographical dispersion, it has not been possible to establish formal 'learning sets'. The potential for learning and develop-ment from action may in consequence have been somewhat diminished. Nevertheless, managers on these courses have reported considerable learning and personal growth.

Knowing what you have done

By understanding the processes involved in experiential learning you will be able to reflect more systematically and insightfully on your experience and thereby gain greater learning and understanding from it.

The story is told of Sir Laurence Olivier, acting in one of his great Shakespearian roles. He had just given an out-standingly magnificent performance. The audience cheered; the cast joined in the applause. But Olivier, just as soon as he had taken his curtain calls, rushed from the stage in a state of distress and locked himself in his dressing room. It was some considerable time before the director was able to persuade him to emerge. 'Larry', he asked, 'What is the matter? You have just given one of the greatest performances of your life'. Olivier replied: 'I know. But I don't know how I did it. So I can't repeat it'.

If you do not understand what you have done and how you have done it, not only can you not repeat it, you cannot develop your performance. Nor can you reap the developmental benefit of knowing that you have reached a new level from which you can progress.

Adapting your learning style

Learning from experience is a skill. It also requires a will to learn in this way. Setting up a developmental experience with the right conditions will not be of much use to you unless you have this will and skill.

We all have preferences, like the Myers–Briggs preferences described in Chapter 2, for learning in different ways. These learning preferences have been described by David Kolb (1984).

Drawing on the work of earlier developmental psychologists, Kolb postulated four learning 'types', which he saw as comparable to Jungian 'archetypes' – such as the introverted and extroverted types, and the other Myers–Briggs types described in Chapter 2. Kolb's types fit within his now well-known 'learning cycle' that incorporates both theoretical and experiential learning (see Figure 5.2).

The abstract-concrete dimension in the model (the vertical axis) represents, in Kolb's words:

> . . two different and opposed processes of grasping or taking hold of experience in the world – either through reliance on conceptual interpretation and symbolic representation, a process I will call *comprehension*, or through reliance on the

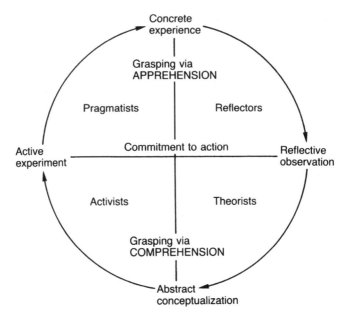

Figure 5.2   The Kolb learning cycle. Adapted from Kolb (1984) by permission of McBer & Company, Inc. 116 Huntington Avenue, Boston, MA 02116. © David A. Kolb, 1984

tangible, felt qualities of immediate experience, what I will call *apprehension.*

The active-reflective dimension (the horizontal axis in the diagram) represents:

> . . . two opposed ways of transforming that grasp or 'figurative representation' of experience – either through internal reflection . . . or active external manipulation of the external world. (pp. 40–41)

Whether one is more oriented to internal reflection or to external manipulation is a measure of one's commitment to taking action (the horizontal axis in the diagram). Part Three of this book is about how you might conduct the external manipulation, while Part Four is about how you might conduct your internal reflection on the experience.

Apprehending and comprehending

In order to understand the distinction between the two modes of grasping experience, comprehension and apprehension, Kolb suggests that you put yourself through the experience of each. First apprehension:

> Pause in your reading for a moment and become aware of your surroundings. What you see, hear, and feel around you are those sensations colours, textures, and sounds that are so basic and reliable that we call them reality. The continuous feel of your chair as it firmly supports your body, the smooth texture of the book and its pages, the muted mixture of sounds surrounding you – all these things and many others you know instantaneously without the need for rational inquiry or analytical confirmation. They are simply there, grasped through a mode of knowing here called apprehension . . .

Kolb goes on to suggest how you can experience comprehension:

> If you put down this book, get up from the chair, and leave the room, your apprehensions of that situation will vanish without trace (substituted for, of course, by new apprehensions of the hallway or whatever new immediate situation you are in). Your comprehension of that situation, however, will allow you to create for yourself and communicate to others a model of that situation that could last forever. (p. 43)

The risk in seeking to learn from experience is that you allow yourself, particularly if this is your preferred style of learning, to become preoccupied with apprehension (the experience) at the expense of comprehension (the understanding). It is vital to move between both. Otherwise you will neither be able to repeat nor build on your performance. Conversely, the risk is to contemplate action at the expense of ever achieving anything. Moreover, gathering experiences is not at all the same thing as becoming 'experienced'.

Types of learner

Drawing on Kolb's ideas, Peter Honey and Alan Mumford (1986) have described four types of learner: the activist, the reflector, the theorist and the pragmatist. The characteristics of each of these types are summarized in Box 5.2

Honey and Mumford have produced a questionnaire which enables people to diagnose their preferred learning style. However, as Honey and Mumford point out, regardless of basic preference, a mature manager should be able to learn effectively by any mode. Some versatility of learning style is essential if a manager is to develop at a personal level. It is not tenable if one is to manage effectively to remain locked into any one type.

Experiments in action

The broad sequence of experiential learning is depicted by the arrowed lines around the circumference of Figure 5.2. You are in effect conducting an experiment to see whether your ideas for achieving your goals will work.

In this experiment you confront the consequences of your choices and actions. You will experience setbacks, and learn from them how you handled the dismay or discouragement.

Box 5.2

Characteristics of the learning types

Activist

Strengths
- Flexible and open-minded.
- Happy to have a go.
- Happy to be exposed to new situations.
- Optimistic about anything new and therefore unlikely to resist change.

Weaknesses
- Tendency to take the immediately obvious action without thinking.
- Often take unnecessary risks.
- Tendency to do too much themselves and hog the limelight.
- Rush into action without sufficient preparation.
- Get bored with implementation/consolidation.

Reflector

Strengths
- Careful.
- Thorough and methodical.
- Thoughtful
- Good at listening to others and assimilating information.
- Rarely jump to conclusions.

Weaknesses
- Tendency to hold back from direct participation.
- Slow to make up their minds and reach a decision.
- Tendency to be too cautious and not take enough risks.
- Not assertive – they aren't particularly forthcoming and have no 'small talk'.

Theorist

Strengths
- Logical 'vertical' thinkers.
- Rational and objective.
- Good at asking probing questions.
- Disciplined approach.

Weaknesses
- Restricted in lateral thinking.
- Low tolerance for uncertainty, disorder and ambiguity.
- Intolerant of anything subjective or intuitive.
- Full of 'shoulds, oughts and musts'.

Pragmatist

Strengths
- Keen to test things out in practice.
- Practical, down to earth, realistic.
- Businesslike – gets straight to the point.
- Technique oriented.

Weaknesses
- Tendency to reject anything without an obvious application.
- Not very interested in theory or basic principles.
- Tendency to seize on the first expedient solution to a problem.
- Impatient with waffle.
- On balance, task oriented not people oriented.

From Honey and Mumford (1986) by permission.

You will recover your ground and learn from this what are the tactics that really do work.

The difference between this 'action experiment' and a research experiment is that you are not just an observer; you are part of the experiment, indeed its principal catalyst. Nor, usually, can you sit back and await the result while the experiment runs its course. You are constantly having to intervene to bring events back on course, or change direction, or perhaps modify your aims.

The time that it takes to complete the experiential sequence – experience–reflection–abstraction–experiment – can be extremely brief, almost simultaneous. Donald Schon has characterized the process as one of 'reflection in action'. Box 5.3 summarizes his description of the moment-by-moment sequence of events in this process of doing–reflecting–adapting.

Both Schon's reflection-in-action and Kolb's more extended learning cycle are models of how we learn to manipulate external events to achieve our ends. Schon is emphasizing how much experiential learning is a naturally occurring phenomenon that may not require you to go through the full sequence of learning suggested by Kolb's model. What we need to do is to learn to catch ourselves 'in action' in order to become good 'reflective practitioners'.

Your purpose–action–accomplishment experiment could be about learning to manage effectively within currently accepted concepts and practices. Or it could be about breaking new ground. Whichever, you will encounter situations that you will need to confront. Some of these, hopefully, will be demanding, really testing your abilities, and these are the experiences from which you will develop.

Personal experiment

In preparing yourself for your developmental experiment or learning project, you need to consider:

- What you want to do;
- What you feel able to do; and
- What resources you believe you could access in order to do what you want.

Box 5.3

Reflection in action: The sequence of 'moments'

1 Routine response

The starting point is a situation in which one is trying to achieve something to which one brings spontaneous, routinized responses – 'knowing-in-action'. These responses may be strategies, under-standings, ways of looking at a problem. Usually they will be delivered without conscious deliberation. As long as the situation is amenable to 'normal' treatment, the 'knowing-in-action' will work.

2 Surprise

Sometimes the routine response will produce a surprise, an unexpected outcome – pleasant or unpleasant. Our routine response may not have worked, or may have worked in an unusual way.

3 Reflection

Surprise leads to reflection. This will in some measure be conscious, though not necessarily in words. We consider the unexpected outcome and the events and actions that led up to it.

4 Question assumptions

'Reflection-in-action' causes us to be critical, to question our assumptions about what works and does not work in these situations. We think critically about the thinking that got us into this fix or opportunity, and in the process restructure our understandings, our strategies for action, our ways of framing problems.

5 On-the-spot experiment

Reflection gives rise to on-the-spot experiment. We think up and try out new actions intended to explore the re-appraised situation and test out our tentative new understanding of it. This on-the-spot experiment may work, that is to say yield the intended results, or it may produce surprises that call for further reflection and experiment.

Adapted from: Schön (1990: 28) by permission.

Each of these is subjective and each influences the other. Your perception of what you feel able to do could be under- or over-estimating your capabilities. Your assessment of yourself will affect your decision about what you want to do. Your perception of what resources you could have, while subjective, is capable of being checked out against reality.

Developmental learning comes at two levels:

* Testing your perceptions of yourself and your world in practice.

    This you will naturally do before you have got to the point of deciding on a course of action. But some perceptions of yourself and the world around you will remain to be tested by the unfolding of events. This process will be discussed further in later chapters.

* Reflection on how far you allowed yourself to be limited in your aspirations by unnecessarily restricted perceptions of the possible.

    Organizational barriers can often appear formidable, indeed insurmountable. Distinguishing between blocks that are real and blocks that are in the mind is an important part of the art of managing.

    Your perceptions could of course work the other way with exaggerated ideas of the possible, but this is scarcely a problem from a development point of view. If you are seeking to learn from experience, the risk of being undone by over-ambitious plans based on an inflated sense of your capabilities is probably worth taking.

When development occurs

You would be grossly misled if at this point you thought that all you now had to do was to get on with some action, and later on turn to Part IV to see how to make sense of it all. Development does not only take place in reflection after the event. It occurs during and in anticipation of it. As will be seen in the ensuing chapters, a large part of the 'doing' takes place in your head, for example formulating your intentions for what you want others to do, or creating within yourself that sense of purpose and commitment that will enable you to carry others with you in your ventures.

Much experiential development in fact comes while anticipating the event. The thought of having to do something provokes you into handling the issue in your mind. The actual doing may then be of relatively minor significance for your development. Or the doing itself may be the development. The point is that not all development takes place during reflection after the event.

This kind of anticipatory learning serves a further valuable purpose for self-development. It gives you a baseline of intentions against which, in later reflection, you can compare what actually happened. Without advance consideration of what you are trying to achieve you can have little basis for evaluating the significance of an event. Through the match or mismatch of purpose and outcome you will learn and develop.

Awareness in action

Learning-in-action demands heightened self-awareness. As well as reflecting on events – before, during and after, you need to be aware of your 'surreptitious agenda'. By this is meant those inner, not always conscious, forces that cause us to handle situations in ways that accord more with the needs of our ego than the needs of the circumstances.

The kind of factors that might come into play – needs, preferences, perceptions, emotions – and divert us from being as effective as we might have been, were discussed in Chapter 2. It is not always easy to be fully conscious of all the nuances of our motives. Nevertheless, some self-reflection, coupled with awareness of the more common forms of distorted managerial behaviour, can be a first step to bringing our surreptitious agenda under conscious control.

Many of the things that we learn from experience are practical skills, clearly observable behaviours, which can be practised and on which a judgement can be made about how well one has performed. Inner competence is less tangible. For example, while exerting power is something you do, you cannot always be certain when or whether you are being powerful. In the final analysis you may only be able to judge whether you have been powerful by the results you get. Awareness of self thus has to be linked to the purpose and task in hand.

Developmental challenges

Implementation of your action plans may not require the intellectual and analytical capacities demanded of the planning stages. But it presents other demands that are equally important for a manager's development – to do with relating to people, engaging with one's organization and using one's personal power to get results. Moreover, implementation impinges on an area that is very much a matter of contemporary concern, i.e. the management of change. It is also concerned with leadership. Formulating vision and direction is only one dimension of leading. Unless the vision is realized, leadership is futile.

Although success in your project will probably be as much due to teamwork as to your own endeavours, you will need, as leader of the project, to ensure that activities proceed in a direction acceptable to you. This is not simply a matter of exercising influence. The objective is that you personally, by whatever means, bring about some action and achieve a suitable outcome.

The implementation phase is treated in the ensuing chapters from the perspective of each of the levels at which a manager operates: organization, group and self. At each of these levels there is a central dilemma that managers and project leaders continually need to resolve:

- How to draw on your organization's resources and facilities and function effectively within its constraints. The central dilemma or challenge here is how to engage in your organization's political life while retaining your personal integrity. This is an issue that often concerns newly appointed managers. It can only grow in importance as society increasingly expects its corporations to give attention to environmental and ethical issues.

- How to get people involved in helping you. This is at the core of your style of a manager. The central dilemma is how you balance your need, often reinforced by powerful organizational expectations, to direct and control events with the sharing and participation that is likely to be demanded by any attempt to generate synergy from collaborative effort.
- How to influence people to do what you want and get events to go in the direction you want. Here the central dilemma is to know how far you can rely upon your personal power as opposed to formal organizational authority and sanctions.

The dilemmas in each case pose a developmental challenge. They cannot be resolved by reference to rule books or text books. Each manager has to work out his or her own salvation for handling the issues involved, and do so in a way that will enhance his or her ability to manage effectively.

Knowing what to do

Striking the right balance in these chapters between 'how to' and leaving it to readers to discover from experience has not been easy. I am sure there will be readers who will feel that I have erred too far in either direction – gratuitously elaborating the obvious for some, cursorily glossing over essential guidance for others. That this should be so is in the nature of learning from experience. Revans' original conception of action learning derived partly from seeing how managers succeeded in solving their own problems, and partly from seeing managers struggling to make use of irrelevant techniques and principles taught them at business school or gleaned from books.

Business-school teaching and books on management have moved on considerably in the half century since Revans was first moved to look for alternatives. Nevertheless, the circumstances of managing remain diverse and each manager still has to work out his or her salvation when it comes to making things happen.

Meeting all your needs

The topics to be covered below in dealing with implementation include being political, gaining autonomy, working relationships, creating synergy, intervening in events, and being personally powerful. This selection is, I recognize, far from comprehensive. There are other aspects of managing that for some readers might well have provided a more relevant vehicle for self-development. However, to the extent that the implementation of any task demands that action is activated, sustained and steered, the selection here would seem pretty central.

Moreover, working through a comprehensive list of managerial activities or competences would be entirely at odds with the spirit of self-development through facing uncertain challenges. In any event, many developmental issues for an individual are likely to be common across a wide variety of managerial activities. For example, a necessity to handle one's urge to be liked or admired, or to practise unpreferred behaviours such as meticulous advance planning, will be thrown up by all kinds of different situations.

Normally it takes only a few unfamiliar and demanding situations for someone to become aware of his or her major development needs. This is not to say that there will not be specific competences, such as report writing or chairing meetings, for which you have a development need which may fully come to light only when you attempt these specific tasks. But if you are aware of particular development needs, there is little problem in finding a situation in which you can put yourself to the test. However, we are more concerned in this book with what might be termed 'strategic development' than with comprehensive coverage of all managerial skills.

Actor Albert Finney once said in an interview that he sifted the many plays and film scripts that he was invited to act in by just reading the beginning and end. If the characters were the same at the end as they were at the beginning he assumed that not very much happened in between. Only if the characters showed development did he bother to read the script in full, expecting then to find some dramatic action.

It is the same in real-life management; not much personal change can be expected without creating some drama in your work. This is one of the main ways in which we can change ourselves – through what we do and achieve. If we can become more aware of how these processes of personal change work, understand better the relationship between our inner self and our actions, we can become more adept at using our managerial capabilities. The next part of this book is about how to create the necessary dramatic action.

Arrival

A final point before you embark on your experience: personal development does not always have to be accompanied by painstaking reflection on experience. Often we develop simply by being someone who has achieved something. No further reflection on what you did or did not do is required. You are aware that you are now a person who can achieve this sort of thing. On the other hand, a setback to achieving your purposed outcome will require reflection so that you can move forward with a changed approach.

Further development may then come from gearing yourself up a notch for your next project. In the course of tackling that, then you might be prompted to reflect on your previous experience to identify what you learned that can now be applied in your new challenging circumstances. But at the time of achievement there may be no point in going over past ground; the arrival is sufficient development.

Reflection and action points

At this point you need to prepare yourself practically and psychologically for the ensuing action phase.

• If you are intending a special development project, use the principles in this chapter to continue the planning begun in Chapter 4. Set up suitable experiences for subsequent reflection.

Regardless of whether or not you are undertaking a special project:

- Clarify your intentions for your development, and consider how they may be realized through your anticipated experiences;
- Be aware of what you are doing during these experiences and take time to draw out the learning; and
- Aim to become a person who has achieved.

Part three
Putting Yourself to the Test

It is by his actions that man learns what his capabilities are, and what he achieves is the most tangible psychological measure of his behaviour.

George Kelly, *Selected Papers*

Personal transformation report 3

Achieving effectiveness through becoming a 'team supporter'

I am a clinical nurse manager, responsible for the general management of two Intensive Therapy Units in a large National Health Service hospital in south-east England, a position I have held for about a year. My predecessor, who had been in nursing for many years, had felt that the old system of care delivery had worked well, providing high-quality care to our patients. But the environment today is changing rapidly and health care practices have to be adapted accordingly. I have been determined, therefore, to ensure that the two Units for which I was responsible kept up to date.

The two Units operate very differently, each with its distinct culture. In Unit 1 the staff are fairly eager to take change on board and are willing to undertake research studies to enable them to improve their practice. Staff in Unit 2, however, need considerable persuasion to accept that change should happen.

Starting the process of change

Two weeks after my appointment I held meetings with the staff in each Unit, at which I stressed the importance of change and that we should all involve ourselves in introducing it in our areas of work. In Unit 1 the staff agreed to various research investigations and to develop plans as appropriate. In Unit 2 when I suggested areas that needed development the staff sounded eager to become involved and set a plan which detailed areas of responsibility for different members of staff. I left the Unit feeling that implementing change was not going to be as difficult as I had originally anticipated.

Two weeks later, when I asked for a progress report, Unit 1 presented details of different topics they were researching. Unit 2, however, could not provide me with any evidence of their progress. I enquired whether there was a problem and if I could give assistance. I was told that they were researching but did not have anything in writing to show me. I believed them, thinking they just needed more time.

Two more weeks passed and there was still no evidence of progress. I then became concerned and decided that I should review my approach.

I set myself the objective of cultivating in Unit 2 staff a positive attitude to change and an enthusiastic willingness to involve themselves in improving our patient care in the Intensive Therapy Unit. My more immediate objective was to ascertain the reasons for their seemingly negative behaviour and form a plan to overcome it.

Before approaching them again, however, I felt that I needed to prepare myself. I needed to review my presentation abilities. It was essential that I portrayed a positive attitude if I was to instil enthusiasm and ownership. I realized that I did not always accept alternative views. I can become demoralized very easily if I cannot obtain the response I would like. Moreover, I knew I did not always present my case in a clear and precise manner which is easily understood.

I spent the next week practising, with the help of a friend, how to be more assertive in my approach and general outlook. At the end of the week I felt I had made progress but was unsure whether I was strong enough to influence my colleagues. Unfortunately, time was pressing, so I decided to try my best and learn from my experiences.

Plunging in

I arranged a meeting with the staff in Unit 2, stressing the importance that as many as possible attend, which they did. I told them that I was concerned about the lack of support in developing the projects as per their agreement. I said that I was aware that this task placed extra pressure on everybody but, nevertheless, any spare time must be utilized to update our practice on the Units.

I then asked why they had not undertaken the necessary work to complete the projects. Initially there was no response. Following a lengthy silence one member stated that they did not have the time. This I thought to be a poor excuse as although the Unit can be very busy at times it had been fairly quiet recently. So I asked what had she had done when the Unit had been quiet last week. She replied that she had done some reading. Immediately another member asked 'What is the point in undertaking this work? When we have helped out in the past the manager got all the credit and none of it was ever implemented.' I gave an assurance that I would not take the credit. As for implementing the results, it was up to us as the experts in our area to improve our service. Another member of staff stated that we already delivered high-quality care so why change. I agreed this was so, but gave some reasons why there was, nevertheless, a need for improvements. This was why I was insisting on these projects.

I then asked for suggestions on how we could work together to plan the necessary improvements. Two staff members started to discuss what they could do and then more joined in. A short time later it had been decided that two members of the Unit would go to the library that afternoon and seek out some information, provided I could stay on the Unit while they were away, to which I agreed.

A week later I met with them to discuss progress. To my delight they had actually made a start. The Unit had been busy during the week and therefore I accepted that progress would be slow. Progress continued, though slowly, but the projects were eventually completed on time.

Personal change

As a result of this experience, I have improved my ability to communicate with my staff, get their attention and convince them of my determination. Although I feel I have achieved a lot, I still have a long way to go. I have not yet 'won over' all of them.

I feel a personal sense of achievement in contributing to the quality of care we give to our patients. I have also improved my self-esteem and feel that I have increased the staff's confidence in me as their manager. As a team we have travelled a long distance from where we were ten weeks ago.

In reflecting upon the course of events, I have gained valuable insights about myself. Initially I went through a phase of delight when the staff agreed in principle to become involved in the projects. This rapidly disappeared when the written documentation did not materialize and a feeling of annoyance took its place. I could feel myself becoming angry with the staff and blaming them for their lack of interest and for being obstructive. I made myself count to ten, go away and think about the situation before approaching the staff in my negative mood.

Thinking about it quietly made me realize that maybe the problem did not lie entirely with them. Perhaps part of the problem lay with my approach to them. The friend who helped me with me assertiveness told me some home truths about how I presented myself, which quite shocked me. She also questioned some of my assumptions about the staff's motives for not cooperating. She asked: did they have the time, the knowledge, the experience? I began to try to see things from the staff's point of view.

I feel that I am now communicating more effectively, giving clear instructions using short and to-the-point sentences. I use an encouraging tone in my voice to help effect enthusiasm.

I have also gained valuable experience in managing meetings more effectively. Along with being clear and to the point with my requests, I have learnt to listen. Although listening has played a very important role in my previous professional work, I found it difficult as a manager just to listen. Another point of value to me was the importance of recording decisions in writing after a meeting has finished, in order to reinforce our agreements.

Undoubtedly this project has made me more effective as a manager. In addition to the communication skills just described, I have become more tolerant of other people, less judgemental and more willing to review my practice as well as that of others. I have improved my ability to support people rather than let them struggle. And I have improved my knowledge of how people can behave and how to respond to them.

6 Managing politically

Introduction

In any organization – and most managers manage within an organization – what you want to do has to be set against what others want to do. Conflicts over priorities have to be resolved, diverse goals accommodated, resources negotiated. If you want to influence this process you need to get involved in your organization's politics.

This chapter deals with how you might appropriately involve yourself in the politics of your organization in order to:

- Draw on its facilities and manage its constraints.
- Secure some freedom of action for yourself and for your supporters or project team.

It sets out different approaches you can take to pursuing your purposes within an organization and discusses how you might avoid political game-playing. Principles of 'positive politics' and managing with integrity are discussed.

The chapter concludes by reviewing some of the outcomes you might seek from the political process:

- Getting your own agendas accepted;
- Having money for your projects;
- Being able to cross organizational boundaries to implement them; and
- Finding the time and space to devote to them.

Your political view

Organizational politics have a bad name. They are associated with in-fighting, empire-building, personality contests – all too often engaged in, so it is suspected, for personal ends rather than the good of the organization. To the outsider political activity may well look like a disorderly scrummage, with everyone jostling to be at the front, regardless of rules or propriety. Because of this poor image, newly appointed managers may try to stay outside the 'politics'. But not to engage in the political life of your organization is to cut yourself off from opportunities to gain help and resources in order to manage effectively.

If an organization worked like clockwork, if all the needed collaboration, co-operation and co-ordination were organized according to an agreed overplan, if resources were allocated rationally and equitably, if everyone had the authority they needed to do their job . . . The reality of course, even in the most well-ordered of organizations, is that the cogs in the clockwork need oiling.

You cannot assume, for example, that because your objectives have been agreed by your boss that the resources you need to realize them will necessarily be allocated to you. You may well need to make your case to other managers who will also be bidding for the same resources. Nor can you assume that because a project has been given formal approval that everyone whose support you need will fall in line. Their co-operation will probably need to be cultivated. Managers pursuing and safeguarding their interests is what organizational politics is all about.

Political games

The need to resolve conflicts of interest is the prime source of all political behaviour. The issue for a manager is to assess whether his or her purposes and those of others are legitimate. Are they narrowly self-seeking or do they serve wider corporate goals?

Mintzberg (1983), in a comprehensive review of power and politics in organizations, has identified thirteen 'political games', listed in Box 6.1.

You can look on organizational politics negatively – as the black art of scheming and devious manipulation, and try to keep your hands clean by staying out of it. Or you can view politics positively – as the natural process of getting things done within an organization or the business world. You

---

Box 6.1

Organizational politics: thirteen political games

Games to resist authority:	The insurgency games – to sabotage the intentions of superiors.
Games to counter resistance:	The counter-insurgency games – more rules, regulations and punishments.
Games to build power bases:	The sponsorship game – hitching oneself to a useful *superior*, a star. The alliance game – finding useful *colleagues*. The empire game – building coalitions of *subordinates*. The budgeting game – getting control of *resources*. The expertise game – flaunting and feigning *expertise*. The lording game – flaunting one's *authority*.
Games to defeat rivals:	The line versus staff game – between units or functions.
Games to change the organization:	The strategic candidates game – informing on an opponent. The young Turks game – enclaves of key rebels.

From: Handy (1985), p. 233, adapted from Mintzberg (1983) by permission of the publisher, Penguin Books.

---

recognize that there will be conflicts of interest, that people will push to get the best deals for themselves, and that they will seek to expand their resources in order the more effectively to achieve their objectives. But you work from the premise that, unless proved otherwise, they are acting in good faith to achieve their objectives.

Lists of political games, such as that in Box 6.1, do, however, provide a source of ammunition for those who like to disparage managerial behaviour and what they perceive to be sectional and self-serving purposes. But all these so-called games can often have a very different interpretation placed on them.

Sabotaging the intentions of superiors may be perceived by subordinates as acting in the best interests of the organization. The most famous example of course is that of Nelson, in the Battle of the Baltic, holding his telescope to his blind eye in order to avoid compliance with Admiral Parker's signal to withdraw. Less famously, I was once involved in a case where failure to place the metaphorical telescope to his blind eye was a contributing factor to an elderly factory manager being forced into premature retirement.

An attitude survey of garment workers had revealed high levels of dissatisfaction with their factory's amenities and consequent low morale. The factory manager's righteous protests that he had already more than once drawn top management's attention to these problems fell on the managing director's deaf ears. The managing director, justifiably or otherwise, took the view that the factory manager had clearly not made his case for expenditure on improved factory amenities forcibly enough. He should have continued to fight his corner and not so compliantly fallen into line when refused the resources he knew he needed to have.

The incident could of course be interpreted as a case of scapegoating. But it nevertheless makes the point that opposing the intentions of superiors can be more than 'game playing'. It can be the right thing to do.

There is a propensity for external observers of political behaviour in organizations to see only its negative, self-serving side. Sometimes this may be a correct interpretation. Managers can be self-aggrandizing and be obsessed with gaining personal advantage. Mintzberg in fact viewed most of his thirteen games, when used in moderation, as having a healthy effect on the organization – helping to keep it on its toes. But they are presented in a negative format, and he observes that if carried to excess, these games can divert the organization from what it should be doing.

Political purposes

Managers seemingly engaged in self-seeking game-playing are very likely to have another side to the story. Many tactics or 'ploys' – for example, referring again to Mintzberg's list of games, building a power base, defeating rivals, changing the organization – may well seem legitimate courses of action to managers seeking to further corporate goals as they see them. Conforming either to top management's or another department's viewpoint may simply not be seen as best for the organization. Organizational politics is the process of resolving these conflicts of view and interest.

There are two primary outcomes to be sought from involvement in your organization's politics:

- Awareness of what is going on around you – partly so that you are aware of plans and events elsewhere in your organization and outside it that could affect what you are doing, but also so that you understand what you need to do and who you need to be talking to in order to bring your own influence to bear on events; and
- Ensure that your activities and projects receive support and resources.

Sheep, donkeys, foxes and owls

A practically useful way of looking at organizational politics has been developed by Kim James and Simon Baddeley of the Institute of Local Government Studies (Baddeley and James, 1987). While light-heartedly characterizing the different political stances that people may take as that of innocent sheep, inept donkey, clever fox or wise owl, they at the same time illumine the dilemmas that face a manager in getting involved in organizational politics.

Baddeley and James' model of organizational politics was originally derived from their observations of local government managers. Many of these took the view that 'politics' was the province of the elected councillors and that they, as employed officials, should confine their activities to the impartial execution of policy determined by their political masters.

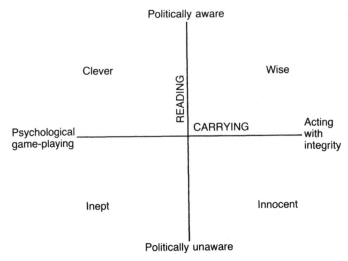

Figure 6.1   Descriptive model of political behaviour. From: Baddeley & James(1987) by permission of Sage Publications

Baddeley and Simon created their model in order to draw attention in a dramatic way to the fact that divisions of work are never that neat. Moreover, the political masters in local authorities were beginning to take an extremely close interest in the execution side of things (this was during the Thatcher era). Local authority managers needed to reciprocate by taking a comparable interest in the policy-formulation process if they were to be effective in implementing it.

The model of organizational politics that Baddeley and James used to get their message across is depicted in Figure 6.1. It is built around two dimensions: 'reading' and 'carrying'.

Reading

'Reading' means reading the organization, being active in finding out what is going on, what is likely to happen and why. In sum, making yourself politically aware.

Donna Lucas (1992), talking with doctors with managerial roles in the National Health Service, found that 'reading' the organization meant for them knowing the answers to such questions as:

- Who are the final arbiters for all the different kinds of decisions, most especially finance, new ventures, staffing, operational targets? What is their agenda? Who advises them? Who do they listen to?
- Who gets on with whom? Who carries weight with whom? How does this affect decision-making?
- What is going on externally and how is this affecting decision-making?
- Who should I be lobbying in my cause? Which arguments would be likely to carry weight?

Specific 'reading' that project managers have been observed to engage in is presented in Box 6.2. The person who does not read their organization will be unaware of its diversities and complexities. Andrew Kakabadse (1983) has suggested that such a manager is liable to respond to situations oversimplistically. Such managers may thus be able to sustain an image of themselves as behaving consistently. But to operate effectively in an organization demands the use of a wide repertoire of behaviours to cope with all its varying circumstances. Managers have to live with the knowledge that their behaviour may not always appear consistent, though from their own perspective it will appear coherent and appropriate.

Carrying

'Carrying' is a less self-explanatory concept than reading. What Baddeley and James mean by it is the propensity that we all have to carry around with us a great deal of psychological baggage that can sometimes lead us into behaving in ways which are more governed by our desire to satisfy our ego than to do what is best in the situation. At one extreme of the carrying dimension, a person will be found engaging in psychological game-playing; at the other, acting with integrity.

Someone driven by the kind of inner needs described in Chapter 2 might well be a psychological game-player, though

---

Box 6.2

How a project manager reads an organization

- Wants to know:
  - Who are the stakeholders, pressure groups, interested parties, potential allies?
  - Who needs to be influenced?

- Asks about them:
  - What are their priorities, goals and interests?
  - What can be predicted from their past behaviour?
  - What specifically do I expect of them, e.g. support for particular tasks, take on new role?
  - What is their attitude to the project (positive or negative)? What are they expecting from it?
  - What is their likely reaction? What issues or snags might they raise?
  - What will be the ripple effects of the project? (You need to map relationships and links to understand this.)

- Looking to:
  - Manage relations outside the team, i.e. gain support, minimize opposition and generally create climate favourable to the change.
  - Spot trouble.
  - Discover how best to concentrate effort.

Adapted from: Boddy and Buchanan (1992; 55–60) by permission of the publisher, Prentice Hall International.

---

not necessarily consciously. Some people deliberately set out to play psychological games in the belief that this is how best to be effective in manipulating the politics.

A variant, which is not game-playing as it is normally understood, is for a manager to fail to tackle a difficult situation because of his or her psychological insecurities, for example avoiding tackling an issue of underperformance with one of your staff because you lack the confidence or ability to do so. But in its own way this is just as much game-playing as the more recognized sort.

The model permits Baddeley and James to characterize four principal stances managers may take with regard to organizational politics.

Four political stances

First there is the manager who eschews all involvement in politics. This is the person who is proud of staying out of all the political machinations, who does not even bother to keep in touch with what is going on. These people may well believe that by staying out of everything to do with politics they are maintaining their integrity. But by being politically unaware, not bothering even to read the organization, these managers are 'innocent sheep'. They risk being herded by more politically astute managers. They may be so innocent that they do not even know this is happening to them.

Then there are the managers who try their hand at manipulating the organizational politics but without taking care to read the organization – playing political games from a position of political unawareness. This is inept behaviour, satirized by Baddeley and James as the 'blundering donkey'.

Next there is the manager who epitomizes the kind of behaviour that has given organizational politics a bad name. These managers are the 'clever foxes'. They are highly politically aware, but use their awareness to fulfil the needs of their ego – for example, to dominate others, to win, to be seen as successful, to expand their 'empire'.

Finally, there is the politically aware manager who acts with integrity – the 'wise owl'. Contrasting characteristics of the four types are presented in Figure 6.2.

Clever or wise

Once these four stances with regard to an organization's politics are pointed out, most responsibly minded managers will no doubt want to ensure that they take up the wise owl stance. This may be far from straightforward. Acting with integrity goes to the root of your self-awareness. We are not

Figure 6.2   Some characteristics of the four 'political' behaviours. From: Baddeley and James (1987) by permission of Sage Publications

always fully conscious of all our motives, and it is all too easy to fall into unwitting game-playing. We do things, so we believe for disinterested reasons, that are really self-serving – and may all too blatantly appear that way to others. There is often no way of distinguishing between 'wise' and 'clever' behaviour by any objective criteria.

Descriptions in the organizational literature of how managers build their power and empires, as for example in Leonard Sayles' (1989) accounts of a manager's organizational life, could equally well be interpreted as examples of managers 'wisely' obtaining the resources necessary to achieve purposes that will serve the organizational good.

My own experience may be cited. At the end of my first year in a new managerial post my written appraisal from my boss consisted of three curt sentences. The first was a pat on the back. Then: 'You need to be more devious. Get in touch with the politics of the third (i.e. the directors') floor.'

In response to my request for elucidation, he told me that I was naive to trust that, just because my objectives had been agreed to, the resources would automatically follow. Other managers were after them too. The only way I was going to get the resources to do all the things that I wanted to do was by being in touch with the politics.

I ignored the advice about being devious. But I certainly opened my eyes to what was going on in the organization and started lobbying, to my great surprise not at all unsuccessfully, for my particular causes. My department grew, to the benefit, so I believe, of my organization.

Integrity

In his caustic book, *The Leaders We Deserve*, Alistair Mant (1985) argues that integrity as a manager has to derive from some purpose, project or cause which is external to the manager. Mant sees corporate life, regrettably, as largely dominated by what he calls 'binary' relationships in which managers struggle to derive satisfactions and rewards from the outcomes of their relationships with each other; for example, win–lose, dominate–submit.

He contrasts this unsatisfactory state of affairs with what he inelegantly calls a 'ternary' model of managing. By this he means that there is a third consideration, a purpose or project, which moderates managers' behaviour and enables them to transcend the petty ego-driven considerations of a binary relationship. Only if, in Mant's view, there is an external referent point can managers hope to act in any way with integrity.

Mant's argument is appealing. But the process of identifying an independent purpose or project is of course political and has to be pursued in good faith.

Positive politics

It is quite possible to act with integrity and at the same time derive personal benefit from doing so – it could be financial reward for high performance or the job satisfaction that comes from controlling a more extensive domain. Integrity does not exclude enlightened self-interest. The issue is one of good faith, and as far as possible being conscious of one's motives. Others of course may cynically attribute you with different, unflattering motives. Whether in such circumstances you judge it appropriate to attempt to justify yourself or to disdain public opinion will be a further issue you will need to resolve.

Enlightened self-interest is at the heart of Peter Block's (1987) vision of how stifling and unproductive bureaucratic mentalities and structures may be overcome. Block castigates the unenlightened pursuit of self-interest:

> When we define self-interest as the pursuit of safety, control, advancement, approval, and territory for its own sake, the bureaucratic way of operating is almost inevitable. Negative politics is created when I feel the organization in some way owns me . . . offers little autonomy . . .

> We see the manipulation taking place around us; in fact, it's so ingrained in organizational cultures that sometimes we hardly know we're doing it . . .

Block has delineated five principles, set out in Box 6.3, by which a manager may pursue positive organizational politics. They all involve in some way balancing personal values and interest with those of the organization or wider community, a re-ordering of the way we view our self-interest:

> It is necessary to give second priority to the personal, career-advancing self-interest that we typically have and to develop the mind-set that our primary self-interest is inevitably linked and interdependent with the self-interest of the business and the other people around us. The major purpose of our work is to build an organization of our own choosing and one that we believe in.

Box 6.3

The road to positive politics: five dimensions of enlightened self-interest for managers

1 Meaning

- Engage in activities that have meaning to you and are genuinely needed. Do those things that express your own values, or those of your unit, while still contributing to the organization:

  We stop engaging in activities designed to defend ourselves, to explain ourselves ... No more ... detailed strategies on whom to meet with and when ... We cast our fate to the wind and do the things that have meaning and depth and substance for our unit, even if we think they may not win approval or blessings from those around us. We commit to the pursuit of substance over form.

2 Contribution and service

- Do the things that you feel genuinely contribute to the organization and its purpose. Make your own unique contribution to the business:

  Our self-interest is best served when we're focused on contributing the things that are of unique value to the business ... No more 'make work' projects, no more committees studying committees on oversight ... We treat this business as it were our own.

3 Integrity

- Maintain your personal integrity in the organization by putting into words what you see happening. Tell people what is really going on:

  Integrity isn't a moral issue; it's not a question of fraud or legally dishonest acts. It is more the issue of whether it is possible for us to tell the truth about what we see happening, to make only those promises that we can deliver on, to admit our mistakes, and to have the feeling that the authentic act is always best for the business.

4 Positive impact on others

- Treat other people well. Care about the well-being of your colleagues and the people around you:

There is a great deal of conventional wisdom about not getting too close to the people around us . . . if we get too close to other people, somehow it will hinder our ability to make objective decisions . . .

All of these beliefs are rationalization for treating people in ways that we don't feel comfortable about. They're based on a very narrow view of what's possible in relationships . . .

- Concern yourself with the nature of the products and services you are offering:

We need to decide what services are of genuine value to other people and become a user- or customer-driven function.

5 Mastery

- Learn as much as you can about the activity you are engaged in:

Performing a function simply for its own sake always serves your best self-interest. To perform a function because it's dirty work that has to be done and somebody has to do it, is a sign that what you're doing may not be worth the effort. This final element of enlightened self-interest involves doing those things that would allow you to be the best and let that be its own reward.

Adapted from: Block (1987: 86–93) by permission.

Block warns managers against thinking that it will all be different when you have reached a higher level in the organization or have more responsibility:

It is possible to be personally 'successful' but in the process to lose a part of ourselves while we support an environment that we really would like to change. Therefore, how we get ahead is as critical as how far we go. (pp. 85–86)

Inner and outer directedness

So far we have looked at political behaviour from a somewhat rational perspective. You make a choice about the kind of stance you wish to adopt: clever–wise, binary or ternary, enlightened self-interest, read or remain innocent.

Andrew Kakabadse (1983) has highlighted a further, more psychological, factor that needs to be taken into account. This is the tendency that we all have to be directed primarily by reference to our inner guiding lights, our values and needs, on the one hand, or to external considerations such as cultural norms and other people's expectations on the other. Kakabadse's summary of the contrasts between inner-directed and outer-directed people is presented in Box 6.4.

The implications for political behaviour of these two contrasting psychological preferences can be considerable. Kakabadse sees the outer-directed managers in terms very similar to those associated with game-playing or empire-building politics. Because their referent point for action is external they both read the organization and act upon its norms. They depend on the judgements of others to evaluate their performance which leads to seeking to improve their position and have public status which will give them

---

Box 6.4

Outer-directed and inner-directed management styles

Outer-directed	*Inner-directed*
Role-oriented	Self-oriented
Status conscious	Personal goals oriented
Checks with others before doing things	Does what he/she thinks is required
Highest reward – improving one's position	Highest reward – recognition for competent task performance
Unlikely to introduce dramatic change	Will introduce changes that are considered necessary
Will take leadership if others give support	Will take leadership to satisfy personal drive

From: Kakabadse (1983: 70).

recognition. This driving force, coupled with skilled management of the organization's politics, will lead some of these outer-directed managers to become, in Kakabadse's phrase, 'company barons'. Those who take a more simplistic view of the politics will be the organization's 'traditionalists', holding to the rules and conforming to the culture.

Inner-directed people, by contrast, are less conformist. Indeed, according to Kakabadse, it is from this group that the visionaries for radical change will be drawn. On the other hand, there is a risk that too much inner-directedness can cause a disjunction between their purposes and activities and broader corporate purposes. Indeed, Kakabadse sees some inner-directed managers forming inward looking teams of like-minded people that are driven by counter-culture attitudes.

All in all, Kakabadse's model does not allow for much wisdom in organizational politics; it is more the traditional, cynical view of politics. But no one is obliged to fall in with the patterns of political behaviour he has observed. You can be aware of what is driving your behaviour. If you are inner-directed, temper your pursuit of personal goals with awareness of corporate needs. If you are outer-directed, seek to emancipate yourself from dependence on knowing what will gain approval and what will not before you act. Finding this out is of course no more than prudent reading of your organization's politics. It is the psychological dependency on knowing, and then on needing to go which way the wind blows, that is the trap.

Time and space

At the beginning of this chapter two primary political objectives for a manager were specified: linking in to the organization's decision-making processes, and enlisting the organization's staff and resources in your projects and causes.

There is a further, rather more personal objective that you will probably wish to consider: securing permanently for yourself a measure of autonomy that allows you to do more of the things you would like, that allows you to be able to manage things more in the way you want.

This means finding ways of freeing yourself to some degree from the day-to-day pressures and the supervision of routines. It means making time and space for yourself so that you really do have an opportunity to contribute what you are capable of.

Organizations can enable the people who work in them to do things beyond the scope of anything they could do on their own. On the other hand, they inevitably restrict freedom and initiative. There are of course good reasons why this is so, but that does not make the constraints less irksome or frustrating.

Having the freedom to do more than responding to immediate pressures, more than 'mind the shop', is at the heart of managing effectively. It is the necessary condition for you to be able to make your distinctive contribution. It is the key to being able to combine managing with leading. Without some organizational 'time and space', not just for yourself but for those you work with too, there can be little opportunity for creative initiative.

Sometimes the necessary time and space may be formally built into one's role. But for many managers it has to be cultivated, negotiated, fought for. In view of all the pressure one is likely to have, this may scarcely seem worthwhile. Why take on extra burdens when there is enough to be done already? There is no good reason really, other than wanting to be a manager who does more than simply respond to events, to be a manager who does more than just get by – who is effective as well as efficient.

Most managers will be aware of ways in which they can create a degree of freedom for themselves. There are four key areas to work on:

- Agendas,
- Money,
- Boundaries, and
- Time.

Agenda setting

Considerable emphasis has been placed in this book on setting your agenda for your personal development. It is expected in many organizations that you in fact do this, i.e. that you should look after your own career interests, and that you should have a personal as well as an organizational agenda. Here we look at organizational agendas.

To make something happen you have to get it onto the agenda of those people who will be instrumental in facilitating the desired action – collaborators, resource-holders, approvers. You need to get your project approved as part of the corporate agenda. What is not on the agenda is unlikely to have much priority.

The implication of this for a manager pursuing a project is that it may not be sufficient simply to get others to assent to your objectives and plans. You have either to make those whose support you need see that what you want is congruent with organizational objectives that they concur with. If these purposes are not already agreed, then you may be faced with the need, unless you choose to act surreptitiously, to embark on the political task of getting organizational purposes modified in a way that incorporates your particular purposes.

Corporate 'agendas' may be written down in the form of mission statements, corporate plans, action points, and similar documents. But ultimately agendas are a psychological phenomenon. They are the ideas and visions that managers carry around in their heads that provide the reference points against which decisions to do or support something are made.

Kotter (1982) has well described this process in his observations of general managers at work:

> Effective executives develop agendas that are made up of loosely connected goals and plans that address their long-, medium-, and short-term responsibilities. The agendas usually address a broad range of financial, product/market, and organizational issues. They include both vague and specific items.

Kotter notes that, while some of the managers' agenda-setting decisions will be made consciously or analytically, some of their decisions will be unconscious or intuitive. The process is:

. . . largely internal to their minds. Indeed, important agenda-setting decisions are often not observable. In selecting specific activities to include in their agendas, GMs [general managers] look for those that accomplish multiple goals, that are consistent with other goals and plans, and that are within their power to implement. Projects and programs that seem important and logical but do not meet these criteria tend to be discarded or at least resisted (pp. 160–161).

General managers, Kotter's research showed, build their networks of collaborative relationships around the people they feel will be useful to them in implementing their agendas. Interactions in their encounters with colleagues and other staff, at least among the effective managers, could be seen to have as their reference point the manager's agendas – glean a relevant point of information, ask a favour, cajole or encourage, influence generally. Virtually all these interactions could be seen to be, in some way or other, to be progressing one or other of the manager's agendas.

The clear message for managers seeking to pursue an objective within an organization is not only to have their own agenda clear, but also to make it their business to know others' agendas. This may not always be easy, as agendas are often unconscious and tacit. But one of your main political roads to freedom in an organization lies in getting your agenda items accepted on other people's agendas. When successful in doing this, you can find yourself expected, even pressured, by others to do the very things you want to do anyhow.

Finding money

Money, available for example through special project budgets or savings on existing budgets which can be used to buy in extra resources or staff help, is perhaps the most advantageous of all the sources of freedom. However, it is a source that tends to come and go with economic cycles and changing buoyancy of revenues. In my own personal experience, when money is available to buy help, creativity and innovation flourish.

The other side of money as a source of freedom is ensuring that you have an adequate budget for the activities you are committed to. Your freedom of action as a manager is probably more at risk from unrealistic budgeting than from any other factor.

Part of the conventional wisdom of management is that managers have to manage with limited resources. Part of managing effectively is not to allow a key determinant of your effectiveness to be settled by reference to platitudinous precepts. It is not effective to succumb to pressure to accept targets that you honestly believe cannot be met within the proposed budget. Successfully to resist such pressure demands three things from you:

- Detailed knowledge about what work is involved in the tasks you are responsible for coupled with a realistic appraisal of the resources, including time, needed to achieve them;
- A determination not to allow fiction to supplant fact (speculating about what is uncertain is another matter); and
- A preparedness to take a stand in order to get your honest judgement about what is possible accepted.

Crossing boundaries

Some organizations encourage people to co-operate in whatever way they see fit regardless of boundaries. In other, more bureaucratically inclined organizations, a request to someone on the other side of an organizational divide to do something may have to pass up one tendril of the hierarchy and down another. Whatever the protocols, you need to establish your freedom to work across the boundaries.

For the purposes of managing a project you can use a manager as a sponsor to effect the necessary introductions and give you authority to request support and assistance. But if you want to gain this freedom of movement on a continuing basis, you will need to cultivate the contacts that arise from your project with a longer term perspective in mind.

There is a risk that on a project's conclusion your 'licence' to operate in different areas of the organization may be revoked. At the end of your allotted time, you are, so to speak, put back in your box as if your few weeks or months of high profile activity had never been.

It is worth citing a particular instance that occurred on an action-learning programme. A head teacher of a secondary school had the approval of his local authority to carry out a project with county wide ramifications. Despite urging from his action learning set he did not work to establish any support for what he was doing that would have extended beyond the life of the project. He deliberately confined all discussion and correspondence with his contacts strictly to the business in hand. On the day that his course formally terminated, his formal 'licence' to operate outside the confines of his school also abruptly terminated. His employers saw his project as an isolated one-off event connected with his course. The head teacher himself also saw it in these self-contained terms, practising some investigatory skills that had no significance beyond the life of the project. So once it ended, he ceased to influence school issues on a county-wide basis.

But project outcomes are not always so unsatisfactory. It is not difficult to seize the opportunities presented by a project to develop long term collaborative relationships. Moreover, a successful project can cause you to be seen in a new light and open up new opportunities.

Making time   log.3

Time is perhaps the most problematic of all the constraints on our freedom to manage as we would like. There is rarely enough of it. In the case of a project, unless you have been assigned to it full-time, it is all too easy for your initial impetus to evaporate in the face of competing pressures. Indeed for some managers, the formidable difficulties involved in freeing themselves from day-to-day pressures of work may be a significant deterrent to taking this route to personal development in the first place.

Organizing your time more effectively, along the lines, say, that you would learn on certain time management courses could no doubt help. A good time management course would get you to review how you presently spend your time and help you devise a more effective way of scheduling it. But more importantly, it would get you to take a strategic look at your priorities. You would also be made to consider how you might delegate or shed some of your present tasks.

An exercise that you might use to help you evaluate your present use of time is set out in Box 6.5. This exercise goes further than simply getting you to analyse your schedule and review your priorities. It gets you to discover how you feel

---

Box 6.5

Your feelings about your time

In order to review your use of time you need to know:

- What you do,
- Why you do it, and
- How you feel about doing it.

To get this information, keep a log of what you do over a working day.

Decide on the day in advance; ideally choose it at random rather than try to select a 'typical' day.

For the whole of the day, from the time you wake up until you go to bed, briefly jot down at 15-minute intervals what you are doing and how you feel (e.g. cheerful, depressed, exhilarated, bored, frustrated, happy, annoyed, pleased, disappointed, satisfied, etc.).

Obviously do not risk safety while driving in order to make your record; if you cannot adhere to the 15-minute intervals record a note of your feelings during the drive afterwards.

On completion of your log jot down against each entry why you were doing that particular activity. Consider how you felt about doing it.

The key to your review is to allow your feelings to tell you how well or otherwise you are handling your work.

Would you have preferred to have spent your time differently? To have been doing different things?

Consider how your day might have been different. Take on board the lessons.

Repeat the exercise two weeks later and see if you have succeeded in changing anything.

about what you do, and then to use your feelings as the basis for deciding how you should be allocating your time.

In deciding whether or not to do anything about your present use of time, you are likely to be influenced by your personality. Different personality types have very differing attitudes to time. Your 'temperament', as indicated by your Myers–Briggs type (see Chapter 2), colours your view of time – its importance to you and whether you tend to focus on past, present or future.

Box 6.6 outlines these differences in preference according to personality type. You may need to refer back to Figures 2.2 and 2.3 in order to relate your own preferred ways of behaving to your use of time.

Box 6.6

Temperament and time

People whose dominant preferences, in terms of Myers–Briggs types, are for:

- Sensing–judging:
  - Prefer to focus on the present and the past. They like timeliness.
  - They like to introduce rules, procedures, routines. Structure is important to them.

- Sensing–perceiving
  - Prefer to focus on the immediate, the here and now.
  - They like to improvise, respond, remodel. Opportunity is important to them.

- Intuitive–thinking:
  - Prefer to focus on planning and forecasting.
  - They like establishing patterns, visioning and inventing. Efficiency is important to them.

- Intuitive–feeling:
  - Prefer not to concern themselves too much with time; it tends to be somewhat immaterial to them.
  - Are concerned with process, and like to personalize things. They are interested in potential and empowerment. Growth is important to them.

Adapted from: Giovannoni *et al.* (1987).

As has already been stated, it is undesirable to become locked into any fixed set of preferences. This applies equally to the use of time. Past, present and future all need to be considered. So you need to be aware of whether your focus in reviewing your use of time is unduly biased and adapt accordingly.

Improving your management of time could well help to reduce significantly any stress you may be experiencing. But whether you ended up with a spare block of time that you could use for new purposes is uncertain.

Whether you choose to free up time for a new project will depend very much on what you regard as legitimate and proper behaviour for yourself. If you believe that your 'real' job is to stay on top of the routines and do the necessary firefighting, then you are likely to have an equivocal attitude towards any task that takes you away from this. On the other hand, if you believe that as well as keeping the show on the road, part of your 'real' job is to do with putting on new shows or new acts, then you are likely to be motivated to find the time for both.

Factors conducive to autonomy

A problem for many middle managers is that their bosses see them as only having one job, namely keeping the show on the road. Attempts to branch out from this may be resisted. This could be due to justifiable anxiety that doing so might be to the detriment of one's attention to the present show. Or it could be due to not wanting to breach organizational norms about what constitutes appropriate roles for someone at your level. Or it could be due to a belief that you are not yet ready to take on an innovatory role. Whatever the reason, your object must be to establish the appropriateness of your having greater freedom.

Your success in securing 'time and space' for yourself will depend on:

- Really wanting to operate with a greater degree of freedom in your organization, and being willing to assert yourself in order to do so;

- Your belief in the legitimacy of upward management, that is to say initiatives coming from people at your level without waiting for cues or authorization from above;
- Your sense of having something worthwhile to contribute;
- Your willingness to experiment, both with your personal style of managing and with your handling of the organizational politics;
- Your wanting to devote your attention and energies to making a difference. The alternative is to seek a quiet life at work and to fulfil yourself outside it.

Finally, others will need time and space too if you are to have any collaborators in your projects.

Reflection and action points

- Review your own political stance in terms of the sheep, donkey, fox or owl model. Are you where you ought to be?
- Review your degrees of freedom in your organization. Can you do the things you want to do?
- If not, consider how you should go about creating the time and space you need for yourself and your ventures.

7   Collaborating

Introduction

To get things done through people a manager needs collaboration. Not just others collaborating with you, but you collaborating with others, and others collaborating amongst themselves.

This chapter looks at some of the issues that you may have to deal with in establishing collaboration with groups, teams and networks in order to:

- Give you the support you need; and
- Generate synergy.

The principles proposed are in effect a further means of implementing 'positive politics', described in the previous chapter. Topics covered include:

- Trust, openness, integrity and ethics;
- Congruence and misalignment in interactions;
- Managing dispersed teams;
- Project leader and project team roles; and
- Generating synergy from team activities.

Relating at work

The way we handle our working relationships is probably more bound up with the kind of person we are than any other aspect of our managing. A key skill of managing, indeed a life skill for anyone, is to be able consciously and deliberately to shape a relationship in the way one wants rather than allow it to develop by default in whatever direction it will.

A first step to consider is the kind of collaboration that you want to establish:

- Do you want collaboration to be on a *one-to-one* basis, with you at the centre of a network co-ordinating all your various collaborators' contributions?

- Or do you want to develop some kind of *team-working*, with your collaborators interacting with each other as well as with you?
- Do you want your collaboration to result in *synergy* – to achieve a combined effect which is greater than that which could be produced by each collaborator working individually?

While you may well have other objectives, these seem to be the principal choices. They can be seen as forming a progression. From one-to-one collaboration you can develop into team-working, which in turn can lead to synergy. The levels are of course not mutually exclusive; you can work on all three simultaneously. Later in the chapter we shall consider some of the distinctive issues involved in working at each of the levels. But first we consider two issues that are relevant to all three: values and style.

Human relations values

Ideas about how managers should conduct their working relationships have been much dominated by the human relations movement. Since its origins in the Hawthorne experiments over half a century ago, its protagonists have been making the case that a style of relating marked by the human values of openness, trust, sharing, involvement and participation is more likely to produce productive results than a coercive and controlling style of management. The example of successful Japanese management, too, has highlighted the value of consultation and participation, not just as ethically desirable human relations practice, but as beneficial to business and corporate effectiveness. After many decades of advocacy, the human relations viewpoint is now widely accepted.

It is not advocated that you uncritically adopt these or any other prevailing norms for yourself. But you need to be aware that they exist as a standard against which your behaviour may be judged. Managers have always had to balance their concern for production with their concern for people. For a manager leading a project these dual concerns provide a continuing tension. You are concerned to complete your project, while at the same time the support of people who do not report directly to you, and usually too those that do, has to be continually cultivated. A foundation of trust and openness has to be laid. It is a matter, as discussed in the previous chapter, of pursuing 'positive politics'.

Trust

Mutual trust is essential for any effective collaboration. The bases of trust include:

- Reliability – keeping your word, delivering on your commitments;
- Believing in others – having confidence in their word and capabilities, being prepared to rely on them;
- Not misusing knowledge you acquire in trust – keeping confidences, being discreet, not exploiting weaknesses that may be revealed to you;
- Feeling safe to disclose information that is embarrassing or could be used to your disadvantage;
- Feeling safe to express doubts or fears, not having to keep up a 'macho' image;
- Telling the truth and believing what you are told; and
- Not being automatically suspicious of motives, always searching for hidden agendas.

Establishing trust can be far from easy in organizations. Parties to a relationship may have differing status or author-ity, or may be in competition with each other, or simply have differing objectives. Such factors can present formidable barriers. Indeed you may feel that only a limited degree of trust is feasible. In which case you have to consider whether this is acceptable or will undermine the level of collaboration you actually need.

In the absence of trust, communications are likely to be restrained, inhibiting the kind of interchange certainly neces-sary for synergy, perhaps even for team-working. At its worst, a lack of trust can so preclude any form of constructive dialogue that the only way forward is by bringing in a third party to help heal relationships. Increasingly, however, managers today are expected to develop for themselves the 'process' skills that will enable them to undertake this kind of role.

Openness

The road to trust is through openness. Complete openness may not of course always be appropriate. Nevertheless it is only through sharing thoughts and beliefs that misconceptions can be clarified, and confidence that confidences will not be betrayed built up. Being open includes:

- Declaring one's intentions, not having a hidden agenda;
- Not concealing information in order to gain advantage;
- Being honest in giving one's opinion;
- Declaring one's true feelings rather than pretending to feelings one does not have; and
- Listening without being defensive.

On the basis of research into the way senior managers collaborate in teams, Kakabadse (1991) identified five elements of behaviour and attitudes that are needed for an open style of management. These are shown in Box 7.1. Kakabadse adds:

> Practising an open style, making oneself available, and working issues through with others in ways they feel comfortable with are demanding in terms of time, commitment and emotional energy. (p. 142)

In a climate of openness managers have to be prepared to handle feedback about themselves and their behaviour. Kakabadse noted that 'psychological hardiness' is needed to handle one's natural defensiveness, particularly if one is to tease out the helpful insights that may be concealed within negative comments. To accept criticism without responding defensively demands active listening. He concluded that practising a genuinely open style of management requires considerable personal discipline.

Box 7.1

Elements of an open style

- Active encouragement to discuss work problems openly.
- Making time available to track progress on key initiatives.
- Acceptance of others' liking/disliking of one.
- Tolerance of differences.
- Personal discipline to practise open style.

From: Kakabadse (1991: Chapter 5).

A major hurdle to building trust in any situation can be the stereotypes of mistrust that you may carry around with you. An overtrusting nature is not necessarily desirable either. As always a balance is needed. But a relationship of trust cannot develop while any party is not prepared to trust another. Openness, taken a step at a time, enables you to validate your perceptions of others as trustworthy or not.

Relating with integrity

The last chapter focused on managing with integrity in terms of having a purpose or project that could transcend considerations of the ego. Effective collaborative relationships can only be based on integrity. Recapitulating what was said in Chapter 6, integrity is partly to do with honesty and sincerity; it is also to do with soundness and completeness. You may sometimes elicit compliance with your wishes through behaviour that lacks integrity. But a moment's consideration about what the opposite of integrity implies – deception, insincerity, unreliability, half-truths – makes apparent that 'game-playing' is unlikely to sustain any relationship except in the shortest term.

But it does not follow that relationships based on integrity will therefore always be unmanipulative, undirective, or even undetrimental to some of those involved. Working relationships are normally instrumental, engaged in for an ulterior purpose. If they are also enjoyed for their own sake that is a benefit, but is not the prime purpose. The issue for managers and project leaders is how to relate to others with integrity in order to achieve a corporate purpose. The solution does not lie in uncritically following glib prescriptions for how to manage, nor in playing clever games.

Integrity, trust and openness have been discussed in some detail as being central to the quality and effectiveness of your collaboration with others. These of course are not the only dimensions of interaction. Box 7.2 sets out a more extensive list. While not exhaustive of all the ways in which you can relate to others, it gives some of the more common concepts that are used to think about our interactions.

On the face of it, you might consider all the dimensions in Box 7.2 in purely negative–positive terms, as good or bad. But managing is never as black and white as this. The art, as is emphasized more than once in this book, is in being able to match style to purpose and occasion, and to be able to handle the resulting incongruities and inconsistencies. Your skill in this is a measure of the degree to which you act with integrity rather than game play.

Box 7.2

Dimensions of interaction

Openness	vs.	Concealment
Trust	vs.	Mistrust
Dominating/controlling	vs.	Allowing freedom and discretion
Directive	vs.	Non-directive
Responsive	vs.	Unresponsive
Caring/sensitive	vs.	Indifferent/insensitive
Close	vs.	Remote
Friendly	vs.	Hostile
Telling/influencing	vs.	Listening/not influencing
Encouraging independence	vs.	Allowing dependence

Ethical choices

It is possible to take the view that there is no such thing as a right or wrong way of relating. Your style has to be judged according to what is appropriate for the circumstances and necessary for achieving your purposes. On the other hand, style can have pervasive effects, and what you do in a working relationship could be deemed right or wrong from an ethical standpoint – whether that of your own, that of others you are relating to, or of an outside observer. In the end, however, you have to be the judge and your ultimate reference point has to be what you consider to be acting with integrity according to your personal values.

Personally, I do not hold with much game-playing behaviour which, in my experience, some people seem to find quite acceptable – for example, not saying what you really think, not really intending to do what you promise, withholding your true intentions. It is not easy to deal with people who engage in this kind of deceptive behaviour since you may not know they are doing it until after the event when it is too late. When it has occurred, your choice is to decide whether it was acceptable in a Machiavellian world and shrug it off, or whether to confront the person and endeavour to build a more open and trusting relationship for the future. Apart from the ethics, I believe that managing effectively demands that you aim to establish collaborative relationships of the highest order. If you accept this, then you· will need to confront the person whose behaviour you believe to be detrimental to effective relations.

Interventions in relationships

Such a confrontation could be a private one between you and the person concerned. There is a very great risk that, if not handled with skill and tact, it could degenerate into a mutual blaming session. Acquiring the skills that enable you to handle such an occasion comes from experience and from courses that deal with handling sensitive interpersonal issues, for example counselling skills for appraisal interviewing or for handling redundancies, or perhaps from

Box 7.3

Case history of a third-party intervention

A member of staff in a small office department was alleged to have taken an action which, not for the first time, had undermined work done by his colleagues.

The department manager, as soon as she was confident of the facts, called all the department staff together for an emergency meeting. She outlined, to the accompaniment of rising tension among those present, what she believed had happened and how she saw the implications of this episode if the feelings it had given rise to were not resolved. In her opinion there had been a breach of trust which she felt jeopardized the continued effective working of the departmental team with the person concerned. (Although she knew from earlier discussions that most of the team shared her view, she did not attempt to invoke this knowledge in support of her own statement.)

She concluded by stating what she wanted as the outcome of the meeting; namely re-establishment of the confidence that we could work with the person concerned. She then invited our colleague to respond. While not attempting to deny his actions, the accused person refuted the motives that had been imputed to him.

The department manager then invited each of the other members of the department in turn to respond to what had been said. Some responded perfunctorily, perhaps not wanting to get too drawn in. But those most closely concerned gave what appeared to be an authentic, heart-felt account of their feelings in the matter and how they felt about their ability to work with their colleague in the future. All said that they felt they could.

For the person being put through this scrutiny it was obviously a stressful experience. One of his colleagues needed to be with him for about an hour afterwards while he expressed his feelings about what had happened and thus help him unwind the emotional tension.

The feeling among the rest of the department afterwards was that it had been a somewhat awkward occasion, though in fact not as embarrassing as had been expected. There was some scepticism as to whether anything had significantly changed as a result of the meeting. It was believed that the leopard had probably not changed his spots. On the other hand, it was felt that should he display these spots again in the future he could the more readily be challenged.

training in assertiveness, negotiating or conflict management. The skills of active listening, helping people to crystallize their thoughts and feelings, giving feedback, and above
all learning how to 'own' your own feelings and avoid
accusation and blame, have much wider application than the
purposes for which they are immediately taught. Thus the
'process' skills of intervening in working relationships, once
the virtually exclusive province of specialist consultants, are
now entering managers' repertoires.

The alternative to a one-to-one confrontation is to involve
the whole group or team, as is exemplified by the case history
in Box 7.3. This example has been chosen, partly because I
have first hand knowledge of the episode, but more particularly because it was handled by an internal manager rather
than by an external third party. Not only does it illustrate well
the simplicity of the principles involved, it also shows that
this sort of intervention can be done perfectly competently by
an ordinary manager. Although the procedure is simple, the
emotional stress involved in undertaking such a confrontation, and the self-confidence required too, should not be
underestimated.

My own conclusions about this particular encounter are
that the department manager, in that she was partly outside
the group of staff in which the conflict had occurred, could to
a degree act as if she were an independent third party; she
was prepared to risk embarking on a meeting which could
have developed in all kinds of unanticipated directions, not
all of them welcome; she structured the interactions; and,
although her demeanour sometimes showed the tension of
the occasion, she generally behaved as she always did.

What I believe to be important for any event of this kind was
that one should not attempt any kind of artificial performance; so that you come over as your natural self. It is also vital
to handle the situation in a way that is not destructive.
Whilst, in order to get through, emotional defences may have
to be breached to a degree, this does not give you a licence to
go to the point of breaking down a person's self-control. You
need to observe some basic rules for ensuring the 'psychological safety' of those involved.

As a manager you are not a professional counsellor. Nor are
you a neutral external third party. You are a boss or a

colleague and you must never lose sight of that. Everyone else stands in a similar relationship. Safety first means that:

- You do not attempt to draw people into making revelations that could be embarrassing or undermining to them later;
- You do not invite or provoke them into expressing emotions that they cannot handle and you are not competent to support them through.

Of course not all third-party interventions to establish or re-establish collaborative relations take the form of confrontations. They can be made in order to:

- *Facilitate* members of a new team in forming their relationships with each other;
- *Bring into the open* opinions and feelings which may be blocking a group's performance;
- *Support* the group members in working through the issues raised by the expression of their real feelings; and
- *Bridge a communications gap*, for example acting as a 'go-between' for interest groups in an organization. Employee attitude surveys often serve this function, providing an anonymous medium whereby employees' real views can be safely conveyed to top management (Reeves and Harper, 1981).

Establishing your role

In building a working relationship you should consider how your interactions with the other persons allow it to be shaped. The aspects of style listed above will be influential here, particularly how directive or non-directive you prefer to be.

Another way of looking at how new working relationships evolve has been suggested by David Keirsey (1987) in his examination of how temperament affects management style. Some people are assertive or proactive in the way they cast themselves and others into roles; others are unassertive and reactive.

The former will naturally and spontaneously initiate role definitions at the start of a relationship, often quite unconscious that this is what they are doing. Keirsey gives the example of someone assuming the role of teacher by instructing another on how to do something, thus defining his or her role as teacher and the other's role as learner. Or one might step into the role of project leader by stating to others what action you expect of them, thus casting them in the role of project supporters or project assistants. If we are a 'role-director', 'we usually speak in a commanding way, give orders, issue directives' (Keirsey, 1987, p. 13).

'Role-informers', by contrast, tend to wait for others to propose the role they are to play and then respond by informing the role-director of their assent or dissent. The example Keirsey gives is of the somewhat trivial situation in which:

> I disclose that I have a headache, whereupon you may advise me to take some aspirin, and in so doing define the reciprocal roles as healer and patient. Whether I respond, 'That's a good idea' or 'Aspirin bothers my stomach', I have informed you of my acceptance or rejection of my assigned action in the role of patient, but I have not rejected your right to cast me into the role of patient. In other words I have responded to your initiative in such a manner as to confirm your right to define the relationship. (p 13)

Keirsey observes that such 'role-informatives' would rarely speak in a commanding way, rarely give orders, rarely issue directives. When they do so it is with some discomfort and usually qualified by an apology. They may disguise their demand by putting it in the form of a question: 'Would you mind writing this section of the report?'

Project leaders who are natural role-informatives may find themselves adopting a role-directive style for dealing with subordinates, because their position gives them a licence to be assertive, but a role-informative one for dealing with colleagues and superiors. What this means in practice is that you cast yourself into the role of grateful recipient of favours with them as benevolent donors. While that may well be the underlying reality of the situation, it is not how you want to structure the relationship. Moreover, it may well be that they do not want the roles defined in that way either. It can be reassuring for a senior manager to be given clear marching orders by a subordinate. It gives confidence that the project is being competently handled.

Alignment in interaction

An altogether different way of looking at how we manage our working relationships, and one that I believe to be quite original, has been developed by Pamela Ramsden from interviews with senior managers and observations of senior management teams in action (reported in Moore, 1982). What she did was to observe how the wires of interaction became crossed as a result of managers attempting to communicate with each other. Her work is especially valuable since she analysed interactions in the context of managers collaborating to work on projects.

Regardless of the actual state of progress of a project, people involved in it may mentally or psychologically be at different stages or phases. Organizations as a whole may also be at different stages, with comparable effects.

Ramsden, according to Moore's report of her work, based her analysis around three project phases, which broadly correspond to those used in this book:

• An initial phase of attending to the environment or to the problem, which is the exploratory, pre-decision stage when information is sought and alternatives explored (*the attending phase*);
• A phase when one decides what one intends to do, which is broadly equivalent to the evaluation and crystallization phases described in Chapter 4 (*the intention phase*); and
• A final phase when one commits oneself to the decision agreed upon and starts to implement it (*the commitment phase*).

When managers are 'coming from' the same phase, this match in their thinking can make the interaction exciting and creative, as can be seen from the boxed scenarios in Figure 7.1. But when the protagonists in the interaction are

SELF	OTHER		
	In attending phase	**In intention phase**	**In commitment phase**
In attending phase	I feel understood, sparked by a mutual sense of interest and discovery. As we clarify points and explore tangents, I feel that I am being needed. I am able to get my ideas across easily.	I feel that I am unable to get a word in edgewise. I feel I am being bulldozed and forced to argue my points.	I feel that I am being rushed into making a decision. I feel unable to get a look at the facts or to establish priorities. I want to slow down, to look into the facts properly and to establish what ought to be done. I feel uncomfortable with the pace he is setting and I want to escape.
In intention phase	I feel I am being given more information than I need. I feel irritated by irrelevancies, impatient and eager to move on to getting things on a more definite level and more action-oriented.	I feel challenged. I feel urged to take a stand on the issues, and confident of saying what I mean with no nonsense. I feel we are coming to grips with the problem and I am very sure of the position we are taking.	I feel as if I am being put on the spot. I sense I am being rushed into action before I have established what ought to be done.
In commitment phase	I feel unable to get anything decided. He is boring me with too much waffle when all I want to do is get the ball rolling. His attempts to communicate are preventing my getting a grip on things and making a decision. I want to escape.	I feel I am not being listened to nor am I able to get things moving fast enough. I feel he is putting pressure on me to agree with his views. I feel bulldozed and want to escape.	I experience an exhilarating sense of pace. I feel we are taking moment-to-moment decisions with urgency or calm precision while alerting ourselves to the next steps. I feel we are able to get things moving.

Figure 7.1 Two-way interactions: matches and mismatches. Scenarios developed by Pamela Ramsden, based on her interviews with senior managers and her observations of senior teams in action. For explanation of phases, see text. Adapted from: Moore (1982: 96–99) by permission of the publisher, Pitman Publishing

mentally or emotionally coming from different phases the mismatch can cause mutual frustration, as Ramsden's other scenarios in Figure 7.1 vividly illustrate.

As an important footnote to the scenarios, Ramsden adds that just because managers are mentally in the same phase does not mean that creative interaction will occur. It does not occur, for example, when one manager wants to share his or her thinking and the other wants to remain private. That kind of out-of-stepness can precipitate scenarios such as:

- In attending phase: 'I sense that he is not paying attention or listening to me. I feel misunderstood'.
- In intention phase: 'I feel unable to come to grips with the problem. I am unable to say what I mean and am confused as to what our position really is'.
- In commitment phase: 'I feel I am not being alerted to what is happening. I feel unable to get things moving'.

Nor does creative interaction occur when managers are forced by circumstances to co-operate. When this is the case, the following kinds of scenario may emerge:

- In attending phase: 'I feel as though we are just informing one another of the facts mechanically. I would much rather be doing my own thing'.
- In intention phase: 'I feel we are just bemusing each other with hollow-sounding statements of intent. I would much rather pursue my private crusade'.
- In commitment phase: 'I feel that we are making a plan of action mechanically, forcing ourselves to stay in step. I would prefer to march to the beat of my own drum'.

These scenarios of how managers interact are salutary. They tell us how difficult effective communication can be even when managers are ostensibly working towards a common objective.*

They highlight the importance too of time. There is often a natural pace of evolution which is different for different

* Adapted from Moore, 1982, by permission of the publisher, Pitman Publishing.

people. As a team leader it is all too easy to underestimate the time it takes for other members of the team to bring themselves to the point that you are at. Some people will need time to divest themselves of the clutter of their last project. Slowness in picking up the essentials of a new project may be no predictor of the level of creative contribution a team member may eventually make. But for the team leader who wants to get things moving, the need for protracted discussions at the outset can prove frustrating.

But perhaps the crucial value of Ramsden's scenarios is that they systematically set the different ways in which communication can go awry in the context of managerial tasks. We are thus offered a mode of thinking, a language, with which to manage our interactions. With this framework it might be possible to explore with someone working on the same project why your interaction is proving ineffectual. You also have a guide to the kind of mutual alignment you need to work towards in order to generate a more fruitful interaction.

Alignment and attunement

Team leaders are often urged to seek 'alignment'. By this is meant having all the members of a team or group of collaborators clear about the common purpose and committed to achieving it. A group can be said to be aligned when all are confident that they are sharing the same understandings and that they are therefore all going down the same path towards the same goal. They understand their common commitment. They will also probably have some appreciation of each other's feelings about working together.

Sometimes a group will reach a point when its members are able intuitively to stay in alignment with each other. They tune into what others are thinking and feeling; they understand without explanation where others are 'at'. Discordant notes are naturally avoided. This phenomenon when it occurs is sometimes referred as 'attunement'. It is difficult to create deliberately. It is, however, extremely easy to sabotage its potential development.

Dispersed teams

It is time to return to the three levels of objective for collaborative relationships identified at the beginning of this chapter: collaboration based on one-to-one relationships with you at the centre of a network, interaction between collaborators to develop team-working, and the generation of synergy.

A distinctive feature of collaborating groups in organizations is that they are very often not structured into teams. At least they are not a team in the sense that a football or similar sports team is a team. Most organizational teams do not work together for a sustained period of time co-ordinating their activities one with the other on a moment-to-moment basis.

Most typically organizational 'teams' comprise a number of people who have agreed to collaborate on a particular task who come together from time to time to plan and co-ordinate their activities. They will all probably have several, perhaps many, other responsibilities or so-called 'team' memberships. This kind of team might be more appropriately called a 'collaborative network' or a 'dispersed team' rather than just plain 'team' which could have misleading connotations.

Leading a network

Holding a dispersed team together and making them feel that they are indeed part of a 'team' can be one of a project leader's more important roles. A 'dispersed team' leader faces distinctive problems. For a start, team members may find it difficult to get to meetings, thus inhibiting the development of a team-wide '*esprit de corps*', and perhaps forcing you into relating with particular members on a one-to-one basis. Because of team members' other responsibilities they will need to juggle priorities in order to give time and attention to the tasks of your particular team. Apart from the occasions when you bring them together for meetings members of the team may not regularly meet with each other. Thus there can be no reliance on chance informal contact either for communications or for mutual idea development or problem-solving. As project leader, therefore, you will need to be exceptionally proactive in enabling your collaborative network to become aligned and develop a shared identity.

Operating your team solely as a network can all too easily be a default position, and you end up having only a notional team. You need then to consider what you should do to turn your committee meetings into real team meetings. Moreover, one-to-one relationships can, for some people, be more comfortable and seemingly easier to handle than the uncertain dynamics of a group. On the other hand, there are some people who are more comfortable with group working and neglect to cultivate the necessary one-to-one relationships. The manager who believes that a committee meeting is an adequate substitute for both, risks losing any opportunity for creative collaboration.

Reasons why people might prefer one mode of operating to another are set out in Box 7.4. It is useful to be aware of your preferences and how they may be diverting you from doing what is best for the project.

Box 7.4

Preferences for one-to-one and group working

- Possible reasons for preferring one-to-one working:
  - Relationships are closer, more personal; you can get a better understanding of each person you are dealing with.
  - Agreements for action can be negotiated to suit each person's needs without interference from others.
  - A leader at the centre of network can have more effective control.
  - Meetings of all concerned not precluded.

- Possible reasons for preferring team-working:
  - Can more readily gain shared understandings.
  - Agreements for action can be based on group consensus.
  - Opportunities for different people to take leading role.
  - Team has life and momentum of its own, which is both enjoyable and creative.
  - More scope for experiment; more likelihood of synergy.
  - One-to-one interactions not precluded.

It is important, however, not to assume that alternatives to team working are second best. David Casey (1993), in his work as a consultant at Ashridge College, has come to realize that many of the difficulties encountered in helping top management teams to work together stemmed from the fact that they had no real need to do so. Armed with this realization, he and his colleagues began to question clients' assumptions:

> So when clients asked us 'Can you help us work as a team?' we countered with a question of our own 'Why *should* you work as a team?' To our surprise this turns out to be a really useful question. It abandons the automatic assumption that all top groups at the head of their organizations ought to be teams and invites them instead to address the question of what kind of work they should be doing. This is a much better place to begin because teamwork is only one mode of working – it is essential for some kinds of work, useful for other kinds, but a sledgehammer to crack a nut for other tasks. (pp. 34–35)

Casey has concluded that a group needs to work together as a team when they are facing uncertainty in their task or tasks. If there is no uncertainty then individuals can get on with carrying out their part of the whole.

Project leader tasks

Collaboration has to be around a practical agenda. This derives from the actual objectives of your particular project, which will be unique, and from the tasks that all project teams or their leaders need to address.

You will want to call on people around the organization, whether on a par, above or below you, for:

- Technical or specialist expertise;
- Sponsorship, political support or commitment; and
- Interest in its outcome.

These three factors have been identified by Colin Hastings and colleagues at Ashridge Management College (1986) as the key criteria for selecting the team of people you will need to help you with your project. They go on to point out that many of these people will be helping you informally and sporadically.

Recognizing that they may therefore be stretching the meaning of the word 'team' somewhat, they have coined the notion of an 'invisible team'. While you may well think about all the people whose support you draw on as being members of 'your team', they may not think of themselves at all in this way. From their perspective they are simply supporters or helpers. They may not even see themselves as active as that. The point, however, is that you will need to draw together a team, both visible and invisible.

Additionally you will need to get:

- Approvals and authorizations for things you want to do that you cannot get done within the bounds of your normal authority or resources. This is important not just to give you the licence to proceed, but to lend legitimacy to your activities in the eyes of people whom you want to involve.
- Agreement on practical support, such as freeing up the time of other staff to help you, agreeing use of facilities, providing additional budget, supplying information, distributing your communications.

What project managers do

Some very pragmatic research has been carried out by David Boddy and David Buchanan (1992) into what project managers actually do. A sample of project managers kept audio-tape diaries recording their reflections on events. These were then followed up with questionnaires and interviews. Six key activities of project managers were identified: shape goals, obtain resources, build roles and structures, establish communications, manage holistically and move things forward. Further description of what is involved in these six activities is given in Box 7.5.

The tasks that confront a project leader and the project team will be affected by the type of project they are undertaking and its status within the organization. Wendy Briner and colleagues from Ashridge Management College

---

Box 7.5

The role of a project team manager: six key activities

- *Shaping goals*: setting or receiving overall objectives and directions, interpreting them, reacting to changes in them, clarifying the problem and setting boundaries to it.
- *Obtaining resources*: identifying them, negotiating for their release, retaining them, managing their effective use.
- *Building roles and structures*: clarifying and modifying their own, and those of other functions.
- *Establishing good communications*: linking the diverse groups or individuals contributing to the project, to obtain their support and commitment.
- *Seeing the whole picture*: taking a helicopter view, managing time and other resources, anticipating reactions from stakeholders, spotting links and unexpected events.
- *Moving things forward*: taking action and risks to keep the project going, especially through difficult phases.

From: Boddy and Buchanan (1992: 41) by permission of the publisher, Prentice Hall International.

(1990) have contrasted three types of project: concrete, temporary and open (see Box 7.6).

The kind of developmental project that readers of this book might be undertaking will most likely have some mix of characteristics from temporary and open projects. Briner and her colleagues note that the leader of a temporary project typically has more choice in how to operate than the leader of a concrete project, which is likely to follow recognized procedures. In a temporary project, there will be uncharted areas which means that the leader is less fettered by precedent. It will cut across normal organizational lines. This may give unusual access to senior people, but it also may engender suspicion and awkwardness at working across unfamiliar boundaries.

In an open project there is likely to be a high level of commitment as individuals take part because of their own motivation. On the other hand, Briner and her colleagues

---

Box 7.6

Types of project and their characteristics

Concrete

- Full-time leader.
- Full-time visible team members with clear roles, special skills and hierarchy.
- Sponsor and client are clear.
- High visibility on the corporate landscape.

- Well-known situation for all stakeholders.
- Well-established systems, for estimating, planning and controlling.

Temporary

- Full- or part-time leader.
- Part-time members – conflicts of priorities, time and interest.
- No clear roles or relationships.
- Cross boundaries.

- Who the sponsor and client are is less clear. What they want will emerge.
- Planning and control systems shaky or non-existent.
- Resources a 'guesstimate'.

Open

- No formal leader. Most interested person will be the focal point.
- Members will self-select – attracted by interest.

- Activities organized and monitored by team members.
- Experimental until something comes together.

From: Briner *et al.* (1990: 35–37) by permission of the publisher.

---

note that time is unofficial, money non-existent, and higher priorities create distractions. All of which means that momentum gets lost and progress is slow. In the case of both temporary and open projects there are likely to be problems of credibility and purpose. Being out of the mainstream of organizational activities there may be suspicion about what the project is trying to achieve. Indeed an open project may be seen as subversive, which of course it may be. In both cases friends and supporters need to be won. As Briner and her colleagues say:

> Creating a sense of team out of previously unconnected specialists with other priorities is a complex skill. Project leaders have to build a committed project group, often against all the odds, and then achieve the full benefits, both personally and to the organization, of this form of cross-functional collaboration. (p. 9)

Team tasks

So far we have been focusing on the project leader's role. Important though that is, what the rest of the team does, independently of their leader, is also vital. A list of team tasks prepared with the whole team in mind has been developed by a group of tutors also at Ashridge College. They have used their experience of working with teams to formulate a blueprint for a 'superteam' (Hastings *et al.*, 1986). Extracts from their list of what superteams actually do are presented in Box 7.7.

What the lists of activities, types of teams and tasks should show is that putting together a collaborative endeavour demands a mix of one-to-one relating and close interactive team-working. What the collaborators – not the project leader on his or her own – have to do is to work together to find a satisfactory mode of operating. From that process effective collaboration will flow.

Team roles   log. 4

No discussion of team-working would be complete without a mention of the well-known 'Belbin team roles', already mentioned in Chapter 2 in the context of behavioural preferences, which seem to have dominated training in team-working ever since the research defining them was published. Meredith Belbin (1981) identified characteristics that marked out successful and unsuccessful teams. He concluded that

Box 7.7

What teams have to do: the superteam blueprint

- Negotiate success criteria:
  - Decide who specifies these;
  - Define outstanding performance;
  - 'Contract', i.e. align and agree around requirements;
  - GET motivated to succeed.

- Manage the outside:
  - Enlist the critical supporting roles outside the team;
  - Build network of other people who may be needed to help;
  - Project a credible and competent image;
  - Spend time developing the key relationships;
  - Mobilize the resources needed.

- Plan the what and the how:
  - Go for excellence in the planning, do not permit mediocrity;
  - Prepare contingency plans for the uncertainties;
  - Set milestones for measuring progress and to motivate success;
  - Develop ground rules that will facilitate a culture of success;
  - Sense where the driving energy is coming from and flow with it;
  - Build the bonds that hold the team together.

- Lead the team:
  - Provide direction and create an environment that stimulates performance;
  - Look inward to monitor performance and reward outstanding performance;
  - Look outward to ensure two way flow of information, resources and support.

- Be effective team members:
  - Be an active rather than a passive follower;
  - Understand what it is needed to support the leader and others in the team;
  - Fulfil your role as specified but flexibly if necessary;
  - Compete to excel without jeopardizing co-operation.

Adapted from: Hastings *et al.* (1986: 12–15) by permission.

Box 7.8

Project team roles

These are the Belbin team roles modified to take account of research into project managers and their teams

Team member	*Team role*
Coordinator	He or she would rather be called disciplined and balanced than expert or creative for it is their job to pick the people, to listen and encourage, to focus and co-ordinate effort.
The shaper	The task leader, outgoing and forceful. His or her strength lies in the drive and passion for the task. He or she is needed as the spur for action but can be impatient.
The ideas person	The source of original ideas and proposals, he or she is a creative and intelligent member, but can be careless of details.
The critic	Better at analysis than creativity, he or she will do the checking and point out the flaws in the argument.
The networker	The popular extrovert contact person, someone who keeps the team in touch with the world around it.
The implementer	The practical organizer and administrator who turns ideas into timetables for action
The team-builder	Likeable and popular, the team-builder keeps everybody going, by encouragement, understanding and support.
The finisher	Without the finisher the team might never meet its deadlines. The relentless follow-through is important but not always popular.

From: Boddy and Buchanan (1992: 110) by permission of the publisher, Prentice Hall International.

successful teams were distinguished by a membership that took on all of a number of essential roles.

A version of these team roles, modified by Boddy and Buchanan (1992) to fit with the experience of the project managers they researched is presented in Box 7.8. Expect, as project leader, to fulfil all of these roles at some time or other. They are all competences that can be learned and practised. Even if you have members of the team with these skills, you still need to take responsibility for ensuring that each of them is attended to.

In developing teams, a questionnaire based on the Belbin research is sometimes used to identify each team member's dominant preferred team roles and their subsidiary preferences. It is then possible for the team to review how well balanced it is, whether any of the roles are missing, and what the team might do to compensate for that.

In an organization, where people are allocated to teams on the basis of their job or skill or for political reasons, it is quite probable that all the desirable team roles will not be covered, and there may be little you can do about it. Boddy and Buchanan concluded from their research that to the extent that any choice exists a team should have content, process and control skills. What they mean by these terms is described in Box 7.9. They observe that:

> It is not sufficient to rely on having a team leader who is skilful at all aspects – though that helps. The skill needs to be more widely present, and it may be worth including some people in the team primarily for their process skills, for example . . . Regard any list of team members' characteristics as a list of targets, a guide to use in putting together a team, not a set of mechanical rules.

It is perhaps worth further noting that the Ashridge staff in their book on superteams, from which Box 7.7 was drawn, only make passing mention of Belbin's team roles, and refer readers to Belbin's book if they want to know what the roles are. Instead, the Ashridge group rely when developing teams on specifying what a team has to do, along the lines in Box 7.7. Its assumption is that if the team understands what is expected of it they will, given the right motivation, find a way of doing what has to be done.

Box 7.9

A team's three agendas: content, process and control

For the **content** agenda, the team needs:

- *Expertise* – in payment systems, planning systems, new technology, or whatever it is that the project concerns.
- *Policy awareness* – someone able to link the work on the project to the wider policies and strategies of the organization.
- *Operating knowledge* – current, accurate knowledge of how the relevant part of the enterprise works.

For the **process** agenda, the team needs:

- *Team-building skill* – able to help the disparate members of the team learn to work together.
- *Awareness of process* – those who are conscious that the way things are done matters as much as what is done; both within the team itself, and in its relations with others.
- *Time and commitment* – willingness and the ability to give the time needed to be an effective team member – and that their boss accepts this.

For the **control** agenda, teams need:

- *Helicopter view* – someone able to see the broader picture, within which the project needs to fit.
- *Time-keeper* – not necessarily in the literal sense, but simply someone aware of how the project is progressing, and how that relates to expected completion or delivery dates.
- *Administrator* – someone with a knack for keeping records and documents in shape, who ensures that reports are done in time, and so on.

From Boddy and Buchanan (1992: 108–109) by permission of the publisher, Prentice Hall International.

Synergy

The original meaning of synergy was simply combined or correlated action. It has come to mean much more than this. In its common usage it means gaining an effect from the whole that is more than would be expected from the sum of the parts. It is an intangible, some would say metaphysical concept.

But when it happens in a group its members will be aware of it: a collective enthusiasm and energy, new ideas emerging as if from nowhere, a seemingly effortless achievement. Group effects of course can also be negative: too many cooks spoiling the broth, duplication of effort, conflict, frustration. The challenge for a project leader is to create positive synergy, to precipitate that driving force that not only keeps the project flowing forward but synergistically enhances the outcome.

Synergy is not something that you can bring about in any facile way using formula-type techniques. It is often as much due to serendipity as to design. You have to work towards it with no certainty that you will get the effects you want. The actions described in this chapter can only set the conditions for it to occur: build networks and teams, hold meetings, align purposes, relate to each other openly and with trust. Further ideas are suggested in Box 7.10. In a team with stable membership and close interaction synergy may come fairly readily. With a dispersed organizational team, or with changing membership, it may be more difficult to generate.

Although it is uncertain what precisely you will need to do in any situation to trigger synergy, one can be certain about what you can do to prevent it occurring. You could use your one-to-one interactions with your team members as a means of 'divide and rule'. In meetings you could bar discussion that is not strictly related to the agenda, divide up the tasks on an individual basis and discourage team members from holding 'extracurricular' meetings which take them away from their individual tasks. You could resist taking on board suggestions that are not in line with original plans. There are many more inhibitors of synergy than those, but they are sufficient to give the picture. What is needed to do the opposite is a certain boldness, a willingness to experiment, be a bit unconventional if necessary.

The notion of synergy has been introduced because seeking to bring it about represents a challenge to a manager from which all kinds of developmental benefits can flow. Management of a project can be looked at in prosaic terms: as a matter of planning, co-ordinating and controlling.

Box 7.10

Suggestions for generating synergy

- Share your own enthusiasm and excitement.
- Draw others out about their potential to contribute.
- Encourage everyone to spend some individual time with everyone else.
- Organize an 'away' day at an early stage, staying overnight if the budget runs to it, in order to accelerate getting to know each other.
- At meetings encourage people to talk to each other rather than address all their statements to the chair or leader.
- Ensure that team members have enough time to think, interact with each other and be creative.
- Make sure everyone understands what team members can do to make the team work effectively – get them all to read *Superteams* (Hastings *et al.*, 1986) or another good book on team working.
- Allow freedom for people to make their contribution in their own way.
- Encourage unconventionality; have a party with a memorable event.
- Keep working away at creating a climate in which it is safe to express feelings, needs and off-the-wall ideas; be sensitive to any blocks to this and deal with them.
- Encourage the questioning of anything that seems like stereotyped thinking.
- Keep everyone aware of what has been achieved to date; when direction seems to be lost crystallize where the team is at.
- Keep working on alignment and attunement.

Those are the underpinning basics. But to manage effectively is to lift what you do above the prosaic. Seeking synergy is such an opportunity.

Reflection and action points

- Use the dimensions of interaction in Box 7.2 to diagnose your own typical behaviour in interactions. Do you need to change?

- Consider the rationales in Box 7.4 and assess your own preferences for one-to-one versus group working. Consider also the version of the Belbin team roles in Box 7.8. Are any of your preferences for a particular style or role getting in the way of your effectiveness?
- Plan to undertake some activities that will demand greater versatility of you.

8 Using your power

Introduction

A great deal of what you have to do as a manager and as a leader requires you to exert power. This chapter looks at the nature of your personal power and how you can use it to:

- Get action started; and
- Keep it moving in your desired direction.

Previous chapters – on initiating, deciding your purpose, determining action, being political, freeing time and space, setting agendas, organizing collaboration – have in one way or another been concerned with building your power.

This chapter considers issues in using this power. Particularly, it looks at how your inner and leadership powers, discussed in Chapters 2 and 3, and your more diffuse organizational powers, discussed in Chapters 6 and 7, coalesce in your overall 'personal power'.

Topics discussed include:

- The meaning of personal power;
- Elements of personal power that need to be drawn upon for a 'project journey';
- Considerations in maintaining control of your projects;
- Knowing when and how to intervene;
- The sources of your personal power and its use in directing your projects; and
- Evaluating your power.

The meaning of power

Power is used in organizations for many purposes: to elicit compliance, to advance one's causes and interests, to acquire resources, to further desired courses of action and block undesired ones. Power is at the core of all organizational politics, regardless of the stance one takes towards them.

'Power', like politics, is another concept with a poor image. Because of its connotations of domination and coercion, some people like to disclaim having or using it. More neutral terms such as 'authority' or 'influence' seem to be more acceptable words for describing managers' ability to get other people to do things. But power has other meanings besides control or command over other people.

It can mean having liberty or permission to act; and in this sense the word 'empowerment' has crept into the management jargon. Empowering people typically means giving them the freedom to do things their way or to pursue their own ideas, often in association with an attempt to establish a climate in which creativity and initiative can flourish.

Power can mean the ability to act strongly or to affect something strongly, e.g. force of character, vigour, energy. This meaning is associated with the idea of someone possessing charisma, i.e. an extraordinary talent or capacity to influence and lead people.

In its broadest sense, power is quite simply the ability to do something. Rosabeth Moss Kanter has defined it as 'the capacity to mobilize people and get things done'. (1985: 213).

If you are a manager you will have power that goes with your position – your formal authority, which is backed up by your organization's procedures for rewarding and disciplining people. Rarely are you likely to have to invoke the latter; most people most of the time comply with what they are expected to do as part of their job. You may have power too because of your control of resources or through other aspects of your authority. But even if you do not overtly make use of these managerial powers, they are always there implicitly, backing you up.

You will also have power that derives from your particular expertise or knowledge. People defer to your directions because they believe you know best.

The basis of managers' and leaders' power, authority and influence, on the one hand, and the reasons people have for complying or following on the other, have been extensively explored by writers and researchers on organizational behaviour, and there many books available on the subject. The focus here, by contrast, is on the basis of your 'personal power' and how you can develop and use it.

Having personal power

Your personal power is your capacity to shape events. This is often a more diffuse and indirect process than Kanter's word 'mobilize' might imply. Personal power includes all the various means by which you get things done through people – from coercing, through influencing to giving others freedom to exercise their own power. It also includes the ways you use your organizational or position power.

Why should managers want power over and above their formal authority? Kanter, reflecting on her research into managers who had been successful in bringing about change, concluded that only managers seeking to innovate, those whom she termed 'entrepreneurial managers', needed it:

> People who are 'just doing their jobs' do not need to 'mobilize' anyone. Little is problematic. They have a job to do; they are told in detail how to go about it or they already know, from past experience with identical assignments; they use existing budget or staff; they do not need to gather or share much information outside their unit; and they encounter little or no opposition. So they can act on their own authority and do not need to seek or use additional power. (1985: 213)

Kanter overstates the case for all people 'just doing their job' not needing any additional power . Managers 'just doing their job' often need to do things that are outside the bounds of their normal authority or budget. This will involve them too in using their organization's political processes to build the power they need.

In Chapter 3 I quoted Kanter's scathing comments about the unexciting lives of managers who confine themselves within the bounds of their formal authority. I could be equally scathing about managers I have worked with who did not even exercise the authority they had got. For whatever reason, perhaps because they were too diffident, too lacking in boldness or self-assertion, they did not do effectively what they were routinely required to do.

The need to use personal power should not be equated solely with innovation. The innovatory manager cannot operate without it; the non-innovatory manager may not be effective without it.

Project journey

From the perspective of a manager seeking to achieve an objective, your personal power is the engine that takes you on your 'project journeys' from A to B. The basis of this power lies very much in the strength of your determination to achieve the goals you set yourself; it is the resultant of the forces that drive you forward and the forces that hold you back.

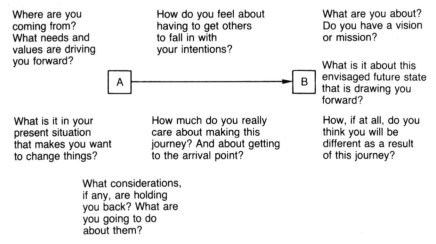

Where are you coming from? What needs and values are driving you forward?

How do you feel about having to get others to fall in with your intentions?

What are you about? Do you have a vision or mission?

What is it about this envisaged future state that is drawing you forward?

What is it in your present situation that makes you want to change things?

How much do you really care about making this journey? And about getting to the arrival point?

How, if at all, do you think you will be different as a result of this journey?

What considerations, if any, are holding you back? What are you going to do about them?

Figure 8.1   Discovering your driving forces: questions for your journey

A guide to analysing these forces, in the form of a series of questions relevant to any project journey, is presented in Figure 8.1. Your answers will tell you much about how motivated you will be to exert personal power to reach your intended destination, and thus what personal power you will in fact have.

Managing tensions

Your personal power can be seen as a function of how you manage your psychology for your journey from A, where you are now, to point B, your desired future state.

You need to understand your present situation so that you know what you have to do to extricate yourself from its constraints and change it. Fritz (1989), whose work was discussed in Chapter 2, calls this 'telling the truth about current reality'. You cannot be effective if you plan the future on the basis of ignorance or, worse still, on the basis of fictions about the present state of affairs.

You need to set up your purposes in a way that draws you forward. This means that your purpose should derive from some kind of tension that seeks resolution (see Box 8.1). Fritz envisages that people journeying from A to B will be driven to oscillate between the forces drawing them forward and the forces drawing them back (see Figure 8.1). The key to progress, assuming you are able successfully to extricate yourself from the binding constraints of the present, is to hold your vision clearly and steadfastly so that it is more powerful than the forces of inertia.

How clear does one's vision or purpose have to be in order to generate personal power? Possessing 'vision' could imply a clearly articulated definition of the outcome. In fact you may have no more than a sense of how things might be different and that you will recognize the 'right' outcome when you see it. If this is the way you are proceeding, you may have to find some way of crystallizing your purpose in a form that can be communicated.

In envisaging the future you need to ask not just 'Where do we want to go?', and the obvious corollary, 'What do we have to do to get there?'. You need also to ask questions about yourselves, such as:

- Will we need to be different in any way in order to get there? Will we need to change our attitudes or our thinking?
- Do we really care whether we get there or not?
- How much do we value the things that are holding us back? Would we really prefer to stay where we are?

Maintaining control

Success in your project journey may require you to intervene to bring the action back on course. Doing this could be

---

Box 8.1

Tension-resolution model

Think of yourself as being drawn forward by your goal or purpose, and being drawn back by forces of inertia which make it feel more desirable to stay in your present state.

The logic of the model goes like this. A discrepancy between a desired state and the state you are in sets up a tension which seeks resolution. You are hungry so you want to eat. You are bored so you seek a challenge. You have a problem so you want to solve it. You see how things could be better so you want to change them. Getting a result reduces the tension.

Tension-resolution effects may also be in a negative direction. You fear failure so you withdraw. You dislike conflict so you avoid confrontation.

There can be circular effects in tension resolution, which can bring you back to your starting point. You are overweight, so you diet. You are then hungry, so you eat. You are in a dead relationship so you leave. You hate loneliness, so you go back. You are dissatisfied with one of your staff's performance so you confront her. This creates conflict so you decide to tolerate his or her performance.

The tension of wanting to get a result may also generate a 'can't have' belief which causes you to abandon your purpose. Not getting the result will of course regenerate the original tension.

You need then to consider whether you should seek an alternative outcome which will resolve the tension, or to work on the blocks that are preventing you from proceeding.

Adapted from: presentation given by John Adams, workshop held at Brunel University, 1987.

---

regarded as a simple matter of managerial control. Unfortunately for anyone seeking guidance from this source, writers on this topic have tended to focus more on the establishment of control systems than on the interpersonal aspects which so dominate in the case of projects.

In any event, you may not think of what you do in order to keep your project on course as 'control' in the formal sense that this term has come to have in management. Nevertheless, a feature of all action that has a purpose to it is that it is 'controlled'. Without control there is no assurance that planned activities will stay on course. Without control you have no means of knowing when you have reached your destination. Without some means of monitoring the results of your action, and redirecting it if necessary, you cannot be said to be acting purposefully in any meaningful sense of that word.

Many of the standard principles of managerial control are of course relevant to a project. Milestones and targets by which you can judge whether or not project objectives are satisfactorily on the road to attainment need to be set. Reports on progress need to be called for. But any attempt at a mechanistic approach to control would be quite inappropriate for 'ambiguous, uncertain tasks in a dynamic context, when it is hard to specify in advance which elements to control and how to do so'. (Boddy and Buchanan, 1992).

Hopefully, all will go smoothly and a satisfactory outcome be achieved without the need for intervention. Time and care given to the preliminary stages can be expected to heighten the prospects for this prognosis. So too will maintenance of a sense of excitement and enthusiasm for what is being done. How the project is controlled will also affect the outcome. Regular reviews are essential, whether to keep the project on its original course, or to adjust the course, or to revise objectives.

In exercising control, a project leader has to:

- Know when to intervene;
- Be prepared to do so; and
- Intervene constructively.

Each of these will be discussed below.

Reckoning progress

On the face of it, knowing when remedial action is called for might appear straightforward. Tasks can be allocated. Deadlines set. Requirements explained. If these can be specified unambiguously there may be little problem. But, as explained above, given the uncertainties and conflicting pressures of many projects that is not always feasible.

For all sorts of reasons, plans may not work out as intended. Moreover, there may have been uncertainty from the outset about the realism of planned activities and the deadlines set for them. Sometimes it is possible to plan only in outline before embarking on the implementation phase.

While 'deciding-as-you-go-along' is often a valid way of proceeding, it can place testing calls on the project leader's powers to keep collaborators in line and the project on course. Deadlines can be argued to have been unrealistic. Whether a task has been completed satisfactorily or not may be open to wide interpretation. These are issues that then need to be discussed and negotiated in the light of project objectives.

A particular problem of feeling your way as you go is that it can be hard even for the project leader to judge whether a point has been reached when corrective action is called for. Moreover even if some kind of intervention is deemed necessary, you are unlikely to have any standard procedure for corrective action that you can call into play. Deviations on projects tend to demand improvised responses.

A control agenda

The project managers researched by Boddy and Buchanan tended to follow one or other of two approaches for 'managing the control agenda'. One was to be explicit about the open-endedness of the project. The other was 'to go with the flow'. The elements of the two approaches, described in Box 8.2, do not appear mutually exclusive.

Resistance to change

What may be more problematical are the wider organizational and political factors that emerge to impede progress. Projects, by definition, are designed to change something. In consequence, many of the resistances that one might expect to arise in the course of change may do so. The outcome of the project may be seen as upsetting existing working arrangements. People may feel that they are being called upon to do

---

Box 8.2

Managing the control agenda: two approaches

1 Explicit open-endedness

Recognize situation for what it is and ensure that others do so. Ask questions such as:

- How can we make everyone aware of the level and sources of uncertainty in this task?
- What can be done to reduce uncertainty?
- Do we have to decide 'X' now?
- Should we plan to review in 'X' weeks time?

Strategies are designed to dispel the impression of muddle.

2 Go with the flow

Keep the broad goal in view, but be ready to change direction:

- Gather 'soft' information that gives the picture;
- Anticipate change in plans and possibilities; and
- Take corrective action which changes course of project in light of external events.

A project manager finds out what is going on, not just progress, but in and around the project.

Adapted from Boddy and Buchanan (1992: 157–158) by permission of the publisher, Prentice Hall International.

---

things for which they lack the skills. They may believe the change will affect their ability to do their job as effectively as they do at present.

It is easy to say that anxieties and apprehensions like this should be talked through, clarified and dealt with at an early stage. What can happen, however, is that the project's implications for staff are perceived by the project leader, and perhaps the team too, as innocuous. Consequently, anxieties are not foreseen.

Danger signals

Monitoring what goes on within the project may also not be as straightforward as it might seem. For periods of time between meetings, team members may be working on their assigned tasks individually, or in subgroups, which can mean that progress is difficult to discern. But there can be danger signals that all is not going well. Once again the Boddy and Buchanan research has highlighted what these may be (see Box 8.3).

The project leader needs to create conditions which enable problems to be picked up before they reach the danger signal stage:

- By making people feel that it is okay to be open about what is really happening, and giving them opportunities to do so;
- Actively listening to what you are told, including being prepared to accept and take on board perceptions and views contrary to your own; and
- Interpreting statements that are couched obliquely, perhaps in some kind of double-speak, when people are hesitant to speak their minds openly.

Your possible responses to deflecting pressures on your project would seem to revolve around two basic options:

- Modify the project to accommodate others' expressed doubts, misgivings, objections; and
- Attempt to carry your opponents in what you want to do.

These are of course not either–or options; there will normally be scope for some compromise position. Indeed, if you have no sanctions to compel compliance, or do not wish to use such tactics, then negotiation and compromise are your only ways forward.

The decision to intervene

There is of course a third option, which is to do nothing. There are many reasons why one might want to avoid

---

Box 8.3

Danger signals for a project

From senior management

- Interfering inappropriately without consultation;
- Not providing support when needed;
- Misunderstandings arising; and
- Making unfounded promises or commitments on your behalf.

From managers at same level

- Giving low priority to project:
  - Over-running deadlines,
  - Not attending meetings,
  - Junior deputies sent,
  - Excuses rather than results;
- Recalling previous failures; and
- Political obstacles raised.

From staff affected by the change

- Refusing to work the new system or equipment, deliberately misusing it or using it as rarely as possible; maintaining old procedures.
- Delaying other changes necessary for system to work.
- Missing meetings about the change.
- Making no effort to learn how to use it; not releasing staff for training.
- Excessive fault finding and criticism, or suggesting new complicating features.
- Endless discussion and requests for more information; bringing other interest groups into the discussion; delaying agreement.

Adapted from Boddy and Buchanan (1992: 78–81, 94–95, 124) by permission of the publisher, Prentice Hall International.

---

intervening. A list of such considerations is presented in Box 8.4.

Amassing reasons why you should not do something could be an instance of the unconstructive side of self-reflection. The risk is that it masquerades as a realistic appraisal of circumstances, and you do not see it for what it is, a

Box 8.4

Considerations that can inhibit intervening to bring project back on course

- Not wanting to have confrontation.
- Diffidence about pushing your objectives or standards.
- Belief that because collaboration is voluntary, assertiveness may destroy goodwill and co-operation.
- Fear that you will not get compliance.
- Doubts about reliability of senior management support, or not wanting to invoke it.
- Sense that the deviation you now want to correct was in some way your fault, e.g. you were not clear enough about your expectations.
- Belief that your collaborator will do it his or her way anyhow – you are powerless.
- Uncertainty about the legitimacy of the project or this particular part of it.
- Acceptance that your opponent has a point/should be allowed to continue in own way.
- Not knowing how to intervene constructively or doubting your capability to make a difference if you do.
- Not caring enough about the project.
- Believing that consequences of not intervening will not be serious – you can get away with it.
- Fearing that you will come off worst in the encounter.

rationalization of an underlying sense of inadequacy about your ability to overcome obstacles. It is sometimes easier to see the obstacles in front of you than to recognize that it is you who are stuck.

Two possible repercussions can be predicted, one positive and one negative:

- The negative one is that team members have an expectation that decisions about action will be clear cut, and are thus intolerant and resentful of the changes made to cope with uncertainties. If any tasks have led in a wrong direction, there may be unpleasant recriminations and loss of good-will and co-operation.

- The positive one is that the uncertainties help build a more creative collaboration as team members work together on solving problems as they emerge.

Holding your line

A further factor to bear in mind when you are working with a group is that others may want to be involved in decisions about the need for and shape of remedial action. Control thus becomes a function of team working.

Regardless of whether plans for your project are well- or loosely-structured, there is a further contingency to be alert for – breakdown of collaboration and support.

For example, there may be collaborators who do not carry out agreements in the way intended. There may be supporters who change their mind about what they once endorsed. There may be dissent among team members about the direction the project is taking. External circumstances may change, resulting in a shift in priorities which causes supporters or collaborators to put their attention elsewhere.

Recourse to one's formal authority, which might be possible if you are taking corrective action for standard routine activities, may be out of the question in the case of a project. Many if not all of your collaborators will work with you voluntarily and by agreement. This makes it difficult to use the heavy hand of formal authority to get someone to remedy a neglect or shortcoming – even if this were your style. Moreover, in the case of deadlines not met, it may be too late to do anything other than accept that you are now behind schedule.

Sources of personal power

The obstacles to making use of formal authority in undertaking a collaborative venture means that you have to rely on your personal power for getting things done and taking remedial action. Personal power is portrayed in Figure 8.2 as comprising three elements: you working through others, others working through you, and preparing yourself to exert it.

Box 1 in the diagram, 'working through others' to achieve your ends is probably what first comes into people's minds when thinking about power, and is where most discussion of power and authority is focused. It is what Kanter was referring to in 'mobilizing people'. This aspect of personal power has implicitly been covered in the course of the preceding two chapters.

Box 2 in the diagram, 'others working through you' to achieve their ends is perhaps a less obvious form of power. But if one thinks about power and working towards a purpose as a collective as well as an individual activity, then it makes considerable sense to think of power in this way. Members of a collaborating group that was well aligned or attuned would probably not find it at all strange to think of their personal power deriving one from another, without having regard to the location of their purpose in any one individual.

Personal power that derives from others can be regarded as a form of leadership. This would be so, for example, if you had placed yourself at the head of a group of people pursuing a cause. Or others, casting themselves in the role of 'follower', may use you as a vehicle for achieving their aspirations. Even though in these examples you might feel you were no more than a conduit for other people's purposes and energy, it is your power that is affecting events.

Preparing yourself

We come now to the third box in Figure 8.2, 'preparing yourself' to use power. This refers to the mental and psychological preparation that you may need to make in order to exert your personal power. Management consultant and counsellor George W. Watts has described personal power as being 'a function of singleness of purpose and lack of impediments' (1993: 107). That succinct summary touches the essence.

Singleness of purpose comprises two factors:

- Commitment to realizing a goal or set of goals; and
- Having specific intentions clear in your mind.

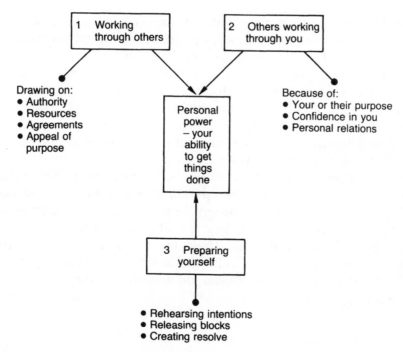

Figure 8.2   Elements of personal power

Each of these will be discussed in turn, prior to looking at what you can do about impediments.

Commitment to purpose

Belief in your purpose and commitment to realizing it are essential if you are to convince others of the worthwhileness of joining with you, or to prevent yourself being deflected from your purpose by other priorities.

Commitment to a purpose is something that is extremely difficult to create artificially. Simulating it through some exercise of will-power is unlikely to prove satisfactory. What you have to create in yourself is a motivation that means something to you and that will thus drive you forward naturally.

You need the will to achieve your purpose. But an exercise of will-power, yourself dominating yourself, is unlikely to provide you with the lasting effects you need to see your project through. Nor could an exercise of will-power be expected to generate the kind of enthusiasm within yourself that you will need to enlist others' support.

Integrating your project goals with your personal goals would help you in generating your commitment. But not all managers will be able to do this, or want to do it. There are many occasions when one simply wants to do a good job without having to concern oneself too greatly with how it fits with some personal purpose.

This raises an important issue: how far can you be effective, and how far can you possess personal power without a strong degree of personal commitment to what you are doing? Some managers may well find they are able to manage effectively without a vision that drives their day-to-day practice. But the risk, I suspect, if one lacks an inspiring cause is to end up as the kind of routine-sustainer on whom Kanter poured her withering scorn.

Rehearsing intentions

Singleness of purpose demands having your intentions clear in your mind. The kinds of intentions that may be relevant are set out in Figure 8.3. They include:

- Specific tasks you want undertaken;
- Agreements you will need for such matters as expenditures or releasing staff; and
- Gaining general support for what you are doing.

Also given in Figure 8.3 are examples of the intentions you might have for yourself in order to strengthen your power:

- Reinforcing your resolution to achieve your purpose, for example, talking with like-minded people, giving presentations about your project to interested parties, exuding enthusiasm for what you are doing – all steps that will help you sustain your 'traction'.
- Dealing with any internal blocks or barriers to realizing your intentions, or which are preventing you from setting them as ambitiously as you might in the first place.
- Drawing more people in to support you; generally extending your network of collaboration and influence.

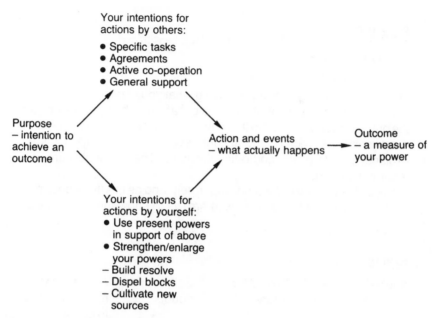

Figure 8.3 Power and intentions

Mapping your intentions along the lines indicated in Figure 8.3 would enable you to rehearse the exercise of your personal power in your mind prior to putting it into force. This awareness in itself can be a contributor to your personal power. Apart from being a useful bit of action planning, it can give you a sense of your power to influence the events that lie ahead of you. There is power in intention.

Dispelling blocks

In the absence of impediments, your personal power should come naturally into play. Exerting personal power is what we do whenever we strive to attain a purpose.

A way of identifying blocks to your power is set out in Box 8.5. The idea is that you contrast a number of different occasions when you failed to obtain the outcome you were seeking, and look to see if you can identify any common pattern.

Box 8.5

Losing your power

The objective of this exercise is to identify any recurring factors that may be preventing you from achieving what you want.

Write down short accounts of three occasions when you did not get the outcome you wanted. So that you can reflect dispassionately upon these episodes, record only actions, events and feelings. Omit all explanations, reasons, and rationalizations. These will obscure any recurring patterns.

Record each step in the story separately, and as briefly as possible, as in the example below. Link with arrows to show the sequence of events clearly.

Example

The pattern that this episode was observed to have in common with others:

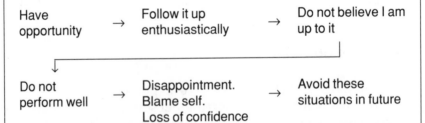

You may need to talk through your accounts with a friend in order to help you discern the underlying pattern. What is obscure to you may be glaringly obvious to someone else. Awareness of the pattern is a first step towards breaking out of it.

This kind of retrospective analysis can be quite difficult to do. It is easy to clutter up one's reflections with all the justifications and rationalizations that one has built up around one's past.

One of the functions served by action-learning 'sets' or support groups is to help managers to attain their outcomes despite adversity, the sources of which can be internal to the person as well as external. You may well find you need to talk to a friend to help you discern the patterns which should result from the exercise in Box 8.5. What you might do about them will often be resolved quite naturally through your awareness of how you are sabotaging yourself by what you think and do. How to let go of more persistent unconstructive beliefs and behaviours will be discussed in Chapter 10.

The point about these kinds of blocking patterns is that as long as you remain locked into them your personal power is diminished.

Drawing powers

Your personal power is in practice, as already noted, the result of both 'push' and 'pull' factors. The push factors are the problems that you want to solve, that are making the present state of affairs unsatisfactory and make you want to improve things. The pull factors are to do with your vision of the future, which you may hold quite independently of any problems that are making the present uncomfortable.

Writers on personal power, for example Fritz and Covey who were cited in Chapter 2, tend to emphasize the pull factors – having a purpose, vision or mission. The proposition is that commitment to purpose will generate in you the power to realize it. You will find the energy you need and will be prepared to take the necessary risks. Obstacles will draw out your ingenuity and you will recover from setbacks and you will not be diverted by events and your purpose will remain a priority. It will become shared by others.

My own experience tells me that there is a lot to this postulated chain of cause and effect. I came into management from consultancy where projects rarely lasted longer than three months. And then I was on to another client and another project. I did not have to think about purposes beyond the immediate deadline and getting the next job. On becoming a manager I was initially dismayed at the prospect of having to sustain my motivation to attain objectives over several years. To my surprise I found that setting my sights on a clear long term future did give me the energy and persistence to keep driving forward. Later on, as a result of attending a workshop where I was exposed to the ideas in this section and the one below, I was able to reinforce this motivation.

Staying in charge

While it is important not to allow yourself to be deflected from your purposes by spurious considerations, you also need to recognize when there are real constraints. To be in control, to be in charge, is as much a state of mind as a set of activities.

It is a matter of caring about the outcome and being prepared to do whatever you see as necessary to bring it about. Sometimes this will require you to be inventive, to use your imagination to find new solutions when planned solutions fail to work. Sometimes it will demand that you assert your will. Sometimes you will need to find compromises. Sometimes you will need to challenge constraints to test their reality.

But always you will need to keep your purposes in sight, whatever deflections or setbacks you encounter. You may need to adapt or modify them as circumstances change. This constancy-cum-flexibility of purpose is the essence of a manager's power to get things done.

Successful use of power

Power is notorious for its abuse. Personal power, as opposed to organizational power, leaves little scope for abuse. Collaborative ventures hinge on the continuing consent of the collaborators.

The approach to power being put forward here is therefore essentially 'transformational'. Transformational leadership was explained in Chapter 3 as gaining compliance by means of getting others to change their viewpoint, attitudes or beliefs. This concept, which has been developed extensively by Noel Tichy and Mary Ann Devanna (1986), is equally applicable to the use of personal power.

Managers, however, are not constrained to use only one form of power or leadership. In practice you will use a balance of different forms of power, organizational as well as personal. Kotter (1983) holds that managers who handle power successfully appreciate that all available power bases have merit. They try to develop their skills and credibility so that they can use whichever type of power is best for the circumstances, and which they and others are comfortable with. This means being sensitive to the source of the power you are using, so that you do not, for example, try to apply your expert power in one field to another field.

Additionally, Kotter notes, managers who handle power successfully act maturely and exercise self-control. They avoid impulsive or egotistical displays of their power, and try not to be unnecessarily harsh on others around them. They understand that power is necessary to get things done, and are comfortable using power.

Knowing your power

For much of our time we are able to take our ability to exert sufficient power for granted. It is usually only when we start a new job, or take on an unfamiliar task, that we are caused to reflect on our power. Box 8.6 highlights some of the factors discussed in this and preceding chapters that can lend you power or detract from it.

Personal power is not a set of attributes or personal qualities. It is what you do in order to get things done through people. Moreover, personal power and group power are far from incompatible. It was suggested earlier that an

Box 8.6

The balance of your personal power

Lending you power	Detracting from your power
Purpose and intention and your communication of these	Lack of sense of direction 'Considerations' for not acting
Collaborators, supporters and their synergy	Illusory obstacles
Your project knowledge	Any 'surreptitious agenda'
Personal values	Lack of alignment
Commitment and resolution	Ambivalence about project, irresolution
Involvement in organization	Lack of contacts to work through
Authenticity	Inauthenticity

important element of personal power was allowing others to work through you. Allowing a group to exert control over its members – for example by putting pressure on each other to meet a deadline, or working together to get yourselves out of a difficulty – is a variant of this. Your personal power lies in having the confidence and strength to allow these processes to run their course.

Reflection and action points

- Review the questions in Figure 8.1 and assess just how powerful you actually want to be in pursuing your purposes. Do you need to strengthen anything?
- Use the checklist in Box 8.6 to review your present use of power. Do you need to change?

The next and final part of this book is concerned with reflecting on experience and developing from it. It is important, therefore, that by this stage you actually have some experiences to reflect upon. This means:

- You now need to take your development project, if you are doing one, well into its action phase.
- If you are not, you should identify some specific experiences that you would like to reflect on.
- You could also profitably identify some forthcoming tasks as opportunities for reflection.

Part four
Reflecting and Evolving

. . . in herself complete, so well to know
Her own, that what she wills to do or say
Seems wisest, virtuousest, discreetest, best.

Milton, *Paradise Lost*

Personal transformation report 4

Achieving effectiveness through becoming a powerful persuader

At present I share a small office with two to three other members of staff. We also share two telephones and one computer. The building is very busy with activities, many of them very noisy, going on all day and into the evening.

The crunch came for me a couple of months ago when I was dealing with a very complex and highly confidential matter. My stress level rose considerably and on a number of occasions when my colleagues left the room I would quickly lock the door so that I could make confidential phone calls. This could not go on.

The constraints

In order to understand how this situation arose it is necessary to appreciate the culture of my organization and of the sector I work in. I am employed as the Director of a local voluntary organization. We are based in a large building that was once a sewage works and is now a listed building.

The organization is a registered charity and a company limited by guarantee. We provide a very broad range of services, including day tuition for people with learning difficulties and training for employment. The organization employs about a dozen permanent staff, two dozen sessional staff and draws on about forty volunteers. As the Director I am answerable to the Executive Committee which is made up of unpaid volunteers who are elected annually. Many of them are also users of our services.

Although, in many respects, managing a charity or voluntary organization has much in common with management in other sectors, it differs in that voluntary organizations, particularly local organizations such as mine, tend to be more directly accountable to their users than other organizations. Many voluntary organizations are underfunded and funders like to see their money being spent directly on service users and not on administration.

As a result of this culture, it is common for workers in the voluntary sector to 'make do' with an inadequate working environment. When resources are scarce and the need for services is on the increase it is difficult to convince some people that spending resources on building office space is a good use of money.

I had been aware of the problem since joining the organization, but I thought I just had to live with it. There is an assumption within my organization that I will take the major responsibility for running it, that I will show the leadership and commitment, but that I can do all this with exactly the same tools as, for example, the part-time Volunteer Coordinator. This is very unrealistic and has great potential for stress and failure.

The project

In this situation I felt that I had a number of options. I decided that I would change myself and my own approach and attitude, and that I would try to change others. If this failed I would leave, but in the meantime I would put up with it.

When I came into the post I inherited an organization with serious financial problems and a poor reputation with users and funders. At this point it would have been counterproductive to have spent money on upgrading the office space. The organization now had an excellent reputation and was financially stable and so the time for change was right. I set myself the following objectives:

1 To improve the quality of my physical working environment

2 To change the culture of the organization with regard to working conditions
3 To change my approach and attitude to my rights and need for a good working environment
4 To increase my effectiveness as a manager
5 To improve the working conditions for other staff.

In practical terms this meant identifying funding to carry out major building works, converting space that was currently used as storage space into office space, and getting the staff and Executive Committee behind these changes.

Personal insight

At this initial stage of the project I gained an insight into how I had undervalued myself. On some level I had thought that I did not have an entitlement to good working conditions. The organization has grown considerably since I started and there are many new legal requirements we have to fulfil. I have just kept on taking more and more responsibility without looking after myself properly.

I am sure it is true that most of the staff tolerate poor working conditions because I do. This has implications for me to use my leadership to set an example. I therefore added some personal goals to my plans:

- To change my approach to how I saw myself as a manager
- To prioritize my need for a good working environment above the short-term needs of others
- To be less self-sacrificing
- To be more assertive in establishing my right to have the tools necessary to carry out the functions of my job.

Gaining support

The next stage was practical: to convert the storage space into office space. I drew up a timetable for implementation. Together with the Assistant Director, I identified savings that could be made in the budget in the current financial year that would allow the building work to go ahead.

Then I started on the process of lobbying organizational members to accept a proposal with which I knew they would be instinctively out of sympathy. I talked through the proposal with other managers in the organization and gained their support. I talked through the plan with the Chair of our Executive Committee and gained his support. I wrote a detailed report for the Executive Committee outlining the proposal and highlighting the impact this would have on the organization, positive both in terms of long-term benefits and alleviating short-term disruption.

Having gained the Executive Committee's full support for the proposal, I discussed the proposition at the Team meeting the following day, making it very clear what the impact on them would be. I gained their support. I then asked the Senior Project Worker to produce draft proposals for managing the impact of the budget reductions.

Learning

The foregoing process reinforced my belief that it is crucial that you involve people during the process of change, that you take them with you. It also reinforced my view that it is important that you are absolutely honest with staff and Executive Committee members about the true impact of what you are asking them to consent to. Because the process was dealt with in an open and above-board way, resentments were dealt with as they arose. Without exception everyone is behind the proposal. Staff have made a commitment to managing the budget reductions as constructively as possible.

As a result of staff having the opportunity to raise their resentments and disagreements openly, my eyes were opened to another aspect of management style that I had not been consciously aware of to date. I realized that I was always ready to take on full responsibility for everything. As a result, a number of staff were more than happy not to take on their own personal responsibility that goes with their job. I also learned about the importance of identifying your own needs and then seeking to find the solutions yourself.

This, of course, was not the end of the project. Severe problems arose in getting architects' plans drawn up and then getting these approved by English Heritage, the local authority's Conservation Officer, the Fire Officer and the Building Control Officer. This exercised all my negotiation skills. In the course of this I also realized that only in the final instance will I call on others for help or support. Part of me believes that as director of the organization I should know everything and that I should be able to cope with every circumstance.

The process of change has started and I am sure it will continue. I feel that I have attained all the personal learning goals I set myself at the outset and most of the outcomes. I learnt a great deal from the process. It was extremely useful to assess my personal learning as I went along. All too often work is so busy and as soon as one task is completed you move swiftly on to the next. This process afforded me the opportunity to look more carefully at my approach and attitude to work and to make conscious decisions to change that approach.

During the course of this project a number of opportunities for further changing the culture of the organization have arisen. I will be working towards implementing these in the coming months.

The model of action described by the 'purpose–action–accomplishment' cycle in Figure 1.1 of this book provides a clear explanation of the process that was involved in the tasks I undertook. However, as Tom Reeves points out, the path to accomplishment and achieving your desired goals rarely runs as smoothly as this would imply. Often many tasks are being tackled at the same time and there may be any number of 'spin-offs' on the way.

9   Landfalls

Introduction

If you are to extract the full potential for learning and development from your experience you need to reflect carefully upon what happened.

This chapter considers how you may look back on your experience: where it has taken you and how you could distil further learning from it. Topics covered are:

* Objectives in articulating the lessons of experience;
* Models to guide your learning, both during and after the action experience;
* Self-evaluation in the light of experience; and
* The process of assimilating new experiential learning and consolidating it into your future repertoire.

Articulating your learning

Managers who have been on action-learning programmes often seem to find it hard in looking back over their action to articulate what they have learned. When asked to write a short piece of reflective commentary on their learning, the examples they give tend to be either very general – for example saying that they now feel more confident or more prepared to take initiatives or more able to work in a team – or very specific – if I had to do X again I would do it differently.

One possible reason for these perfunctory accounts is that the exercise is felt to be intrusive. Managers are reluctant to disclose to a tutor or to fellow managers information about their learning that might be personally revealing. Or they may be reticent about seeming too boastful about what they have achieved. Or writing about one's development is felt to be embarrassing. For whatever reason, managers may well not want to say or write very much publicly about their personal development.

A further possible reason, I believe, is that we do not have many concepts and words for describing personal development and its outcomes. It is not difficult to describe what knowledge or skills we have learned. Statements beginning 'I now know . . .' or 'I now can . . .' are easy enough to write. It is less easy to describe how we have changed or what we have become. Sentences beginning 'I now see . . .' or 'I now feel . . .' or 'I now understand why . . .' or 'I have become . . .' are rather more difficult to complete. There are no obvious ready references for the words and concepts needed to describe the experience of personal development. But, whether privately or publicly, you need to articulate what you have learned, at least to yourself. This chapter will give you some concepts and language with which you can do so.

The conclusion of a successful project or management task can be a time of great personal satisfaction, exhilaration even. It may seem rather mundane now to spend time going back over what you have done. For those not naturally given to introspection and reflection it may seem a somewhat dubious use of your time. But to neglect this stage would probably mean that you fail to get anything like the benefit you could from your project or experience. It would be comparable to studying for a qualification and dropping out at the point when you were meant to start revising for the exams. In all learning experiences, whether courses or projects, it is often only at the end, in concentrated retrospection, that your really significant learning takes place.

Moreover, the sense of 'eureka' that may accompany successful achievement is unlikely to last. As some of the managers, reported in Chapter 5, who felt they had discovered 'it' later ruefully commented when anticlimax set in: 'The feeling was fleeting'. 'It has evaporated'. In fact their attitudes and behaviour gave the lie to what they were now saying. To external observers, the course tutors, these managers appeared to have changed quite dramatically. That their sense of a high point should fade was inevitable.

What needs to be done is to consolidate the achievement, and more particularly the journey to it, in prosaic but lasting terms. This requires that, as well as distilling any further learning still to be drawn out of your experience, you:

• Appreciate fully what your experiential learning tells you about managing and about yourself; and
• Carry over the practices that you have experimented with successfully in the course of your experiences into the way you manage in the future.

Getting feedback

If you are serious about developing yourself you will need feedback. Your own reflections on your experience may or may not be sufficiently insightful. You cannot know this without some feedback from people who work with you about whether your performance and impact are what you think they are. You may get this in the normal course of events. Or you may need to seek it out. You may therefore wish to consider enlisting the support of a trusted colleague to give you the feedback that will aid you in your development.

There is another issue to be considered here. The foregoing observations assume that you know that you need to develop. On the other hand, you may believe that you do not need any development at the present time. Which may be so. Or it may not be.

A manager's decision to work on himself or herself is often triggered by some explicit and inescapable feedback. This could have resulted from some setback in the course of your work. Or it could occur on a course you are sent on. Most management development courses are designed to put you in situations where the feedback you need for yourself will emerge. Your performance in carrying out a challenging task, probably in a team, perhaps outdoors, possibly on a mountainside, reveals aspects of yourself and your behaviour that you were hitherto unaware of or had refused to acknowledge. Feedback from other members of the team and from the course leader is unequivocal and inescapable. You simply have to consider why you acted the way you did.

But in these off-the-job exercises there is a let out. It was an artificial exercise. This is not the way you normally behave. A good course tutor will be unlikely to let you get away with specious rationalizations. But there is no evading the issue when the behaviour happens at work.

The task that confronts you if you are serious about making use of this book for self-development is getting honest and accurate feedback on your performance to aid you in your self-reflections. My experience of action-learning sets is that, valuable as these are, they do not give the feedback that can only come from someone who sees you in operation at work. On the other hand, an effective set, in that it will get you to address personal obstacles to achievement at work, may indirectly lead to the kind of observational feedback that you need.

How you engineer this feedback from work colleagues only you can determine. The point has been made that you will probably need it.

Feedback will of course be positive as well as negative. But being positive does not necessarily make it any easier to accept. It is not unknown for people to attempt to cling on to a poor self-image in the face of contradictory positive feedback; they may need help in getting the penny of success to drop.

For example, a manager in the probation services had produced a report of an action project which was full of achievements. Yet when he presented it to me he simply had not grasped at a psychological level what he had done. He sat in front of me talking just as he had done six months earlier when he had perceived his project aspirations as a hopeless cause, doomed to failure by insuperable bureaucratic obstacles and lack of resources. Yet he had circumvented most of these hurdles. But at some inner, emotional level he seemed determined to hang onto his old self-image as someone who could not really achieve anything.

Eventually, confronted with indisputable evidence of his success, illumination suddenly began to dawn. His face lit up. 'You're right', he said with growing astonishment at himself, 'Six months ago I never dreamed I would have Home Office officials interested in following up what I am doing . . .'. He subsequently asked me to write references to support his applications for senior appointments.

It may be important for readers of this book seeking to take the purpose–action–accomplishment route to development to have a mentor who can give positive feedback when it is needed. It is sometimes difficult to blow our own trumpet even to ourselves. In British culture particularly, great value is placed on modesty; the British tend to be self-deprecating and to down-play praise. But recognizing one's achievements, even celebrating them, is important for self-development.

Learning from surprises

Much development through experience takes place at the time of the experience. Often it is intuitive, virtually unconscious. You have done something, so you know it. Something happens and you absorb its meaning. But some experiential learning will need more deliberate and calm reflection after the event.

Schon's notion of 'reflection-in-action' was described in Chapter 5 (see Box 5.3). You try something. It does not work. You try something else. It works. You have learned. In Schon's model of reflection-in-action, learning experiences start with a routine response, which, when it does not work, precipitates a 'surprise'. In the case of managers pursuing a developmental project, the whole point has been that you should not have been trying out routinized responses.

Indeed a primary purpose of Parts Two and Three of this book has been to get you to rethink the way you normally approach tasks. You were structuring your experience so that it would throw up surprises to trigger learning. You should thus have had many opportunities for reflection-in-action.

Not all learning from experience requires conscious reflection even at the time. Sometimes we just do things, and having done them know that we can do them. It might be difficult to explain your knowledge or skill, but you know that you can, for example, plan a work schedule, control a budget, or intervene in conflicts. Managers often say that what they have 'gained' is 'the experience'.

Making learning explicit

Much of a practitioner's knowledge results from what Schon calls 'knowing in action'. It is comparable to the kind of tacit knowledge that we have of how to ride a bicycle or cross a road. It may of course become necessary to try to make our tacit knowledge explicit if we want to pass it on to someone else. But often it may be sufficient just to be aware that you 'know' it. Where this is the case, you do not want to spend time on further reflection.

You might feel that this was the case with your achievement of your project purposes. You are now a person who knows that, working in an organization with other people, you can achieve what you intend. If this is as far as you want to take your learning, you may be justified in not engaging in any retrospective reflection.

On the other hand, there will be those who feel in some way dissatisfied with what they have achieved or how they have achieved it. They have a sense of still needing to tease out from their experience that insight or lesson that will enable them to progress.

Retrospective reflection

Reflection, it will be recalled from Chapter 5, is one of the four major learning styles identified by Kolb (1984) and elaborated by Honey and Mumford (1986). Despite this attention, there is remarkably little guidance around on how to go about reflecting on experience. Most of what little has been written has taken the perspective of the tutor or facilitator helping someone to reflect rather than that of the learner. Possibly it has been assumed that reflection is such a natural process that it needs no explanation or guidance. Or it may be simply a legacy of the domination of learning by teachers who have been more interested in how to impart knowledge than in helping learners to discover it for themselves.

This neglect of the learner's part in reflection is, however, beginning to be remedied. David Boud and colleagues in their own contribution to their edited book, *Reflection: Turning Experience into Learning* (1985), have set out what I believe to be the first attempt at a comprehensive description of the reflective process in experiential learning. They note that:

> As yet little research has been conducted on reflection in learning and that which has been undertaken offers few guidelines for the practical problems which face us as teachers and learners. (p. 21)

The kind of retrospective reflection that Boud and his colleagues are referring to is somewhat different to Schon's reflection-in-action. There are similarities with the processes described in Box 5.3, but also important differences. Retrospective reflection is of necessity a much more deliberate process. In the absence of any particular 'surprise' to trigger it, retrospective reflection depends on a systematic searching of experiences for significant events to ponder. Boud and his colleagues describe reflection as

> . . . an important human activity in which people recapture their experience, think about it, mull it over and evaluate it . . .
>
> Reflection in the context of learning is a generic term for those intellectual and affective activities in which individuals engage to explore their experiences in order to lead to new understandings and appreciations. (p. 19)

An outline of Boud and colleagues' model of retrospective reflection is presented in Figure 9.1. The process of reflection iterates between experience and contemplation, resulting eventually in outcomes. These are as much to do with new behaviour as with knowledge or understanding.

'Experience' is not just the actions and events which the individual experiences. It includes the individual's 'experience' of these experiences – that is to say his or her thoughts, feelings, conclusions and other responses to the situation or event being experienced.

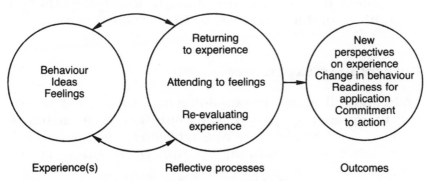

Figure 9.1 The reflection process. Adapted from: Boud et al. *(1985) by permission of the publisher, Kogan Page*

Reflection, at least for adults, should be triggered by the normal events of life rather than be some kind of contrived activity. Such events can be positive or negative, and might well include achievement of a managerial task:

> Probably, for adult learners, most events which precipitate reflection arise out of the normal occurrences of one's life. The impetus may arise from a loss of confidence in or disillusionment with one's existing situation. This could be provoked by an external event, or could develop from one's own reflection on a whole series of occurrences over time, causing a dissatisfaction which leads to a reconsideration of them . . .

> Reflection may also be prompted by more positive states, for example, by an experience of successfully completing a task which previously was thought impossible. (p.19)

The foregoing quotations note some of the conditions that may provoke adults to learn and change. It has to be admitted, however, that some people seem extremely hard to provoke. They simply continue with their existing management style, be it dictatorial or permissive, regardless of appropriateness for circumstances. A manager who is extremely egotistical may remain unmoved by events which cause others to question their most basic assumptions. It is unlikely, however, that such a person will be reading this book.

Figure 9.1 has provided a source of headings for the discussion of reflection that follows. However, in order to take account of the particular issues likely to concern managers, the content discussed under these headings departs considerably from that discussed by Boud and colleagues.

Returning to experience

Boud and colleagues, in explaining their category of 'returning to experience' simply say that this is a matter of recollecting the salient events, replaying the experience in your mind or recounting to others features of the experience.

Reflecting on experience demands that you mentally stand outside yourself and the situation you have been managing and reflect dispassionately on what has occurred. This skill is essentially the same as that of research, where one also seeks to record and analyse events objectively. The only difference is that in experiential learning a large part of your subject of study is yourself and your own actions. These are things that it is not always easy to be dispassionate about, especially when self-image or self-esteem may be at stake.

What you will need to do is to 'research' what you have just been doing, using the kind of objective approach that you would take in any management investigation. Your research 'data' will necessarily be very 'soft', and you will need to use a qualitative approach. But, as in any qualitative study, you can still be thorough and exacting.

Starting points for reflection-in-action arise naturally from the surprises. But in looking back over a whole project or experience your starting point may be less obvious. Should you reflect on whole or part? What should you be looking for? How thorough and systematic should you be? How will you know when you have done enough reflecting?

You have a choice of a broad or a narrow focus. You can:

- Seek to review the entire experience, seeking to discover the lessons that can be drawn from all its different episodes; or
- Focus your reflections just on those episodes that are relevant to particular learning outcomes which you feel you need in order to round off your development at this time.

Managers are likely to be drawn to the second option. There are likely to be particular events that you know you want to reflect upon – things that worked well or not so well, unexpected difficulties or anticipated difficulties that did not materialize, feelings of satisfaction or frustration, relationships with particular individuals or with a group, and so on. If you have any sense of what you ought to be looking at, it seems sensible to be guided by that at least initially.

Reflection is essentially about looking backwards. If it is to be more than just an exercise in writing your personal history, it should be tempered by some looking forward to your future directions.

Boud and colleagues emphasize the importance of the learner's intent in guiding the way experience is approached and processed, and note three particular intentions one might have:

- Exploring organized knowledge;
- Self-exploration; and
- Examining the environment or context in which you are operating.

Analytical skills

The first of these, exploring organized knowledge, might seem to a practising manager something that he or she need not be especially concerned with. But one of the things you will have been doing in the course of your experience is test out the validity of ideas and practices you have culled from books, journals, other managers and other organizations. It is sensible that, if you have not already done so as part of your reflection-in-action, you now take time to evaluate these ideas and practices so that you may qualify, adapt or reject them.

Some readers may be on an academic course which demands that you write a report or dissertation in which you relate your experiential learning to the wider body of management theory and knowledge, perhaps even develop your own theories or principles. The process of relating your experience to organized knowledge involves analysing the events you have experienced, to produce:

- First, a descriptive account of what occurred; and
- Second, an explanatory interpretation in which you identify chains of cause and effect, and the conditions that favoured or impeded these causal sequences.

This needs to be done at two levels: firstly, at the level of the particular events that occurred; and secondly, at a more abstract level, describing events and processes in terms of more general concepts or categories than those you used to describe the particular. In moving to this more general or abstract level, you can draw on concepts and explanatory models (or theories) that you have come across in the body of organized knowledge to be found in books and journals. Or you can develop your own concepts and models to fit the circumstances and events you wish to describe and explain.

Systematically setting out your experientially based knowledge and understanding enhances considerably your ability to manage situations you are responsible for. The processes of abstract conceptualization and logical thought involved in going through this kind of analysis gives training in an invaluable intellectual discipline.

This style of thinking is the key to manipulating situations and events from a perspective of knowing what you are really doing, and understanding the factors that could make things turn out differently.

It is failures of conceptualization and analytical thought which lead to half-baked attempts to implement popular nostrums intended to put the organization and the world to rights without any proper understanding of their relevance, or all too often irrelevance, to particular circumstances.

Self-evaluation

As a practical, regular routine, it is worth spending an hour or so every six months reviewing progress on your key job objectives, and highlighting the successes and not so successful elements. Analyse why tasks went well or not so well, paying particular attention to tasks where you relied on others for their achievement.

Looking back over your experience will lead you into a variety of post mortems. You will often kick yourself for not having done things differently. Sometimes these 'mistakes' will be errors of judgement. It is important to understand these and know where your analysis of the situation went wrong, what assumptions were misplaced, what you could have done to make things turn out differently.

Things may have gone wrong, however, as a result of a way you have of responding to situations that you keep repeating regardless of appropriateness. This recurrent pattern of behaviour sabotages your intent.

This kind of failure to get the outcome you wanted was looked at in Chapter 8 (see Box 8.5) in the context of habitual behaviour undermining your power. In reflecting on experience, you should give further critical attention to your behaviour patterns. There is always a different way you could respond if you so choose.

In this connection, it is worth bearing in mind an assertion by George Kelly, a psychologist who developed a theory of behaviour based on each individual's 'personal construct' of their world:

> We take the stand that there are always some alternative constructions available to choose among in dealing with the world. No one needs to paint himself into a corner, no one needs to be completely hemmed in by his circumstances; no one needs to be the victim of his biography. (Kelly, 1955)

The learning experiences you have confronted may be likened to the questions in a questionnaire on your style of managing. The purpose of the review in Chapter 2 of your internal processes was to heighten your awareness of aspects of yourself that you should be attending to in the course of the learning experience to come. It is now time to take stock of how well you were able to manage yourself:

- Did I break out of accustomed patterns and experiment with new ways of doing things?
- Did I allow unvalidated assumptions about situations or misplaced perceptions of people to affect what I did?
- How aware was I of how my inner needs were driving what I did, and how well did I handle them?
- Did I use my feelings constructively or allow them to block me?

Telling the truth to yourself

It is not always easy to be honest in one's self-reflection. Habitual patterns of behaviour may not readily come to consciousness. Or all the self-justifications and other defensive reactions that we have for concealing from ourselves the true nature of our behaviour may come into play. The key will lie in your 'experience of your experience'. Your feelings about events, if you can see behind your own defence mechanisms, can tell you much about how you are being self-defeating.

Getting feedback from a trusted friend may be helpful. I emphasize 'trusted'. You may find it difficult enough to listen and to accept home truths, even in the most propitious of circumstances.

Too much should not be made of these potential difficulties in knowing yourself. Most people do know themselves, often better than they care to admit to themselves. When managers get feedback from questionnaires about their personality or behaviour they will often express astonishment at how accurately the questionnaire has diagnosed them. The results of course are really only confirming what they already knew about themselves. The questionnaire has, through a series of seemingly innocuous questions, 'tricked' them into disclosing an overall picture which they may have been loath to articulate too explicitly. But they are now confronted with this self-knowledge and have to think what to do about it.

If, during the course of your learning experience, you have allowed yourself to be aware of the interaction between your psychology and your outward behaviour, you will have been similarly confronted.

In reflecting on experience your attention will inevitably be drawn to the negative aspects of your behaviour. Managing these will lead you to break old patterns. The issue is essentially whether any of your behaviour is proving counter-productive. A large part of the reflective process should be concerned with making that judgement.

Some pairs of words that may prompt you in your reflections are to be found in Box 9.1. The cautionary note in Chapter 7 advising that the pairs of opposites in Box 7.2 are not to be interpreted in black and white terms is relevant also to this box.

Often simple awareness is sufficient for you to manage a counter-productive behaviour. But if the pattern is deeply engrained some work on yourself may be called for – this is discussed in the next chapter.

In this context, Boud and colleagues refer in their model in Figure 9.1 to 'attending to feelings'. By this they mean

Box 9.1

Productive or counter-productive behaviours?

Competitive   –   Collaborative
Avoiding   –   Confronting
Accommodating   –   Uncompromising
Perfectionist   –   Unobsessive
Independent   –   Dependent
Supportive   –   Destructive
Understanding   –   Critical
Enthusiastic   –   Unexcitable
Dominating   –   Compliant
Friendly   –   Hostile
Aggressive   –   Even-tempered
Caring   –   Indifferent
Loner   –   Team worker

utilizing positive feelings and removing negative ones. This too will be discussed in the next chapter.

Re-evaluating experience

The entire process of reflection is in a sense concerned with re-evaluation. The simple 'I won't make that mistake again' is a re-evaluation. Boud and colleagues' model is referring to something more profound than this. They argue that the re-evaluation which takes place immediately after the event risks being clouded by false assumptions, inadequate comprehension of events and, last but not least, the feelings that the events provoked. A period of time to reflect dispassionately and analytically and to work through feelings is needed before a reliable re-evaluation can be made.

The process of retrospective re-evaluation is in large part one of re-perceiving and re-judging. It is also a psychological process. By redefining our account of what happened we reach a new understanding, which allows us to let go of the past and move in new directions for the future.

Boud and colleagues see this as a four-stage process of association, integration, validation and appropriation. What they mean by these terms is explained in Box 9.2. The process and its four stages should be recognizable by anyone who has ever been conscious of the way they have learned

---

Box 9.2

Assimilating learning

Association

Connecting the ideas and feelings you had during your experience and your reflection on it with normative views on what these should be. You may decide that your own ideas and attitudes are outmoded, or vice versa.

Integration

Your associations need to be made meaningful and useful for you personally. If you can integrate them with your existing conceptual frameworks, a new synthesis of ideas and attitudes will begin to develop.

Validation

You need to subject the new ideas and attitudes you are developing to 'reality tests'. You need to try out your new perceptions in new situations. You need to assess the consistency between your new appreciations and your other knowledge and beliefs.

Appropriation

In the case of learning which you are going to make use of in a major role, such as managing, a further step is needed. You have to make the learning your own. Some learning of this kind can be so personally significant that it becomes part of your sense of identity. There is likely to be a strong emotional element in this process. The learning may become part of your value system. In colloquial jargon, you 'own' what you have learned.

Adapted from: Boud *et al.* (1985) by permission of the publisher, Kogan Page Ltd.

something of significance. Awareness of the process should assist in future learning from experience. It could also have relevance to the process of generating commitment.

Outcomes

The outcomes set in the circle in Figure 9.1 are certainly among those that a manager might seek from reflection on experience: new perspectives on experience, change in behaviour, readiness for application, commitment to action.

From the point of view of being effective, changes in behaviour may be critical. However, the importance of a 'new perspective' should not be underestimated. The orientation to action in management can be so all pervading that the value simply of knowing and seeing in new ways can be overlooked. In the same way that managing effectively is more than the aggregation of a repertoire of competences, it is also more than the progressive refinement of one's practice in the light of experience. The way you see the world is of the essence.

Versatility

You need to think too about the range of circumstances in which your experiential learning would be relevant. When competences are assessed for a qualification, the range of circumstances in which you are able to exercise the competency is taken into account. So one outcome you may seek from your reflection is to extend the range of circumstances in which you can use the competences you have acquired.

Competency has been defined (Edmonds, 1992) as:

> . . . predispositions in people to behave in ways shown to be associated with getting successful outcomes.

The word 'predisposition' in this definition draws attention to the fact that

> . . . competency refers to behaviour which is characteristic of a person. This means it is not situation-specific but occurs over a wide range of different and unrelated situations.

This view of competency as characteristic behaviour re-emphasizes the need to work on those aspects of yourself that drive your behaviour. Practising competences in different situations may not enhance your effectiveness unless accompanied by modification of your predispositions.

Consolidating gains

There is a further outcome not listed in Figure 9.1 that managers are likely to be concerned with. Progress that you may have made to push back organizational frontiers for yourself needs to be consolidated. You will perhaps have acquired authority to work across boundaries, you may have created a new network of contacts, have set up new collaborations, or set a new direction for some part of the organization. These 'organizational gains' must not be lost, as was the case with the head teacher described in Chapter 8, just because your project has come to an end. You do not want to end up more knowledgeable but less powerful.

Your aspirations for yourself

A further outcome to consider is the kind of manager you now want to be. You need to define how you want yourself to be in the future. What epithets would you like to describe you? Some prompts are given in Box 9.3. The point about all these possibilities, unlike personality traits, is that they are all things that you can do or be.

Confidence in yourself

One of the most valuable indicators of the worth of your experiential learning is your sense of whether or not you have been doing, or are now doing, the right things. Looking back you have a sense of 'that was it'.

You may listen to the opinions of others about how well you have done but you are no longer psychologically dependent on knowing these opinions. This does not mean that you have

---

Box 9.3

What do you want to be? How do you want to be?

Visionary?
Resolute?
Director?
Discoverer?
Purposeful?
Excited?
Leader?
Follower?
Confident?
Powerful?
A draw?
Autonomous?
Initiator?
Sponsor?
High profile?
Innovator?
Team-worker?
Resource holder?
Energetic?
Self-controlled?
Achiever?

---

become arrogant and insensitive to others' views; simply that you have reached a point where you are confident of making your own independent judgements about whether you have succeeded in achieving your intentions.

Reflection and action points

- How far have you developed in your desired direction? What more do you need to do?

Comparing yourself now with how you were before embarking on your developmental project or task is an essentially subjective assessment. Ask yourself:

- What new things do I now feel able to do?
- What did I feel apprehensive about then that I would now have no qualms about doing?
- In what ways do I now see things and people differently?
- Do I feel different?

Ask yourself questions for the future:

- What would I want to do differently next time? How?
- What would I want to repeat? Why?
- What ego drives and misplaced perceptions do I want to stop 'carrying'?
- What organizational 'gains' made during the project do I want to consolidate, and how should I do this?
- What new directions do I want to take? In my present job? In my career?

10   Personal alchemy

Introduction

Having distilled some practical and personal learning from your experience, the next step is to work on the source of any counter-productive behaviour you have become aware of. This means working on your psychology and accustomed style of behaving so that more productive behaviour becomes second nature to you.

The first half of this chapter gives some developmental and behavioural benchmarks against which you can compare yourself:

- A model of the stages of development that managers typically pass through, together with quotations from managers that illustrate the nature of the progression from one stage to the next; and
- A set of five vignettes describing certain managerial archetypes which you can use to hold the mirror up to your own style of managing and its effectiveness.

The second half of the chapter then suggests some practical steps to help you in working to develop, improve, and change yourself. It covers:

- Witnessing and influencing yourself;
- Handling your emotional responses as you move through the cycle of personal change;
- Changing your behaviour as a means of changing yourself;
- Letting go of outmoded beliefs and feelings; and
- What changing yourself means and how to retain your personal integrity in the change process.

Personal transformation

A great deal of learning from experience is to do with discovering how to manage your external world – what to do and how to do it. You also need to be personally adept in this external world – to know yourself and how you need to be.

'Adept' means to be 'completely versed in', 'well-skilled in', 'thoroughly proficient'. It comes from the Latin word *adeptus*, meaning 'having attained', used in medieval times to describe someone who had attained the great secret of alchemy. This historical connotation is appropriate for managers who use their insight to transform themselves.

'Personal growth' means becoming more mature, better able to relate to others, more able to cope with the world and to influence it – in sum, a 'bigger' person. Box 10.1 sets out some of the changes in yourself that you might expect to experience.

You may not always be conscious of growth happening to you, except perhaps when you take stock and look back at how you were. In terms of the dimensions of self presented in Chapter 2, you are aware that you think differently, see things differently, feel differently, act differently.

Not everyone wants to grow; there is comfort and safety in staying as you are. There are basically two reasons why you might want to grow:

- Dissatisfaction with your present self and your current abilities – your learning experience has perhaps made you aware that you are not living up to your expectations, or has made you conscious of inner impediments to performance.
- A sense of being capable of more, able to attain more ambitious goals – you do not feel yourself to be at all inadequate but want to realize more of your potential.

Gaining insight was discussed in the last chapter. Acting on the insight often follows naturally. It just needs the will to do so. Indeed, personal development workshops normally stop at the point of having helped you to the point of gaining insight and wanting to do something about it. It is assumed that you will be able to take your development on from there yourself.

Box 10.1

Elements of personal development and growth

- Change in perspective or outlook:
  - new beliefs and attitudes; and
  - less cause for stress and tension.

- New insights and self-understanding:
  - confidence and sureness of self.

- More in control of oneself:
  - self-knowledge;
  - better able to handle and direct emotions;
  - conscious of inner forces; and
  - more ready to let go.

- Relating to others with fewer barriers:
  - more at ease; and
  - more open and trusting.

- Directing oneself more purposively:
  - creating and holding personal vision;
  - utilizing inner resources; and
  - being whole-hearted about what you do.

- Able to go further, do more:
  - not deterred by barriers;
  - more energy and enthusiasm; and
  - new view of the possible.

- Take on the 'mantle' of management:
  - act and think like a manager; and
  - be a manager.

- More one's own person.

Usually this will be a valid assumption. Skill in managing our behaviour is something that we all learn for ourselves naturally. So often all that is needed is to have our attention drawn to behaviour that we may not have been fully aware of. We are then quite capable of taking the necessary remedial action.

Sometimes, however, it is less easy than that. Some patterns of behaviour can be well entrenched and supported by beliefs that are difficult to let go of. Those of you who did the exercise in Box 8.5 will probably be aware how difficult it can sometimes be even to see recurrent patterns of counter-productive behaviour, let alone break out of them. It can sometimes be similarly difficult to adopt a new style of behaviour that you see is needed.

In deciding that you want to grow, there is a risk that you start to see your present self as inadequate. This may be how you feel but it is not always a constructive way of looking at yourself. Counter-productive behaviour is what you do; it is not who you are. If it were you could not change. So do not allow new insights about your behaviour to undermine your self-esteem. Deleting unproductive practices from your repertoire or introducing new ones will not make you a 'better' person.

It is more constructive to think of yourself as 'okay' as you are, even though you want to change, and that you are simply going to move from one 'okay' state to another. This kind of positive thinking is often maligned as being facile. It is not the solution to everything, but it can have a useful part to play. It is usually more constructive to have positive thoughts in place than negative ones.

Stages of personal development

It can be helpful in thinking about personal change to see your present state of development, not in terms of good or bad, okay or not okay, but simply as a stage in the natural evolution of a manager.

The stages that managers progress through have been researched by a team from development consultants, Transform, and the then Sheffield City Polytechnic (Leary *et al.*, 1986). Their view of managerial effectiveness as straddling input, process and output was presented in Chapter 1 (see Box 1.6).

The Transform/Sheffield team postulate seven levels of managerial development. An alternative version of this model is to found in Pedler and Boydell's self-help book, *Managing*

Yourself (1985: 70–71), where the problems for a manager of being 'stuck' at any particular level are described.

The seven levels divide into three broad stages, to which I have given my own labels.

Stage One: conformist implementer

Level 1
Static, rigid, standard – adhering to rules and procedures; obeying those in authority.

Level 2
Responding by adapting, modifying or controlling rules, procedures, systems and people

Level 3
Sensitive, aware, in tune with what is happening, thus relating to norms and conventions.

In these first three levels in this model of a manager's development, the manager's behaviour is basically controlled by outsiders, at the first two levels by rules and procedures, and, at the third level, by conforming to 'correct' behaviour.

Stage Two: independent experimenter

Level 4
Experiencing things and prepared to learn from this experience

Level 5
Experimenting and deliberately trying to find out more, to add to the stock of knowledge, to improve on the status quo, to advance 'the state of the art'.

Level 6
Connecting, making large scale links, leading to much wider understanding, including the realization that most things are somehow connected. 'Sense of oneness'.

These three levels are marked by the manager moving away from doing the approved thing and starting to find out for herself or himself what is true, right, and correct. Your behaviour is now controlled from within yourself rather than by external factors. You learn to find out for yourself, to do things your way – even though this may mean deviating from norms, being different, being yourself. It is these three levels with which the experiential learning in this book has been primarily concerned.

Stage Three: autonomous agent

Level 7
Integrating yourself with the outside world and with the task of the times. Making part of this your own life task, and dedicating yourself, with full commitment, to it. Fulfilling yourself within the constraints of also having to meet corporate purposes.

This seventh and final level has considerable overlap with level 6. Managers' sense of connectedness and holistic view of the world is now drawn upon to integrate themselves with the world around them. It is about doing something important and constructive, about changing the world.

Within each of the seven levels, the Transform/Sheffield team saw managers as having distinct modes of

- Thinking;
- Feeling or sensing; and
- Willing or doing.

Managers' histories

To test the model, biographical data were obtained from a sample of over 50 managers in six different organizations – covering different industry sectors, different managerial levels, different functions. A selection of comments extracted from these managerial histories that illustrate the thinking, feeling and doing characterizing each developmental stage are presented in Box 10.2.

Managers in the sample were asked to relate their experience directly to the model, which they were all apparently able to do. The model thus provides a tested framework which other managers can use to help make sense of their past experience and see the direction in which they need to develop in the future.

Box 10.2

Stages of management development

Levels 1–3: the conformist implementer

Thinking

'If I don't know what to do, I look to see what others have done in the same situation.'

'As far as I'm concerned a person is either good or bad. Generally, if I see a man as bad then he's all bad. You can have a thief who sings in the choir, but he's still a thief.'

'No, I don't ever recall seeking a wider understanding of anything. I'd be more likely to narrow it down to something small.'

'You learn by asking questions, checking, asking why do we do things this way? What's the reason for that procedure?'

A manager at this stage initially operates from memory, using rules, check-lists, set procedures, 'correct' ways of doing things. Then starts thinking through various 'what if' scenarios that may temper strict adherence to rules and procedures, eventually developing quite a sophisticated understanding of cause-and-effect relationships, but mainly using other people's ideas and theories to do so.

Feeling or sensing

'I like to do things by the book.'

'It's a big worry to me, not knowing what the organization wants.'

'It's very threatening, having to go outside your boundaries.'

'If I worked strictly to the rules this would cause more problems.'

'I like to check things out with others – mirror what I'm doing in someone else's mind . . . so as to see if my ideas will fit in.'

'I sometimes feel annoyance at the fact that I haven't time to get into a body of knowledge that would help.'

The world feels threatening. Security is at first sought through adherence to rules and set ways of doing things, later through control and domination of the environment, systems and people. As the world appears safer, the manager will seek to tune in to situations, to sense what is expected, and want to demonstrate that he or she 'belongs' by behaving in the 'appropriate' way.

Willing or Doing

'I use what I call "coping skills" – looking for standard solutions.'

'When someone makes a mistake in this section, they blame it on rotten luck, or on the weather, or something like that.'

'I don't apply the rules to a T, but apply common-sense; that's one of my strong features, common-sense – knowing when to bend the rules.'

'I use the "Law of the situation" – do what seems most appropriate.'

'If I disagreed with my boss, and felt strongly about it, I'd . . . try to persuade him. If I failed to do that I'd do what I was told – after all, he's got a better overall picture.'

'I try to work with a sense of what is needed at that moment.'

Initially do as told and stick to the rules, but as a wider range of competences is acquired start to manipulate situations. Practical skill coupled with an ability to tune into situations leads to efficiency, effectiveness, virtuosity – a polished performance but sticking basically to established or approved scripts. This is the manager developing from apprentice to craftsperson.

Levels 4 – 6: the independent experimenter

Thinking

'I've realized that I've got to make my own value judgements, based on my own experiences, even though these sometimes seem in conflict with the accepted norms of the company.'

'I distrust experience but cherish the memory; by that I mean that the experience itself is often horrid, but the learning is useful.'

'I like to think things through, where things are new, where do they need to move to.'

'By meaningful I mean getting something from experience that you could learn, apply to other experiences and make them work, and explain to others.'

'Identifying the things the organization does not care about, has not the skill to do, not going to get much out of immediately – but which are important.'

Consciously reflects on events and creates one's own understanding, which is internalized as having personal meaning. Thinking for self, generating own ideas, and beginning to know self as a manager. This independent thinking provides a platform for experi-

menting to find out more, both about how the external world works and to gain new personal insights. This leads away from compartmentalized thinking to seeing connections and making syntheses. Boundaries that once appeared clear-cut – e.g. manager–subordinate, teacher–taught, masculine–feminine, appear less so. Beginnings of holistic thinking. Knowing yourself.

Feeling or sensing

'I've begun to have confidence in the worthwhileness of my own knowledge.'

'I have to stick up for what I believe, to be positive, if I am to retain my self-esteem.'

'I often find I'm in a dilemma between situational demands and my own inclinations.'

'If I were in charge of this, different quality standards would apply. The time-scale would change. I would have more freedom to act.'

No longer content to rely solely on outside sources for direction. Self-esteem and self-respect now demand that one thinks for oneself and comes to one's own opinions and conclusions. Untoward events precipitate reflection and a search for meaning, rather than a prescribed response. Time is spent finding out, making things work better, even though this may sometimes be an uncomfortable, even painful, process. A need to see and feel the whole picture emerges which leads to understanding and experiencing oneself as part of an integrated whole. This sense of connectedness creates awareness of the moral consequences of actions. You value yourself and others.

Willing or doing

'Skills and knowledge alone don't make a manager; you need to be able to negotiate, make cases out, alter your behaviour, put a different face on things.'

'One of the great skills is being able to manage others who expect managers to have the answers.'

'You need methods for yourself, methods set down by you for others to follow . . . explained and passed on in such a way that others can identify with them, make their own.'

'We can do top-down budgets, can we do bottom-up? Or create a mid-point? Appreciate both top and bottom. Establish links between the two.'

Starting to express individuality and personality through the way one does things – to be oneself. Experimenting with new and better ways of doing things, logically testing out, passing on ideas to others – this is the manager as 'scientist'. As skills and abilities progressively extend to whole fields of activity, systems and strategies, managing acquires a satisfying form (aesthetic, timely, balanced, integrated). This is the manager fulfilling himself or herself – the manager as 'artist'.

Level 7: the autonomous agent

Thinking

'Perhaps I didn't choose (my career) . . . perhaps it chose me, one of those coincidental/chance happenings? That's been a theme in my life.'

Having penetrated through the complexities and struggles of the earlier levels, have become aware of some fundamental, basic and simple idea or ideal, around which beliefs, values and purpose in life are built.

Feeling or sensing

'I now see that the acquisition of knowledge and skills is only valid if these can be *used* for some really useful purpose; that's what I want to do now.'

Searching for a higher ideal or task, outside of self and purely personal ambition. If it is found, will dedicate self to it with deep conviction about the need to do the things the ideal or task dictates, if need be making personal sacrifices.

Willing or doing

'It's easy to say what aspect of the managerial role I enjoy most – it's developing subordinates and probationers. When I was in the "women's force" I developed ways of helping women subordinates; now I have adapted these for helping men.'

Now have ability to conceive visions, grand aims, according to the imperatives of the time, and to realize these aims over a long period, often against indifference, resistance or hostility. This is the manager as change agent, practical visionary.

Adapted from: Leary *et al.* (1986: 46–47, 144–180).

Research carried out by Transform/Sheffield City Polytechnic and sponsored by The Manpower Services Commission. Quoted with permission.

Progressing through levels

This does not mean that all managers will pass through all stages in the order specified, though the authors do seem to believe that a progression along the lines of the model is a fairly universal experience.

Key points they make about progression through the levels are:

- Managers do not have to finish developing in one stage before moving onto the next;
- But at any given time a manager will have moved definitely into a particular stage, and his or her behaviour will reflect the characteristics of that stage;
- While in a particular stage a manager may display precursors of the next stage, prior to stepping into it; and
- Conversely, he or she may temporarily regress under pressure to an earlier stage.

The Transform/Sheffield model provides a way of looking at development. It may be useful in helping you to place your own development in context. It may be reassuring to know that your experiences and mode of progression have been shared by others. You may find in its higher levels a vision of managing that you can aspire to.

On the other hand, you may feel that your own progression as a manager hardly corresponds with the model at all. This would be particularly likely for people entering management roles later in life when their development to maturity has taken place in another context, for example in a professional specialism or by raising a family.

Archetypal characters

Instead of thinking about your development in terms of a progression through levels, you could compare yourself with a managerial 'type'. You need to consider whether acting out characteristics of a particular type is something that you are happy with doing. On reflection you may conclude that you are doing so for inappropriate reasons.

There are many typologies of management that you could compare yourself with. The characters portrayed by Flamholtz and Randle (1989) in *The Inner Game of Management* (see Box 2.5 in Chapter 2) are one example. The types of political manager described in Chapter 8 are another.

Often types are constructed from two or more divergent aspects of human behaviour, for example 'people-orientedness' vs 'production-orientedness', or 'perceiving' vs 'judging' as in the Myers–Briggs personality types described in Chapter 2.

'Profiling', in which a battery of questions measures your position on a range of behavioural or attitudinal factors, may give you a more comprehensive picture of yourself, though without defining you as a 'type'.

An alternative to comparing yourself against constructed types or profiles is to compare yourself against archetypal characters. An archetype is an original model, a prototype, a universally recurring type. In this sense the Transform/Sheffield authors saw their levels of management development as archetypes.

There are certain human types or characters that have been recurrently observed. They have been repeatedly depicted in drama and reported in the literatures of both analytical and clinical psychology.

Five managerial types

Five such archetypal characters, redrawn slightly so that they are recognizable as managerial types, are described in Box 10.3. Probably all of us can recognize some aspect of our self in at least one of these archetypal characters, possibly in several of them.

Comparing yourself against these archetypes can help you be more aware of different facets of yourself. The trap is to allow yourself to be locked into any one of them, so that your behaviour lacks versatility.

The descriptions of the archetypes are of course stereotypes and as such cannot be regarded as a completely accurate portrayal of any single individual. But stereotypical behaviour is easy to fall into. Like writing in clichés,

Box 10.3

Five character archetypes

The fixer

Fixers are wheeler-dealers. They are adept manipulators who use their social and negotiating talents to fix things, and most especially fix people, to achieve their ends. Archetypal fixers have been recognized down the ages, appearing in plays and fables as tricksters and foxes.

As well as cunning, they have enormous vitality which they put to use in deploying their not inconsiderable social skills. They are charmers and beguilers, with sometimes a certain lack of scruple.

The Fixers' goal is to win. Their fear is not to be the master of any situation. Consequently, they will go to great lengths to avoid themselves being tricked or taken for a ride.

As project leaders they can be most effective in securing co-operation and resources. They are usually good negotiators. The risk is that they use their personal power for their own ends rather than the common good – that they play political games.

To experience what it feels like to be a Fixer:

Stand with your feet slightly apart. Hold your chin with your right hand (if that is your dominant one) and with your left hand hold your right elbow. Turn your head to look past your left shoulder, smile slyly and let your eyes twinkle.

The improviser

Improvisers respond to the here and now. They can thus deal well with unexpected predicaments.

But these skills in improvising can be a function of not anticipating events. Improvisers tend to believe what they want to believe about the world around them – until it is upon them.

They are usually highly imaginative, sensitive and creative people, with an intuition that enables them to appreciate other people's feeling and desires.

The Improvisers' goal is not to be troubled. Their fear is to be responsible for events. By engineering themselves to be victims of circumstance, they are not responsible.

As project leaders, Improvisers are adept at sorting problems as they occur. But they can be overoptimistic, believing that somehow events will turn out their way, and allow warning signs of problems to go unnoticed.

They can be powerful when their improvising is effective. However, they may fail to see that, with their head out of the sand, they could be more foresighted. They are the archetypal 'innocent', neither reading situations nor playing games to win advantage.

To experience what it feels like to be an Improviser:

Stand with your feet close together, hands by your side. Rock back slightly on your heels. Momentarily, open your eyes wide and let your jaw drop, looking as if you have been taken by surprise. Then quickly recover your posture and look business-like.

The bearer

Bearers seek to serve, support and care for others. They like to be responsible for others and their problems.

Although these others may not always appreciate what they do, Bearers have a sense of worthwhileness, indeed an inner strength that comes from their private knowledge that they are carrying the world on their shoulders. At the same time they may inwardly resent the compelling sense of obligation that causes them to do this, and even explode with anger if their goodwill is presumed upon too far.

But most of the time Bearers are uncomplaining in their desire to please others. They may at times feel manipulated, put upon, but nevertheless they carry on bearing their self-inflicted load.

The Bearers' attitude to the world, therefore, is essentially one of submission in the service of others. Much of their potential energy is consequently suppressed. They are the archetypal martyr or beast of burden. In mythology, they are symbolized by Atlas. Such characters can even get to look as if they are permanently carrying the world on their shoulders.

The Bearers' goal is to be regarded. Their fear is to lack a cause in life, without which they would feel worthless.

As project leaders, Bearers' desire to assume burdens makes them reluctant to delegate and share responsibility. They can thus find themselves too overworked to give proper attention to the longer term needs of their project.

To experience what it feels like to be a Bearer:

Stand with your feet slightly apart, your knees sagging slightly, and bow your head exactly as if you were carrying a burden on your shoulders. Keeping your shoulders bowed, look up with your lips slightly parted. Although that posture is somewhat exaggerated, in modified form you can frequently observe it, even lapse into it yourself when the world seems on top of you.

The protector

Protectors look after and support people. They are usually warm friendly, open and accessible. They will often be seeking to fulfil themselves vicariously through others' achievements.

Manifestation of their protecting can take diverse forms. They can be listeners or mentors, the people that others go to with their problems. They can be 'carers', providing a haven of comfort and security in an otherwise demanding and hostile organization. They can be patrons or lieutenants, working to help people above or below them to achieve.

They have a capacity to draw people to them. They are good listeners, and readers, knowledgeable professionals. But they tend to be withdrawn rather than outgoing.

There is often an ambivalence in the Protector's character. Although they seemingly protect and support others, they themselves like to be taken care of, have their affairs looked after. This dependency can cause them to be demanding of attention, which drains and exhausts others. They are the archetypal parent.

The Protectors' goal is to see others achieve. Their fear is not be looked after or to have to achieve on their own – in fact to be the archetypical 'orphan'.

As project leaders, Protectors enable team members to flourish and use their potential. Their latent concern to be looked after themselves can make them very demanding with regard to results.

To experience what it feels like to be a Protector:

Stand with your feet apart and your hands by your side. Now raise your hands slightly with palms turned outwards as if you were just going to greet someone warmly. Part your lips and look intently with your eyes.

The determiner

Determiners like to get their way in the world. They tend to be indeflectable in pursuit of their ideas or plans.

Metaphorically they will stride through whatever is their domain, confident that they can bend it to their will. They are manipulators, but, unlike Fixers, when persuasion fails will use power to get their way. They are proud, ambitious, often aggressive, competitive people.

Determiners are very much in touch with world around them, and, unlike Improvisers, plan to shape events. They are extremely reluctant ever to let go of a purpose, or give in to others. Determiners can be very stubborn and lacking in sensitivity towards others.

They have a high energy level, manifested in an aliveness of gesture and movement. While they can be effective in getting things done, Determiners may restrict themselves to a rigid, narrow, safe outlook on life, in which emotions have little part.

The Determiners' goal is to dominate. Their fear is for events or people, including themselves, to be out of control.

They are the archetypal hero or warrior, overcoming all obstacles to achieve their intent.

As project leaders, Determiners will bulldoze their way through all difficulties and opposition. Wariness about being used or controlled by others may result in a reluctance to listen or give way, even when plans now appear inappropriate. While their style can be effective for achieving goals, their goals may be confined within a limited vision.

To experience what it feels like to be a Determiner:

Walk about holding yourself as upright as you can, the more rigidly the better. Look slightly over one shoulder and stride determinedly, assuming that there will be no obstacle ahead to obstruct your progress.

Note on sources: These archetypes derive from a drama workshop on mime run by Olly Crick using archetypal masks devised by John Wright of Middlesex University, and the work of Alexander Lowen (1958) on character archetypes. Some refinements come from Relph (1980), Keirsey (1987) and Bellin Partnership notes.

archetypes provide a ready-to-wear response for handling different roles and situations.

It is possible that one particular archetype dominates our behaviour. If so, our *persona* may be so wrapped up in it that our repertoire of responses to varying situations is blinkered and limited. The greater risk from these stereotypes, however, lies not so much in falling into their patterns, but by not being aware that one is doing so, and being blindly attached to that style of behaving. But normally we all from time to time play most of these archetypal characters.

If you do identify strongly with any one of the archetypes, or any other managerial type, you should ask yourself some searching questions:

- Is this really how you want to be and to present yourself to the world?
- Is your range of responses overly limited by the repertoire of your particular type?
- What inner needs are you satisfying when you behave in the manner of this particular type?

Each of the archetypes has great strengths, and these can be capitalized upon. But each also has a serious weakness.

Bearers may need to consider why they never serve their own needs. Improvisers may need to ask themselves why they are so often in a state of unreadiness. Fixers may need to consider why they always need to win. Protectors (and their Lieutenants) may need to ask themselves why they do not seek to succeed in their own right. Determiners may need to ask themselves why they are so fearful of allowing others to have control.

To be a particular type is not 'right' or 'wrong'. It is a matter of consciously choosing your management style rather than allowing yourself to be driven by your psychological reflexes. Often you may be able to measure your development according to your ability to regulate more consciously your resort to archetypal characteristics.

Witnessing

It is through consciousness, and our ability to stand outside ourselves and 'witness' our thinking and behaviour, that we are able to change ourselves. Boud and his colleagues (1985), whose model of reflecting on experience was described in the previous chapter, have given a useful summary of the varieties of witnessing that we may engage in – they call it 'reflectivity'. These are presented in Box 10.4.

It is through witnessing or reflectivity that we gain the insight which enables us to work on ourselves to change our behaviour or assumptions about the world. Boud and colleagues suggest that the insight can come as a sudden flash; or result from an accretive process, until as a result of constant small revisions to perceptions and assumptions, a threshold is crossed and we have a new awareness of ourselves.

Box 10.4

Types of reflectivity or witnessing

'Reflectivity' is the act of becoming aware of ourselves, our behaviour, our habits, etc. Types of reflectivity include:

- Affective reflectivity – becoming aware of how we feel about the way we are perceiving, thinking or acting, or about our habits of doing so.
- Discriminant reflectivity – assessing the efficacy of our percep-tions, thoughts, actions and habits of doing things. It includes identifying immediate causes, recognizing the realities of the situation we are operating in and identifying our relationships in that situation.
- Judgemental reflectivity – making value judgements, and being aware of them, about our perceptions, thoughts, actions and habits. We like or dislike them, regard them as beautiful or ugly, positive or negative.
- Conceptual reflectivity – becoming conscious of our awareness and critiquing it, as for example when we question the criteria we use to make judgements about another person.
- Motivational reflectivity – recognizing the personal interests and drives which influence the way we perceive, think or act. This includes recognizing how such interests and drives may lead us to make precipitant judgements about other people on the basis of limited information about them.
- Societal reflectivity – becoming aware of how our behaviour may be shaped by taken-for-granted cultural or psychological assumptions.

Reflectivity can be expected to lead eventually to 'perspective transformation'. This is when we become critically aware of how our assumptions and perceptions constrain the way we see ourselves and our relationships. This may happen through sudden insight or through a series of revisions to assumptions.

Adapted from: Boud *et al.* (1985) by permission of the publisher, Kogan Page Ltd.

Here, a more directed and expeditious approach is recommended. Managers who need to develop cannot rely on sudden insight to occur, though it may. Nor can they wait for the slow accretive process to occur, though they should not impede it.

As a result of your learning experience you have taken a new look at yourself and what you do. You very likely have new insights about yourself that you now want to work on. The remainder of this chapter looks at ways you can do this.

Working on yourself

By 'personal change' is meant making some change to the way you behave, think, feel, see yourself or your external world. It does not mean some radical shift in personality which makes you virtually a different person. On the other hand, a shift in some aspect of your behaviour or in how you see yourself or the world can be experienced by you – and others – as profoundly transforming. You see your world differently. You may literally feel that you are living in a different world. You may feel that you have a new self.

The process of personal change involves three broad elements:

- Influencing yourself to change;
- Working on yourself to change your behaviour, thinking, perceptions or motives; and
- Handling the transition.

Influencing yourself

Insight is not always a sufficient impetus to change. We all tend to be attached to our existing ways of thinking, feeling and doing things. It can sometimes take a considerable shock, such as a failure, to achieve what we intended, to break us out of our old, comfortable patterns.

In the absence of any such shock, an important first step in changing yourself is cultivating the will to do so. Your insight indicates that you should change. You now need to influence yourself to make the change.

The idea of 'influencing yourself' has come from a self-help book on personal therapy. Tom Rusk and Randy Read, in a postscript to *I Want To Change But I Don't Know How* (1986), have set out their views on what constitutes best psychotherapeutic practice. Their conclusions are based on extensive observations, using videotape, film, and one-way mirrors, of therapeutic sessions.

Their conclusions about 'worst' practice go a long way to explaining the ineffectualness of much therapy. What they concluded about 'best' practice has relevance to the process of personal change in any context.

One of their conclusions about 'best' therapists was that, regardless of their particular brand of therapy, they tried to influence their patients to heal. In doing so, they used general principles of influencing rather than techniques specific to therapy. They:

- Fostered hope and expectation of things becoming better;
- Used acceptable theoretical rationales to serve as frameworks for insight and behavioural change;
- Encouraged non-destructive emotional release; and
- Deliberately used discomfort or pain to promote change.

Each of the above influence tactics is commented upon below from the perspective of you attempting to influence yourself.

Moving forward

The best therapists established a clear sense of direction for the process as a whole and for the steps within it so that the client could know where he or she was going next. They also worked on making their clients believe that they could get there.

This is obviously immensely important for you working on yourself – it is not just a matter of 'putting yourself to rights', but of positively knowing where you want to go. You also have to see that you will not be able to attain your aspirations unless you change.

The theoretical rationale had to be acceptable to both therapist and client. Credible explanation gives a sense of personal control, thereby making co-operation in the therapy more likely.

If you try and fit an explanation to an event or insight that you are not fully convinced of, it is improbable that you will want to do anything about it.

You have no means of validating theories about yourself other than your own intuitive sense of fit. Making sense to you is all that matters. You can never be certain that your explanation of how your inner processes have been driving your behaviour is 'true'. But if your 'theory' enables you to release some attachment to your past and move forward, it has served its purpose.

Emotional release

Emotional release needs to be constructive. It can be brought about through confrontation in the 'here and now', or by using recall, fantasy or role play to create emotionally laden experiences. Development workshops will often make use of such techniques. The emotional release not only enables you to let go of the past, it can also help dispel emotional blocks you may have had to going forward in a new direction.

It is difficult when working on your self by yourself to contrive emotional release. But should reflection on events bring up feelings of, for example, regret or anger or elation, it would be appropriate in a suitable moment to give vent to that feeling.

Expressing your feelings by writing them down can be an effective way of releasing your emotions in solitude – for example, drafting a letter to someone who has upset you, as long as you do not send it. Laughing at yourself is another useful form of release and has the advantage that if you tell the story against yourself to a friend you can also be committing yourself to change.

Remember always that the object is to express and release a negative feeling, not to wallow in it. You want to remove feelings that are obstructing you from moving on, not to reinforce stuckness.

Detachment

Earlier, the notion of witnessing yourself was introduced as a technique for helping you to gain insight. Witnessing is of equal value in the process of releasing emotion, or a belief, or a perception. Jagdish Parikh (1991), in a book that bridges Eastern and Western approaches to development, explains how witnessing, standing outside yourself, can give you greater control over yourself:

> The process of observing or witnessing yourself creates a psychic distance or detachment from that which you are witnessing. That gives power to you as the observer or witness. (p. 100)

Parikh describes how, by repeatedly witnessing yourself, you can go beyond – transcend – your ego. You are thus able to operate from a higher level of consciousness or self.

> The basic tenet is that *you manage that from which you are detached; you are managed by that with which you are attached or identified.* You must remember that you are neither your thoughts, nor your beliefs nor your feelings or behaviour: you are the manager of all these. However, if you identify with them you will find it almost impossible to alter them: any effort to do so would imply attacking your self-identity. (p. 100)

The point is simple: if you wish to let go of a belief or feeling, stand outside it. Distance yourself from it. The difficulty is that all too often we allow our ego to be bound up with what we believe or feel. We feel it is right to have these feelings or beliefs; having them and expressing them is part of our self-identity. This identification can often be of great value: it is what drives people to pursue altruistic causes. But it can also drive them to feed their ego.

Often we recognize such behaviour for what it is and seek to let go of the negative feeling that drives it. This recognition is an initial step in the witnessing process. It is important in this context, Parikh points out, to realize that any resistance to an emotion in fact makes it persist:

On this basis, the formula for misery would be: M (misery) =
NE (negative emotion) × R (resistance). If the resistance is zero,
misery also becomes zero.

As he has explained:

. . . noticing, witnessing and allowing eliminates the negative
emotion. (p. 101)

Dealing with negative emotions is, of course, only one side
of the equation. Positive feelings need to be harnessed.
Expressing enjoyment, satisfaction, excitement, enthusiasm
can be a powerful influence on you, and on others, to take on
new challenges.

Working to change yourself

People are not usually motivated to change when they feel
good. If you have taken no risks in your learning experience,
you may have succeeded in avoiding the pain of making
mistakes and the discomfort that comes from anxiety about
whether plans will turn out as intended. But you may now be
lacking any impetus to change.

In working on yourself you can err to one of two extremes.
You can be overly critical of yourself, thus undermining your
self-esteem. Or you can be too complacent, failing to be aware
of areas where you should be developing yourself. Preventing
yourself from erring in either direction may well demand that
you talk your self-perceptions through with a trusted
friend.

Changing yourself demands first that you actually want to
be in some way different, to be able to do greater things. It
then means abandoning inappropriate behaviours, perceptions, modes of thinking and adopting new ones that will
serve you better.

The literature on how managers change themselves has
been dominated by the notion that the impetus for change
can only come from depression or crisis. The sequence of
events typically postulated is shown in Figure 10.1. (See, for
example, Adams *et al.*, (1976) and Carnall (1990).)

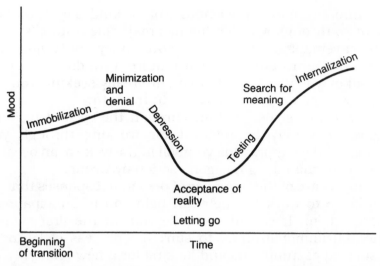

Fig 10.1 Self-esteem changes during transition. Source: Adams et al. *(1976)*

The idea is that the manager is overwhelmed by events or the task ahead, say as a result of unfamiliarity with a new job, or pressure to go beyond previous proven capability, or experience of a failure. In consequence, he or she is 'immobilized' – is unable to take the action needed to cope with the situation.

Initial response may be to put one's head in the sand and deny that anything is wrong, or minimize the effects in one's mind. But eventually as one is forced to face up to one's immobilization, depression ensues.

Eventually, in the trough of despair, perhaps having reached some inescapable crisis point, one starts to pull oneself together and embarks on the hard process of relearning. Depression is replaced by hope as one accepts reality and lets go of one's false assumptions.

Then, as one experiments with one's 'new' reality the process of re-mobilization gets under way. New meanings are found to replace one's misplaced interpretations. As these new understandings are 'internalized', one is ready once more to move forward effectively.

This scenario rather assumes that only depression and crisis are sufficient to motivate people to change themselves.

It is probably more representative of the kind of cycle that one might go through in adjusting to a major life trauma such as a bereavement or divorce or redundancy. Surviving such major upsets in one's life can require a fundamental reappraisal of who you are, what you are really seeking from life, and how you are going to lead it in the future.

On a lesser scale, working through the cycle depicted in Figure 10.1 may be relevant for working through your feelings and re-appraising yourself in the wake of an occasion when your managing has gone seriously wrong.

Being aware of the sequence of personal responses that you may have to work through can help you to anticipate and handle them. It can also enable you, at the first signs of potential immobilization, to start the process of letting go misplaced assumptions and looking for a new reality.

Alternative cycle of transition

If you are putting yourself through a learning experience, or starting a new job, you do not have to wait until immobilization and depression force you to face reality.

The idea of carrying out a project was that the resulting achievement should bring you to a new high point in your feelings about yourself, as depicted in Figure 10.2.

Testing your perceptions of reality en route to achievement could force you to re-appraise original assumptions. Or surprise events could put your plans in temporary disarray. Either eventuality could engender dismay or depression as you face up to their implications. This possible deviation from your progress towards achievement has been indicated by a broken line adjacent to the upward slope in Figure 10.2.

Achievement could be followed by temporary anti-climax – another dip in the broken line in Figure 10.2. But there is no reason why you should not aim to remain more or less on the new plateau as you reflect upon your experience.

It is from this plateau, rather than from a trough in your emotional fortunes, that you should seek to undertake such letting go and searching for new meanings that your reflections upon experience indicate are necessary. What is being advocated is that, rather than wait for events to force you to

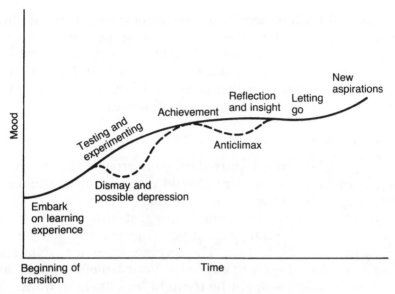

Figure 10.2   Transition through a learning experience

change, you are as proactive with regard to your personal growth as you are with your other areas of managing.

Growth vs therapy

Working on your personal growth has some affinities with the processes of psychotherapy. In both cases you are seeking greater self-understanding and to change your behaviour. To the extent that you are trying to 'cure' yourself of unwanted attitudes or behaviours, the objectives may appear similar. But there the parallels end. It would be unfortunate if you were to be deterred from attempting to realize your potential in the mistaken view that you would be engaging in some kind of 'therapy'.

Psychotherapy is usually concerned with helping people who are not functioning adequately in their world. Or perhaps, despite an outward appearance of functioning adequately, they do not feel adequate. Or they have been through a traumatic crisis from which they are unable to recover on their own.

What is written here does not attempt to address these kinds of personal problems. It is assumed that you are already functioning reasonably well as a manager, and that your learning experience has confirmed to you that this is so. Your starting point for change is therefore to develop further from this level of achievement, as illustrated in Figure 10.2.

Starting points

Where and how to get started on your growth? How can you take your insights further? Should you work from the inside outwards or from the outside inwards?

Conventional wisdom might suggest the former – that through understanding your psychology you will best be able to change your behaviour. The reverse sequence – changing your behaviour first and expecting your beliefs, feelings and motives to follow – might be thought less likely to work.

Contrary to popular belief, either sequence can be made to work. An obvious example of the latter sequence is using achievement as a basis for development, with success in action leading to a changed self-image.

Resistance to change

Wanting to develop further does of course depend on you recognizing a need to do so. Which you may not. We are all skilled at deflecting, discounting or ignoring evidence that has negative implications. This skill is sometimes described as defence of the ego. Eight of the more common 'ego defences' are listed in Box 10.5. All are likely to be familiar to you, if not from use of them by yourself, then from your observations of others.

You should watch out for your own use of these defences. They are likely to be a warning sign that you are avoiding or resisting awareness of the need for change in yourself.

Eliminating defensive reactions will make you a more effective listener. You will become more open and accessible to others – and be perceived as such.

A further defence is to believe that people are not capable of changing themselves. It is perhaps unfair to call such a belief a 'defence' since it may be genuinely held. Nevertheless it is a block to change.

Box 10.5

Eight common ego defences

- **Denial** – you deny the validity of feedback that is coming to you about yourself. This could be feedback that someone has given to you, or which results from you not getting the outcomes you were seeking. Denial is in effect putting your head in the sand.

- **Distrust** – you discredit information about yourself in your mind by not believing the integrity of its source.

- **Blaming** – the fault is not yours, but someone else's.

- **Projection** – you attribute your own behaviour and thoughts to other people, while failing to recognize them in yourself. A subtle variant on blaming.

- **Rationalization** – you produce excellent explanations of why you are acting so inappropriately, which deflect, to your own satisfaction at any rate, any criticism.

- **Humour** – you treat your manifestly inept behaviour as a joke. Or you recognize a criticism as having some validity but laugh it off.

- **Going blank** – you pretend you are unaware of what you have been told, what you have done, or the consequences of what you have done. This defence usually fails to convince even yourself.

- **Changing the subject/creating a distraction** – you deflect attention or potential criticism away from yourself. A more socially skilled version of going blank. The technique is much used by politicians, though not necessarily as an ego defence.

Source: the list of eight defences derives from Helena Cornelius of the former Bellin Partnership. The notes describing them are mine.

Can you change yourself?

In some senses it is true that you cannot change yourself. We have a fundamental personality which may well not be amenable to any significant change. We also have an inner core, a sense of our permanent 'self', our sense of the essence of who we are and the purpose of our existence, which we might well not want to change even if we could. These fundamental enduring aspects of our 'self', in part genetic, can be expected to survive most of life's vicissitudes – except, tragically, pathological personality changes resulting from disease, for example schizophrenia.

Personal evolution, rather than change, might be a better term to describe what this book is about. Nevertheless, to the extent that you do believe or feel different things, you will have changed as a person – and hopefully in the direction of growth rather than regression.

Perceptions and beliefs, preferences for particular ways of behaving, needs and motives, feelings – were highlighted in Chapter 2 for the very reason that they are amenable to modification. You can do something about them in a way that you cannot about your personality traits or inner core.

One could debate whether change in behaviour or beliefs represents 'real' personal change. Certainly it does not change the fundamental, enduring 'you'. On the other hand, it will cause you to experience yourself as different and to be experienced differently by others. You will appear to have changed.

Moreover, a change in what you do, believe, or feel can seem to have the effect of changing your whole being. If you stand outside the change you have made, saying to yourself 'I am doing this, but it is not really me', then you will probably not experience changing as a person. But if you identify with what you are doing new, you very likely will.

Working on behaviour

To change your behaviour you simply need to start doing things differently. There is no more to it than that. You either do something new or stop doing something. Or you reverse your behaviour, thus doing both these at the same time.

A frequent prescription in self-help guides is what might be called 'behaviour reversal'. In fact in one particularly pragmatic guide, examples from which are presented in Box 10.6, over a third of the recommendations are of this nature. Many further examples of suggestions for behaviour reversal could have been cited, but there are probably enough in Box 10.6 to convey the point.

Box 10.6

Suggestions for behaviour reversal

- If you tend to be hide-bound by habit and routine, overconcerned to stick to convention:
  - Try doing something to break out of your rut (e.g. drive to work by a different route, eat an unaccustomed food, look for ways to do things differently);
  - When blocked by a rule that you would normally comply with unquestioningly, look for a way round it.

- If you are someone who prefers to work on your own:
  - Start teaming up with others;
  - Get to know people – listen to them and share something of yourself.

- If you are someone who avoids confrontation and conflict:
  - On the next suitable occasion do not back off – assert your interests and ideas.

- If you tend to look to others for approval:
  - Take more initiatives of your own;
  - Judge for yourself whether you are being successful rather than look for approving feedback.

- If you have a propensity to be negative about new ideas:
  - Curb your tongue until you are sure that your response will be more than an automatic reflex.

- If you tend to use language that implicitly puts you down, for example 'I'm not very good at this sort of thing, but . . . ' 'My opinion, for what it's worth . . . ' 'I'll try . . . ' 'Would you mind doing . . .?':
  - Delete from your vocabulary and keep alert for these kinds of phrases slipping back in. It can be helpful to appoint a friend to be your 'monitor'.

Source: Human Synergistics-Verax (1989) by permission.

This kind of advice may seem elementary, banal even. But once you have grasped the basic principle, you can invent a behaviour reversal to suit virtually any development need and get on with doing it. Refraining from certain behaviours, for example being overly critical, overly garrulous or overly self-deprecating, demands not just a resolution to stop, but also persistent self-observation to avoid relapses.

The question of course is: does this kind of behavioural approach work? Or is it necessary also to look inwards to understand the causes of your behaviour? If your objective is simply to change your behaviour, and you are able to do so, then this behavioural approach has served its purpose.

Common sense advises that you should take your behavioural modifications a step at a time. Do not expect to revolutionize your management style overnight. Comprehensive action plans for change with dates are likely to be unrealistic. One or two small steps may be realizable. More can come later.

Behavioural change is not always the appropriate way forward. If you feel the new behaviour will be too alien for you to adapt to, some prior work on your psychology may be indicated.

Self-counselling

You do not need to understand theories of psychotherapy and psychoanalysis in order to manage your own psychology. On an everyday basis, it is something that we all do naturally, though perhaps with varying degrees of skill.

Managing your own psychology can be viewed as a process of 'self-counselling'. There are two basic stages:

- 'Self-searching' or 'self-interrogation' to realize why you behave, feel or think the way you do; and
- Resolution of the insights generated by your self-searching.

At the simplest level you need to make use of the insight to manage yourself.

More profoundly you need to be able to manage the psychological driving forces you have become aware of. You want to reach a state where you are free to act without undue interference from unconstructive forces, and are able to harness the constructive ones.

Self-searching

To discover how your behaviour is being affected by your psychology, you need to ask questions of yourself. Examples of self-interrogatory questions produced by a firm of consultant psychologists for use by managers are to be found in Box 10.7.

Box 10.7

Questions for self-searching

- For someone who has identified that he or she has an excessive need for approval by others:
  - Examine your need for approval and think about how you may have developed it. Ask yourself why you accepted this need in the first place, and why you continue to accept it.

- For someone who conforms unduly to rules and others' expectations:
  - Ask yourself if your life is how you want it to be, or if it has become merely adherence to routines and directions imposed from without. If so, question the effectiveness of continuing to behave in this way.

- For someone who avoids confrontation or other types of difficult situation:
  - Determine what is threatening you and provoking your avoidance behaviour. It could be a reaction to a traumatic life event such as the loss of a significant relationship, or a disturbing exposure in childhood to the kind of situation you are now trying to avoid.
  - Focus on your feelings. Examine only the current reasoning behind your feelings of holding-back. Ask yourself: 'What's bothering me right now?'

- For someone who needs to be right:
  - See others' criticism of you in a more positive light. Evaluate what the person is saying. Is the criticism valid and constructive? Can you gain something from this feedback that will help you improve your performance?

Source: Human Synergistics-Verax (1989) by permission.

Answers to why we strive for particular goals, or avoid particular outcomes, may lie in events that occurred in infancy or early childhood. Becoming aware of these unconscious influences, contrary to some popular belief, does not always require deep psychoanalysis. Many of our unconscious motives and forces are only unconscious because we have never taken the time to allow them to surface. Once we examine our behaviour and start the process of self-questioning, much will come into consciousness. You may not plumb the bottom of your psyche. But all you are seeking is sufficient awareness and understanding to provide a lever for change.

Resolution of insights

Before you can act on an insight you may need to use the new understanding it has given you to modify your existing understandings of yourself. In this aspect of self-counselling you may have to accept facets of yourself that you had not adequately recognized before, to accept perhaps that your view of the world has not been correct, and to let go of beliefs and perceptions that are no longer serving you well.

Some examples of this form of self-counselling are to be found in Box 10.8. Notice how the injunctions start 'Recognize . . .' or 'Accept . . .' or 'Realize . . .' as you are exhorted to take on board a different view of yourself or see the world differently. As in Box 10.6 you are being asked to do something. But this time what you 'do' is in your head.

It is easy to take a superior attitude to these down-to-earth homilies. But they simply express what people do intuitively all the time in order to manage their psychology. Set out explicitly, the advice seems self-evident, almost banal. But this seemingly elementary self-counselling can be effective.

The examples of self-counselling given in Box 10.8 are all geared to specific diagnoses that would have resulted from completion of a management-style questionnaire. You will have your own diagnoses of your self, for which you will need to devise your own injunctions and advice to yourself. Usually what you have to do will be self-evident, though

---

Box 10.8

Self-counselling to resolve insights

Recognize that you are a valuable person simply because you're you – *not* because people like you or approve of you.

Accept the fact that not everything you do will meet with approval.

Realize that approval-seeking can result in one-sided relationships. Others may take advantage of you knowing that you won't complain and risk losing their approval.

Talk to yourself when you encounter disapproval. Tell yourself that the words and actions of another are just that; no more, no less. They do not affect your feelings of self-worth unless you allow them to.

Recognize that conventionality is a way of hiding yourself and avoiding developing as a person. By giving up control of your life to outside factors, you become a mirror that reflects the expectations of everyone but yourself.

Continually remind yourself that your sense of self-worth is not tied to how well you 'blend in' and follow the rules.

Listen to yourself. Decide what you want out of life and go after it. Live your life for *you*.

Realize that no one can make you happy or unhappy. Only you have the power to determine how you *feel* by controlling what you *think*.

Accept that you live in an imperfect world and that the outcome of things will be less than perfect.

Acknowledge your accomplishments and achievements, even though they may not be perfect.

Source: Human Synergistics-Verax (1989) by permission.

---

you may not always want to do it. The key is to develop your own style, one that is true to yourself, and not be tempted into copying the alien styles of others.

'Affirmations', in which you repeat positive statements about yourself or your intentions in order to embed them into your consciousness, are a variant of self-counselling.

Emotional responses

Self-counselling is an emotional as well as an intellectual process. Looking inside yourself can stir up feelings, not always comfortable ones. You may need time for your feelings to align with your intellectual understanding.

For example, although you may 'know' that your personal worth is independent of particular accomplishments, that is not what you feel. Self-evident 'truths' can take time to permeate at the emotional level. Talking with a mentor, friend, or professional counsellor can sometimes help enormously with this process of emotional assimilation.

Sometimes you may feel the need to express feelings that you are not sure you can handle. You might on occasion feel that your self-exploration has left your ego defences undermined with nothing in their place.

These sorts of reactions are perhaps more to be expected at those developmental workshops where the intention is to confront you with new self-knowledge. But even in the course of everyday managing, events can be upsetting. As a manager you are ever at risk of experiencing anxiety, anger, stress, regret and other forms of emotional disturbance. Which is why 'emotional resilience' is so often cited as a quality that managers need.

There is an unfortunate propensity for emotional expression in management to be seen largely in negative terms. The very use of the phrase 'emotional resilience' illustrates this point. Emotions are seen as having to be endured and survived.

Emotions can be a positive force. And not just the obviously positive emotions – excitement, joy, happiness. A certain degree of anxiety is good for stimulating adrelin. Anger, so often regarded as unacceptable to display, has been called 'God's fire for change'. Depression can be a route to personal change. If one did not feel the peaks and troughs of managing there would be precious little job satisfaction. The only way to learn how to handle one's emotions and feelings is through experiencing them.

Expressing an emotion is something that you do. But because emotions so often appear as spontaneous reactions to situations they can seem outside our control. So people see themselves as having a quick temper, or easily upset, or easily depressed, believing these feelings to be a 'natural' response to circumstances.

Rather than suppress or deny their emotions, managers need to learn how to direct and use them. It is not so much a matter of being emotionally resilient, as being able to flow with one's emotions and harness their energy – like a surfer riding the breakers. If you do not ride your emotions, they may indeed batter you.

Changing beliefs

The way you see the world and see yourself shapes what you do possibly more pervasively than anything else. Altering your beliefs and perceptions is thus the key to changing your behaviour.

Beliefs about the external world can usually be checked against reality. Beliefs about yourself and your internal world are less easy to confirm or disconfirm.

Beliefs about other people can also be difficult to validate. An element of self-fulfilling prophecy can be at work. If you perceive someone else as, for example untrustworthy, that perception is likely to be reciprocated in the way he or she relates back to you. You are thus confirmed in your original beliefs, or at least you get no evidence to disconfirm them.

The only way open to you to break out of this kind of vicious circle is to behave as if you trusted the other person. To do this you have to trust him or her. Which means replacing a belief of mistrust by one of trust. Put another way, it means 'letting go' of your old belief and probably too the feelings that attached to it. This is not always easy.

Letting go

One way to manage your psychology is by consciously controlling and directing the various inner forces that you sense are driving you. The other way is to remove the driving force – let go of it.

Thus, you abandon a self-limiting belief. You let go of a need. You forget your stereotyped views. You dispel a negative feeling. Fear, though, may need to be faced in the world before it is dispelled.

Many of your out-moded feelings and attitudes will fade naturally as you do new things. But sometimes you will need to work on a belief, or need or feeling in order to eliminate it from or reduce its effect on your life.

We all have our own strategies for letting go, for breaking our attachment to old patterns of doing things or old patterns of thought. Indeed the colloquial label, 'letting go', reflects what a commonplace activity it is.

Sometimes letting go is a gradual process of which we are scarcely conscious. Eventually we realize that we are no longer living by our old lights. Or letting go can be a deliberate decision consciously taken at a point in time. You simply stop holding on to a belief, a principle, a way of doing something. There are a number of clichés used to describe such an event: 'swallowed my pride', 'gave up worrying about it', 'was bigger than the situation', 'controlled my ego'.

Awareness of having let go can bring a sense of relief, of lightheartedness. You may wonder what drove you to hold on to the past so tenaciously. You may even be able to laugh at your old self. A further outcome is likely to be a new release of energy. Resistance to change absorbs energy; letting go releases it. It is a paradoxical process that has to be experienced to be believed.

Blocks to letting go

How does one stop 'resisting'? The answer is quite simply that you stop. A great deal of time and discussion in counselling or therapy sessions is often focused on enabling the 'client' to get to just this point – to want to stop resisting change. Self-counselling too will in large part need to be focused on this objective.

You need to reflect carefully on the considerations that are holding you back – the self-talk along the lines of 'Won't changing my mind be seen as weakness?' 'Once I stop fighting my corner people will take advantage of me.' 'This is a principle that I cannot compromise on.' 'I'm not the sort of person to change my mind.' Self-counselling is about working your way through such self-talk and letting go of it.

Our sense of identity can be bound up with our present way of thinking or doing things. The more it is bound up, or the more it seems like a matter of principle, the more energy we are likely to invest in resisting change.

All of us can no doubt think of pressures or expectations that we have at one time or another resisted on principle, or still are resisting – for example complying with a procedure we disagree with, obeying an instruction that we regard as high-handed, doing something that we believe to be inappropriate, or simply perhaps doing something we do not feel we ought to be asked to do or that we dislike doing.

Or we can recall our resistance to letting go of a style of behaving that we felt to be an important part of ourself but now recognize as counter-productive – for example wanting to oversee everything we are responsible for in detail, or insisting on an unreasonable perfection in everything we and others do.

Box 10.9

The process of letting go

- Stop attaching value to the outmoded behaviour or thought.
- Recognize that you do not need to do or think this.
- Be aware of the importance to you up till now of maintaining this belief or behaviour, or of maintaining your aversion to behaving differently.
- Understand why this has been so important to you.
- Consider what would be the worst possible outcome for you if you change.
- Consider your higher values and purposes and the benefits of changing.
- Spend adequate time on self-counselling.
- Let go. Cast off.
- Do not tie up again at the first signs of bad weather.
- Make yourself aware of the benefits of having changed. Give yourself positive feedback.

The dividing line between resistance on the grounds of genuine principle and resistance because of the uncomfortable emotional adjustment involved cannot always be easily drawn.

If you see your resistance as a matter of principle you will believe right to be on your side. The choice is between betraying or standing up for one's principles. 'Letting go' is not an issue. We know we must 'resist'. But there are also instances where we know we are clinging on to out-moded behaviours and beliefs. We want to be rid of them, and just need to know how.

The danger is that we all have a propensity to elevate our inclinations into principles – that is to say we kid ourselves. It needs a fine judgement sometimes to tell the difference between genuine principle and spurious rationalization.

As long as one sees one's behaviour and beliefs as being in the 'principle' category, there is small prospect of letting go. To do so would be 'wrong', a betrayal. A first step in letting go of anything therefore is to be able to see the change in non-ethical terms. The process of letting go is summarized in Box 10.9.

Authentic role-players

Personal change, particularly letting go of seeming principles, may appear to some as compromising one's personal integrity. How can one be oneself yet change?

Changing your behaviour or beliefs may convey the impression, to others as well as yourself, that you are acting a part. You feel ill at ease in it, 'phoney' even. You may be tempted to hold back from new roles and new behaviours for fear that they will somehow be betraying your 'true' self.

Taking on a new role can in fact be an opportunity for you to display more of your 'real' self. On the other hand a new style of behaving, even acted, changes you. So where is the real self?

In addition to the five archetypal characters described in Box 10.3, we need also to compare ourselves with the archetype of the wise owl. 'Wise owls' were described in Chapter 6 as managers who can handle the politics of their organization without playing ego-driven psychological games. They managed with integrity.

This integrity was best achieved, so it was argued, not just by being true to yourself, but by reference to an external touchstone, an agreed purpose and project. Indeed, as should be becoming apparent, your 'self' can be somewhat of a shifting sand.

As a manager you will evolve your own distinctive philosophy of how you want to manage, the kind of manager you want to be, the principles that will guide you. These personal values, like external purposes and projects, provide further touchstones that guide your integrity.

What a manager has to do is to bring self, values and project together. He or she needs to be an 'authentic role-player'. This might seem a contradiction in terms: authentic means being real or genuine, while roles are 'played'. In practice there need be no contradiction.

'Authentic role-players' are adept in managing the tension between acting a role and being their 'self'. An effective manager is willing to experiment with new 'personas', new selves. In doing so they are as much true to the vision of their emerging self as to the self they are leaving behind. They are also true to the roles they have to take on in order to be effective managers.

Reflection and action points

- Use Boxes 10.1, 10.2 and 10.3 to review your managerial behaviour and assess your present stage of managerial development. Draw also on earlier chapters to help you in this self-appraisal.
- Consider whether you need to change, and if so decide whether you are going to do anything about it.
- Think through how you would like your behaviour, thinking or feelings to be different, and use the processes suggested in the second half of this chapter to help you achieve these changes.
- If necessary, search out other activities designed for management self-development. The references cited below should be useful for this.

The book by Pedler *et al.* (1986), *A Manager's Guide to Self-development,* has long been virtually the only source for self-development exercises aimed specifically at managers. However, new books with work-based activities and other exercises designed to meet the growing interest in developing management competences are now coming on to the market, for example Quinn *et al.* (1990), Stott and Walker (1992) and a series of books from staff at Middlesex University Business School which take a 'skill and activity' approach to managerial learning – see particularly Anderson (1995).

11   The developing manager

Introduction

It is customary in a final chapter to draw together the threads of the previous chapters and reach some overall conclusions. However, it should be you, the active learner, who should now be weaving the threads together. Each learning experience is unique and what each manager gets from it is unique. It is not possible for me to draw conclusions that only you can draw. The whole point of experiential learning is that the learners should discover for themselves the meaning of their learning journey.

Nevertheless, I do have some views about where the kind of learning experience advocated in this book may have led you. One purpose of your journey was to reach a greater understanding of 'managing effectively' and implement this understanding in your work.

The first part of this chapter reviews what some of these understandings might be:

- Five precepts that you might take away from your experiential learning *and* incorporate in your everyday managing are suggested.

Another purpose of your learning journey was for you to reach a greater understanding of yourself and how your managing is a reflection of who you are. There is nothing at all that I can put in this concluding chapter that would add to this understanding which only you can reach. The book therefore concludes by looking beyond your immediate learning to your wider life and career.

It is not customary to end a book by introducing new ideas and material. But in a book which is about a learning journey that you will inevitably continue, it is appropriate to end with an introduction to its next stages:

- A model of men and women's archetypal journey through life is presented to enable you to take a simple overview of where you may have been and where you may now be going.

The project spirit

Many of the things that you do in the course of a project are common to all management – planning, collaborating, leading and influencing, managing time, operating politically, monitoring progress, evaluating results. You should have little difficulty in transferring your experiential learning in these areas into your everyday managing.

There are, however, certain other aspects of project management which may be more problematic to transfer. Once your learning project is over, assuming you have done one, the gains you have made could lapse with it unless you take deliberate steps to ensure the contrary. A developmental project is the start not the end of your development.

You will no doubt be aware of any such gains that you wish to perpetuate in your everyday managing. The precepts or principles to be derived from a successful learning project that I believe to be worth perpetuating are:

- Manage with one hand free;
- Lead from below the top;
- Direct without domination;
- Succeed in imperfect organizations; and
- Promote learning.

Each of these precepts will be discussed in turn below.

Managing with one free hand

There is a precept amongst seafarers who have to go aloft to work in the rigging: 'One hand for the ship and one hand for yourself'. It is a useful precept for all managing. If you give both hands to your organization or to your boss, you will have no hands for any initiative of your own.

One of the distinguishing features of your learning project or other developmental experience will have been finding the time and space to do it. That may well have been a challenge. Now that is over it would be all too easy to relapse into your old routines.

If you believe that you can manage effectively while totally locked into responding to other people's requirements and expectations – from your boss, colleagues, subordinates, customers, suppliers – then no action is required. It is unlikely, in the wake of a successful project, that you now believe this, if you ever did. So you need a strategy for keeping one hand free.

For some readers this freedom will already be an integral part of their job. Even so, it is easy to allow oneself to become the slave of day-to-day pressures. Other readers, however, may find they are expected, implicitly or explicitly, just to be 'implementers'. Whatever your circumstances, with a successful project or achievement behind you, you will be aware of the practical hurdles that you will need to overcome in order to break free of day-to-day pressures.

Whether you do so or not will depend very much on how you want your managing to develop in the future. It can be a difficult choice. Being a wholly responsive manager can often be the easy option. It may be the one that is rewarded in your organization. Working on the consensus priorities, especially if you are seen to put in long hours doing so, may be your best route to survival and promotion. Who knows?

One thing only is certain. To manage with one hand free you need to believe in yourself and your ideas. If you did not have this self-confidence before your learning project, and if your project achievements have not since given it to you, gaining time and space for your own ventures is unlikely to be a consideration for you.

Your view of managing and your own particular role will also be relevant. You need to believe that managing is about more than just 'minding the shop' and implementing your boss's directives. These have to be done of course. But you also have to believe that you are employed – regardless of what any job description may say – to make your own distinctive contribution. Which leads to the next precept.

Leading from below the top

Leading is integral to managing effectively. A principal reason for advocating a project as a means of self-development was that it would involve you in 'leading'. If you have now initiated a project of your own and seen it through to the end you will have done the things that leaders do – create vision and direction, initiate, enlist support, and influence 'followers' to achieve a purpose. Whether you possess what are considered to be the 'right' personal qualities for leadership is irrelevant. You have done it.

If you are to continue to make use of these leadership skills you will need to keep initiating projects. This of course turns traditional hierarchical practice on its head. Change is as much initiated from the bottom and the middle as from the top.

There are some very real organizational dilemmas to be resolved. Unfettered initiation from the middle could be chaotic. On the other hand, the complexity of modern organizations and the speed of response needed to keep abreast of market and technological change means that traditional top down styles of planning can no longer be effective – if they ever were. So 'leading from below the top' may be essential for the future.

Writings on leadership, as was seen in Chapter 6, have a schizophrenic quality. They are based on research into what the top person in an organization does, and the qualities he or she is seen to possess. On the other hand, they appear to be written for a wider audience. Are they advising managers how they should be preparing themselves for that time, which most of course will never reach, when they are in the top position? And in the meantime, should they refrain from being a leader? Or at least refrain from leadership that would take them outside the boundaries of their small team within the organization? Books which invidiously contrast what leaders do with what mere managers do serve only to perpetuate this schizophrenic approach.

In designing your learning experience you selected a project that served worthwhile corporate objectives. You were advised against taking on board some harmless proj-ect your boss thought might be a low risk development exercise for you. If you have now successfully led a project of corporate significance, you may not now wish to be relegated to playing mere 'manager' to your chief executive's 'leader'.

In many organizations there may be no problem in moving into an initiating role, indeed it may be encouraged. Moreover, as a result of your project success, you may be seen in a new light and be expected to continue initiating and leading change.

On the other hand, if you were only allowed to undertake your learning project on a 'grace and favour' basis, you may have to work at bridging the gap between what you are now capable of and what is permitted to you in your everyday managing.

You were urged in Chapters 3 and 4 not to allow your learning project to be seen merely as a training exercise. If it was, you may find that collaboration received in the course of it was not real collaboration; you were simply being indulged to help you in your 'development'. It is all over now. What is vital is that, if this was not already so, you use the occasion of the project to establish initiation and leadership of change as an intrinsic part of your management role.

Leading from below the top means that you have to be a direction-finder. You need to keep your antennae well tuned to your external and internal environments to determine relevant priorities for action. You need to be able to conceive new projects, and be able to shape adopted projects.

Directing without domination

Leading change requires that you communicate your ideas about the direction to be taken and convince people that this is the way to go. To the extent that your learning project took you outside your normal organizational boundaries you will have had to elicit voluntary co-operation.

The issue now is how far you want to rely on voluntarism in your managing generally. When managing within the normal bounds of your authority you may not feel it so necessary to attend to all the communication and persuasion that were essential for establishing co-operation in your project. You need to be aware of what you did in the course of your project that generated commitment to it.

Work on your project will often have gone on without you. What did you do that made this happen? Should you now be doing similar things in your everyday managing?

Actors sometimes talk about their director 'giving them direction'. By this they mean that the director tells them what he or she is trying to achieve in the production and suggests how their role should be interpreted. If they agree they will 'take the direction'.

Giving direction implies leadership – communicating a vision of what you believe should be achieved, having ideas about how to get there should anyone need to know, and nudging people in the right direction to arrive. The role is essentially that of impresario of the action.

When it works, as you may well have discovered from your project, things happen that go beyond anything you might have imagined for yourself.

Succeeding in imperfect organizations

Conventional wisdom has it that the organizational climate has to be right for training and development to work. You cannot expect, so the wisdom goes, a trainee to implement new principles or skills in a hostile organizational culture. Taking managers away for off-the-job development and then allowing them to return to an unsupportive environment is seen as a recipe for failure.

One of the great virtues of using a project as a vehicle for development is that you have to overcome obstacles to achieve. You start off with the assumption that the culture may be unsupportive. Indeed you design a project that will not be straightforward to implement. So you have to win over the 'culture', or rather the people who operate within it. You do not wait for the culture to be 'right' before you embark on your learning. Indeed you learn from it being 'wrong'.

The risk is that in the wake of your learning project you make less sustained and persistent effort to overcome the obstacles that the organization puts in your way. Because, for example, you do not have an adequate expenditure budget you give up on trying to introduce improvements that will cost money. Yet for your project you were probably prepared to seek a special budget.

It is all too easy to interpret lack of routine organizational support as a statement about the organization's expectations of you. You can then blame the organization and its rules and constraints for your unwillingness to take initiatives. But if you are to manage effectively you have to be guided by your purposes as you see them, not by the constraints of the bureaucracy. Organizations are always 'imperfect'. The skill of managing effectively is to achieve, regardless of these imperfections.

Promoting learning

Having brought yourself to a new level of development, you may feel honour bound to consider how you might help others to develop. You have had an exhilarating learning experience. How can you enable others to attain something comparable?

The recommendation here is not to work towards any visionary dream, but to focus just on what you can initiate yourself. Establishing a small ring of learners could be feasible. From your experience of developing in an imperfect organization you could help them do the same.

At this point you will be stepping into a role that you may not have had direct experience of in the course of running your project. You will need to think through how your experience of learning worked for you and what this signifies for facilitating others in their learning.

This may lead you to think in terms of acting in the first instance as a 'mentor', though this need not be to the exclusion of 'coaching' and 'instructing' roles. How to develop yourself in such roles is well described in an excellent guide to facilitation skills for managers by David Megginson and Mike Pedler (1992).

You could also consider passing on this book. The point is that you work at developing your staff by whatever means you are comfortable with. You will be doing so in the knowledge that at least on your patch the climate will be right for learning.

The learning organization

Ideally there should not be a gap between an organization's culture and the training and development of its managers. The training and development of everyone in it should be seen as intrinsic parts of an organization's own development. Each organizational task should be viewed as an opportunity for developing new, shared understandings of the organization's purposes and how to achieve them. The organization is thus in a state of perpetual and constructive evolution as it makes itself ready and fit to tackle its tasks.

This is the concept of the 'learning organization', defined by its original proponents as:

> . . . one that which facilitates the learning of all of its members and continually transforms itself as a whole. (Pedler *et al.*, 1991: 1)

The conditions that need to be established for a learning organization to come into existence are considerable. There has to be a climate of openness, trust and co-operation in which people can share their learning, admit mistakes and give each other honest feedback. There has to be a willingness to allow the organization's own development and evolution to be led from the grassroots – or wherever the germane learning is taking place. And above all there has to be commitment to the notion of organic, collective learning at all levels.

That is the concept. But it is important to remember, as my colleague, Peter Critten (1993), has pointed out, that the learning organization is not something that exists 'out there':

> It cannot be created by following a series of steps.

In Critten's opinion,

> It is the *embodiment* of a thousand 'incremental changes' that occur every day in every department but which we are not attuned to because we are looking for consequences of learning we can recognise against standards we have used before. (p. 231)

The learning organization in this view is not so much created by deliberate planning, but emerges from the myriads of interdependent learning activities that go within an organization when all its members are committed to learning.

A more formal, deliberately creative perspective on the learning organization is taken by Gordon Wills (1993), Principal of International Management Centres. The opening sentence of his book has been used as one of the introductory quotations to this book.

Wills has a vision of what he sees as an 'enterprise school of management', in which there is a corporate policy of learning from experience. The chief executive is the 'Professor' of strategic purpose and integration. Other senior managers are 'professors' of finance, marketing, human resource management, operations.

The syllabus in this 'school' is formed from the questions, challenges and problems that the management (or professorial) team faces. Their lessons from experience go to form the corporation's 'body of knowledge', continually being added to as new experiments in action are evaluated.

It may sound fanciful, but International Management Centres, through its action-learning programmes is seriously endeavouring to create this kind of ethos in its client companies.

Your own learning future

The vision of a thriving learning organization may seem remote and unrealistic to a manager who is a lone learner and developer within his or her present organization. But if many others besides yourself were equally assiduously pursuing their own development, and sharing the learning from their experience, the ideal could become a little closer. You, by displaying your own enthusiasm for your development, can motivate others to follow you down the experiential learning path.

The learning organization is a great ideal to work towards. Judging by the popularity of the idea among management developers, I suspect that for many of them the 'learning organization' is their ideal of a perfect organization in which people can develop without fear of molestation by an antipathetic culture. But learning is only a means to an end. For line managers the ideal might be the 'achieving organization'. Learning is simply a step on the road to managing effectively.

In the meantime, most of us work in organizations that are a long way from the ideal. The risk is that in seeking to create the true learning or achieving organization you fail to get on with the more immediate learning and development that are possible. The whole drift of this book has been to focus on what is immediately practicable and can be instigated by one person wherever he or she happens to be in the organization.

Weighing anchors

Ever since Edgar Schein (1978) coined the phrase 'career anchors', the phrase has recurred in books on careers. Schein meant by his metaphor those talents that we see ourselves as possessing which, together with our values and motives, guide our career choices, and serve to stabilize and integrate our careers over time.

Careers today are less secure. The waves of managerial redundancies in recent years mean that the safe corporate career is a thing of the past. In these stormy times 'anchor' is perhaps no longer an appropriate metaphor. Or if it is, then we need perhaps to weigh the appropriateness of our current anchors.

Gone too today is any assurance that your development will be taken care of by a benevolent employer seeking to foster talents for future promotion. Sponsored management development and training still of course continues, but the context has irrevocably shifted. It is we as individuals who must now take the prime responsibility for our development and for managing our careers.

Re-appraisal of our career anchors demands that we look at our needs and what we are seeking from our careers. This book has looked at needs primarily from the point of view of how they affect your management practice. Dave Francis (1985), elaborating on the five career anchors originally propounded by Schein, has identified nine 'career drivers'. These are listed in Box 11.1.

Francis' book goes on, as do most other books on careers, to consider how you might shape your career to meet these needs or drivers. Most readers of this book are probably at a point in their career when its broad shape has already been determined.

Box 11.1

Nine career drivers

- **Material rewards** — seeking possession, wealth and a high standard of living.

- **Power/influence** — seeking to be in control of people and resources.

- **Search for meaning** — seeking to do things which are believed to be valuable for their own sake.

- **Expertise** — seeking a high level of accomplishment in a specialized field.

- **Creativity** — seeking to innovate and be identified with original output.

- **Affiliation** — seeking nourishing relationships with others at work.

- **Autonomy** — seeking to be independent and able to make key decisions for oneself.

- **Security** — seeking a solid and predictable future.

- **Status** — seeking to be recognized, admired and respected by the community at large.

From: Francis (1985: 60–61).

Career stages

Michael Arthur and Kathy Kram (quoted in Herriot (1992)), drawing on the theory of others, suggest that we go through three stages.

Up until the early or mid-thirties, we are *exploring*, developing competence at the job and forming an occupational identity. In this stage, we largely learn by doing, especially by performing technical or functional tasks. During the middle career stage, *directedness*, we become clear about some of our career anchors. Managerial competence may supplant technical and functional competence as a career anchor at this stage. After the mid- to late-forties, we enter the *protecting* stage. We need to secure and maintain our status, experience continued affirmation of our work, and pass on the benefits of our learning to others.

Whatever career stage you are currently at, it could be valuable to apply the same kind of critical appraisal to your career drivers as you have applied to the needs driving your managerial behaviour.

In the light of where you want to go, and more especially where you know yourself to be going, which drivers are productive and which counter-productive? At this stage in your development you should not need guidance on recognizing and dealing with any unproductive ones.

Career management is beyond the scope of this book. The point being made in this section is that you must take responsibility for the development that you need to support your career. You may want to take this into account in your future experiential learning.

Being your own hero

An altogether different way of looking at your management development in the context of your life and career is provided by a unique book by Carol Pearson entitled *The Hero Within* (1989). Subtitled *Six Archetypes We Live By*, the book describes characters we may inhabit as we move through life. Within each archetype Pearson sees a 'heroic' element, which we need to discover and bring out in ourselves.

Three of Pearson's archetypes, the Innocent, the Orphan and the Martyr, broadly correspond to the archetypal managerial characters, Improviser, Protector and Bearer, described in Box 10.3. The difference is that Pearson has focused more on depicting the negative or 'shadow' sides of these archetypes than I have. But three of her archetypes, the Wanderer, the Warrior and the Magician, described in Box 11.2, are of a different order. These are the 'heroic' archetypes.

Box 11.2

Three heroic archetypes

The Wanderer

Wanderers are on a quest to discover what the world will bring them.

Consciously taking their journey, setting out to confront the unknown, marks for them the beginning of life lived at a new level.

The archetype of the Wanderer is exemplified by stories of the knight, the cowboy, and the explorer who set off alone to see the world. During their travels they find a treasure that represents the gift of their true selves.

Wanderers may be self-made men or women of business, or hippies living on the edge of society. They define themselves in direct opposition to a conformist norm.

They are likely to distrust orthodox solutions, choosing instead to be very conservative, very radical, or just idiosyncratic. As learners, they distrust the answers given by authorities and search out their own truths. The Wanderers' identity comes from being the outsiders.

The Wanderers' goals are independence and autonomy. Their worst fear is conformity.

The Warrior

Warriors are fighting to make their way in the world.

Warriors take charge of their lives, eliminate problems and make a better world. It is the archetype of the Warrior that is our culture's definition of heroism. The Wanderer identifies the dragon and flees; the Warrior stays and fights.

At the physical level, the Warrior consciousness includes self-defence, a willingness and an ability to fight to defend oneself.

At the psychological level, it has to do with the creation of healthy boundaries, so we know where we end and other people begin, and an ability to assert ourselves.

Intellectually, the Warrior helps us learn discrimination, to see what path, what ideas, what values are more useful and life-enhancing than others.

The development of Warrior capabilities is essential to a full life.

The Warriors' goal is strength and effectiveness. Their worst fear is weakness and ineffectuality.

The Magician

Magicians hold their position in the world simply by virtue of who they are.

Magicians take full responsibility for their lives and for their impact on the world.

The archetype of the magician teaches us about creation, about our capacity to bring into being what never was there before. It is about ordering and arranging life.

When we enter the terrain of the Magician in our journey, we discover that the Magician is not a witch or a wizard who by their magic causes the war to be won or lost. That is how people who are still in dependency positions see it. The Magician is ourselves.

The Magician as hero understands that the world is not something fixed and eternal, but is in the process of being created all the time. We are all involved in that creation, and thus all of us are Magicians.

We cannot *not* be Magicians. We cannot live without ordering and arranging life. But until we resolve our warrioring issues, we run the risk of using the power of the Magician to demonstrate our superiority or to try to control other people.

The seductive idea is that we can solve our problems by magic instead of taking our learning journeys. (This corrupted vision of the Magician archetype has been widely articulated by the New Age movement.)

The Magician's goals are authenticity, wholeness, balance. Their worst fears are superficiality, alienation from self and others.

Adapted from: Carol Pearson (1989: 20–21, 51–52, 74–75, 116–117) by permission.

Pearson originally wrote her book to help women understand how their own archetypal roles related to those
associated with the careers of men. But men apparently
found her book so enlightening, that in the second edition
additional material aimed at helping men to understand their
archetypal roles and life journeys has been added. Each
archetype is in fact relevant to both men and women, the
more so as women take on traditional male jobs in managing,
and men, influenced by seeing the way women work, now
seek to move into the women's archetypal roles.

I should perhaps add that Pearson treats the Martyr or
Bearer, so often adopted as a role by women, as one of her
heroic archetypes. She believes that men too have to learn the
lessons of this archetype. In Box 10.3 in the previous chapter
I have endeavoured to present the positive side of each
archetype without implying associations with any gender.

Embarking on experiential learning will inevitably draw
you, at least to some degree, into the behaviour and thought
pattern of the Wanderer archetype. It is scarcely possible to
explore your world and your self without raising questions
about where you fit and seeking to change.

The starting point for this exploration could be dissatisfaction with any of the less heroic archetypes – Fixer,
Protector, Determiner, Improviser. Or it could be that you
went from one of these archetypes, or combination of them,
to becoming a Bearer (most typically if you are a woman,
according to Pearson) or a Warrior (if you are a man).

In terms of the stages of management development described in Chapter 10, you would have moved on from a state of
dependency on others and their expectations, i.e. being a
Conformist Implementer, to becoming an Independent
Experimenter.

The ideal is that you should then develop towards the final
stage of management, to become an Autonomous Agent, a
state of being that has close affinities with that of the
archetypal Magician. It is the point at which you can say, as
Clint Eastwood has said of his acting: 'I don't just do
something. I stand there'.

Many people, however, remain stuck as Bearers or Warriors, or even as Wanderers, never attaining the state of being
of Magician.

To become an Autonomous Agent or a Magician, you must, as Pearson puts it, 'take your journey'. You cannot be a Magician until you have learned the lessons of the other archetypes.

For women the sequence of the journey has typically been:

Orphan   →   Martyr   →   Wanderer   →   Warrior   →   Magician
(i.e. a pattern   (i.e.
of dependency)   Bearer)

For men it has been:

Orphan → Warrior → Wanderer → Martyr → Magician

But these sequences are by no means fixed and may be changing as men's and women's roles change. Pearson observes:

> A career woman who strives to be independent early in life may work on warrioring and martyring simultaneously, being tough at the office and all-giving at home. Many men also organize their lives this way as well. Whether male or female the pattern reduces to this:

```
              Martyr
           ↗        ↘
Orphan                  Wanderer  →  Magician
           ↘        ↗
              Warrior
```

> In this case, identity issues are forced when the split seems untenable and conflicting values of the Martyr and the Warrior find enough integration that we feel whole again. (p. 8)

The key to growth, whether you interpret it in terms of archetypes or in other ways, is to take your journey – not to remain stuck.

> Heroes take journeys, confront dragons, and discover the treasure of their true selves. (p. 1)

This book has been about a journey to discover how to be a manager. Seeking the hero within is an apt metaphor for the whole of it.

Reflection and action points

- What gains from your experiential learning do you wish to consolidate into your everyday practice? Will you be able to do this? Are there any further steps needed?
- Consider where you are now and where you want to be in the future – both in terms of job or career and your personal growth. What do you need to do to achieve this? Will you?

References

Adams, J. Hayes, J. and Hopson, B. (1976). *Transitions – Understanding and Managing Personal Change*, Martin Robertson.

Adams, J. and Spencer, S. (Eds) (1986). *Transforming Leadership*. Miles River Press.

Anderson, A.H. (1995) *Effective General Management: A Skills and Activity Approach*, Blackwell.

Baddeley, S. and James, K. (1987) 'Owl, fox, donkey or sheep: Political skills for managers.' *Management Education and Development*, **18**(1), 3–19.

Belbin, R. M. (1981). *Management Teams: Why They Succeed or Fail*. Heinemann.

Bennis, W. (1989). *Why Leaders Can't Lead: The Unconscious Conspiracy Continues*. Jossey-Bass.

Block, P. (1987). *The Empowered Manager: Positive Political Skills at Work*. Jossey-Bass.

Boddy, D. and Buchanan, D. (1992). *Take the Lead: Interpersonal Skills for Project Managers*. Prentice Hall.

Boud, D., Keogh, R. and Walker, D. (Eds) (1985). *Reflection: Turning Experience into Learning*. Kogan Page.

Boyatzis, R. (1982). *The Competent Manager: A Model for Effective Performance*. Wiley.

Briner, W., Geddes, M. and Hastings, C. (1990). *Project Leadership*. Gower.

Bryman, A. (1992). *Charisma and Leadership in Organizations*. Sage.

Burgoyne, J. and Stuart, R. (1976) 'The nature, use and acquisition of management skills and other attributes'. *Personnel Review*, Autumn.

Burton, C. and Michael, N. (1992). *A Practical Guide to Project Management: How to Make it Work in Your Organisation*. Kogan Page.

Carnall, C. (1990). *Managing Change in Organizations*. Prentice Hall.

Casey, D. (1993). *Managing Learning in Organizations*. Open University Press.

Conger J. A. and Kanungo, R. N. (1988a). 'The behavioural dimensions of charisma'. In: J. A. Conger, R. N. Kanungo and Associates (1988), 78–97.

Conger, J. A. and Kanungo R. N. (1988b). 'Training charismatic leadership: a risky and critical task.' In: J. A. Conger, R. N. Kanungo and Associates (1988), 309–323.

Conger J. A., Kanungo, R. N. and Associates (1988). *Charismatic Leadership: The Elusive Factor in Organizational Effectiveness*. Jossey-Bass.

Covey, S.R. (1992). *The Seven Habits of Highly Effective People: Restoring the Character Ethic*. Simon & Schuster.

Critten, P. (1993). *Investing in People: Towards Corporate Capability*. Butterworth-Heinemann.

Drucker, P. (1988). *The Effective Executive*. Butterworth-Heinemann.

Drucker, P. (1989). *The Practice of Management*. Butterworth-Heinemann.

Edmonds, P. (1992). AMED London Regional Network meeting, October. Reported in Newsletter by Jennie Kettlewell.

Evans, R. and Russell, P. (1990). *The Creative Manager*. Unwin Hyman.

Fayol, H. (1949). *General and Industrial Management*. Pitman.

Flamholtz, E.G. and Randle, Y. (1989). *The Inner Game of Management*. Business Books.

Francis, D. (1985). *Managing Your Own Career*. Fontana.

Fritz, R. (1989). *The Path of Least Resistance: Learning to Become the Creative Force in Your Own Life*. Fawcett Columbine.

Giovannoni, L. C., Berens, L. V. and Cooper, S. A. (1987). *Introduction to Temperament*, 2nd edn. Telos Publications.

Handy, C. B. (1985). *Understanding Organizations*, 3rd edn. Penguin.

Hardingham, A. (1992). *Making Change Work For You*. Sheldon Press.

Hastings, C., Bixby, P., Chaudhry-Lawton, R. (1986). *Superteams: A Blueprint for Organisational Success*. Fontana.

Herriot, P. (1992). *The Career Management Challenge: Balancing Individual and Organizational Needs*. Sage.

Honey, P. and Mumford, A. (1986). *Using Your Learning Styles*. Peter Honey.

Human Synergistics-Verax (1989). *Life Styles Inventory: Self-development Guide*. Verax, Odiham, Hants RG25 1LN.

Jay, A. (1987). *Management and Machiavelli*, revised edn. Hutchinson Business.

Johnson, R. (1991). *Transformation: Understanding the Three Levels of Masculine Consciousness*. HarperCollins.

Kakabadse, A. (1983). *The Politics of Management*. Gower.

Kakabadse, A. (1991). *The Wealth Creators: Top People, Top Teams and Executive Best Practice*. Kogan Page.

Kanter, R. M. (1985). *The Change Masters: Corporate Entrepreneurs at Work*. Unwin.

Kanter, R. M. (1989). *When Giants Learn To Dance*. Simon & Schuster.

Keirsey, D. (1987). *Portraits of Temperament*. Prometheus Nemesis Books.

Kelly, G. A. (1955). *The Psychology of Personal Constructs*. Norton.

Kolb, D. A. (1984). *Experiential Learning: Experience as the Source of Learning and Development*. Prentice Hall.

Kotter, J. P. (1982). 'What effective general managers really do'. *Harvard Business Review*, **Nov–Dec**, 156–167.

Kotter, J. P. (1983). *Power and Influence*. The Free Press.

Kotter, J. P. (1986). *The General Managers*. The Free Press.

Kotter, J. P. (1990). *A Force for Change: How Leadership Differs from Management*. The Free Press.

Leary, M., Boydell, T., van Boeschoten, M. and Carlisle, J. (1986). *The Qualities of Managing*. Report on a Project carried out by TRANSFORM Individual and Organisational Development Consultants Ltd and Sheffield City Polytechnic, Manpower Services Commission.

Lowen, A. (1958). *The Language of the Body*. Collier Macmillan.

Lucas, D. (1992). Paper presented at NHS Training Directorate conference, London.

Majaro, S. (1992). *The Creative Gap: Managing Ideas for Profit*. McGraw-Hill.

Mant, A. (1985). *The Leaders We Deserve*. Blackwell.

Margerison, C. (1991). *Making Management Development Work*. McGraw-Hill.

MCI (1990). *Occupational Standards for Managers*. Management Charter Initiative, 10–12 Russell Square, London WC1B 5BR.

McGill, I. and Beaty, L. (1992). *Action Learning: A Practitioner's Guide*. Kogan Page.

Megginson, D. and Pedler, M. (1992). *Self Development: A Facilitator's Guide*. McGraw-Hill.

Mintzberg, H. (1983). *Power in and Around Organizations*. Prentice Hall.

Mintzberg, H. (1991) 'Managerial work: forty years later'. Commentary in reprinted edition of: S. Carlson, *Executive Behaviour*. Uppsala University.

Moore, C.-L. (1982). *Executives in Action: A Guide to Balanced Decision-Making in Action*. Macdonald Evans.

Morgan, G. (1993). *Imaginization: The Art of Creative Management*. Sage.

Myers, I.B. (1980). *Gifts Differing*. Consulting Psychologists Press.

Murdock, A. and Scutt, C. (1993). *Personal Effectiveness*. Butterworth-Heinemann.

Nash, C. and Vis-a-Vis Productions (1988). *A Question of Service*. Hotel and Catering Training Board.

Ninomiya, J.S. (1991). 'Wagon masters and lesser managers', In: *Managers in the Middle*. pp 24–30. Harvard Business Review Paperback Series/McGraw-Hill.

Parikh, J. (1991). *Managing Yourself: Management by Detached Involvement*. Blackwell.

Pearson, C. (1989). *The Hero Within: Six Archetypes We Live By*, expanded edn, HarperCollins.

Pedler, M. (Ed.) (1991). *Action Learning in Practice*, 2nd edn. Gower.

Pedler, M. and Boydell, T. (1985). *Managing Yourself*. Fontana.

Pedler, M., Burgoyne, J. and Boydell, T. (1986). *A Manager's Guide to Self-Development*, 2nd edn. McGraw-Hill.

Pedler, M., Burgoyne, J. and Boydell, T. (1991). *The Learning Company*. McGraw-Hill.

Peters, T. J. (1989). *Thriving on Chaos: Handbook for a Management Revolution*. Pan Books.

Peters, T. J. (1992). *Liberation Management*. Macmillan.

Peters, T. J. and Waterman, R.H. (1982). *In Search of Excellence*. Harper and Row.

Pinchot, G, III. (1985). *Intrapreneuring: Why you don't Have to Leave the Corporation to Become an Entrepreneur*. Harper & Row.

Plant, R. (1987). *Managing Change and Making it Stick*. Fontana.

Quinn, R. E., Faerman, S. R., Thompson, M. P. and McGrath, M. R. (1990). *Becoming a Master Manager: A Competency Framework*. Wiley.

Reeves, T. K. (1970). 'The control of manufacture in a garment factory'. In J. Woodward (Ed.) *Industrial Organization: Behaviour and Control.* Oxford University Press.

Reeves, T. K. (1992). 'Making Born Managers', Middlesex University Inaugural Lectures, 1.

Reeves, T. K. and Harper, D. G. (1981). *Surveys at Work: A Practitioner's Guide.* McGraw-Hill.

Reeves, T. K. and Turner, B. A. (1972). 'A theory of organization and behaviour in batch production factories'. *Administrative Science Quarterly,* **17**, 1.

Relph, P. (1980). 'The bodily expression of emotional experience'. In L. S. Rubin (Ed.), *Movement for the Actor.* Drama Book Specialists.

Revans, R. W. (1971). *Developing Effective Managers.* Longmans.

Revans, R. W. (1983). *The ABC of Action Learning.* Chartwell Bratt.

Rosener, J. B. (1990). 'Ways women lead', *Harvard Business Review,* **Nov–Dec**.

Rowe, D. (1988). *The Successful Self.* Fontana.

Rusk, T. and Read, R. (1986). *I Want to Change But I Don't Know How: A Step-By-Step Programme for Mastering Your Life.* Thorsons.

Sayles, L. R. (1989). *Leadership: Managing in Real Organizations,* 2nd edn. McGraw-Hill.

Schein, E. H. (1978). *Career Dynamics: Matching Individual and Organizational Needs.* Addison-Wesley.

Schön, D. A. (1990). *Educating the Reflective Practitioner: Toward a New Design for Teaching and Learning in the Professions,* Jossey-Bass.

Smith, B. (1993). Work-based project guidelines at Sundridge Park Management Centre. Item in *Personnel Today,* **23 Mar**.

Stott, K. and Walker, A. (1992). *Making Management Work: A Practical Approach.* Prentice Hall.

Tichy, N. M. and Devanna, M. A. (1986). *The Transformational Leader.* Wiley.

Watts, G. W. (1993). *Power Vision: How to Unlock the Six Dimensions of Executive Potential.* Business One Irwin.

Wills, G. (1993). *Your Enterprise School of Management: A Proposition and Action Lines.* MCB University Press.

Index

Achievement, 9, 24, 27, 31, 32, 44, 52, 57, 69, 82, 102, 113, 118, 129, 144, 202, 222, 247, 270, 289
  outcomes from, 239–44, 280–2, 298–9
Action learning, 9, 27–9, 107, 116, 122–3, 141, 171, 223, 237, 240, 305
Adams, J., 210
  et al., 279
  and Spencer, S., 74, 75, 76
Agenda, 1, 23, 45, 74, 88, 119, 151, 157, 193, 202
  control, 213
  hidden, 178
  personal, 103
  setting, 24, 167–9, 205
  surreptitious, 139, 226
  team, 201
Anderson, A., 296
Archetypal:
  journey, 298, 311–12
  roles, 311–12
Archetypes, 256, 271, 294, 309
  character, 266–71
  heroic, 309–10
  Jungian and Myers–Briggs, 131
  learning, 131–4
  see also Types
Arthur, M. and Kram, K., 308
Ashridge Management College, 193, 194, 197, 200
Attitude(s), 13, 15, 35, 61, 69, 74, 76, 85, 96, 114, 158, 165, 172, 173, 208–9, 224, 238, 251, 258, 269, 281, 291–2
  of leadership, 70–2
  of open style, 179–80
  surveys, 154, 185
Autonomy, 18, 39, 53, 142, 162, 166, 309
  factors conducive to, 174–5

Baddeley, S. and James, K., 155, 156, 157, 160
Behaviour, 36, 41, 58–62, 77, 81, 114, 139, 145, 158, 174, 177, 180, 203, 238, 239, 243, 247–8, 259–61, 264, 277, 287–8, 311
  avoidance, 287
  changing, 252, 272, 274–5, 281–6, 291, 293

counter-productive; unconstructive, 34, 223, 248–50, 256, 259, 278
  distorted, 36, 139
  exemplary, 81
  game-playing, 182
  inappropriate; outmoded, 53–4, 293
  managerial, 35, 53, 160, 295, 308
  measures of, 145, 266–7
  open, 179–80
  organizational, 207
  need driven, 53
  political, 152, 155, 158, 160, 165
  reversal, 284–6
Behavioural preferences, 34, 59, 61–2, 103, 134, 204, 284
  for interacting, 192
  ✓ for managing time, 172–3
  for political style, 165
  for relating to one's worlds, 45–8
  ✓ for team working, 197, 199–201
Being:
  able to do things; active; prepared to act, 17, 35–6, 61, 74, 85, 88, 151, 158, 166, 174, 206
  adept, 74, 143, 257, 268, 294
  a boss, 1
  creative, 37, 76–7, 91–4
  driven, 52–8
  effective, 31, 34–44, 58–9, 141, 220, 252
  efficient, 10–11
  political, 142–3, 159–60
  powerful, 143, 223
  successful, 36–7, 50, 56
  a team member, 198
  yourself; true to self; natural, 32–6, 60, 114, 185, 258, 261, 293–4, 309–12
Belbin, M., 45, 46, 197, 199, 201, 203
Beliefs, *see* Perceptions
Bellin Partnership, 269, 283
Bennis, W., 71, 72, 73
Block, P., 162, 164
Blocks, 51, 202, 208
  dispelling them, 221–3
  inner, 46, 221, 276
  to letting go, 292
  organizational, 21, 138
  see also Considerations
Boddy, D. and Buchanan, D., 158, 194, 197, 199, 200, 201, 209, 210, 211, 212